Face/ Fetty Boy

Published by
Etched in Stone Publications
756 South Orange Avenue
Newark NJ 07106

http://www.Etchedinstone-Books.com
Copyrights reserved in 2014
Printed in Canada

Fetty Boy
Written by Face

This work and all of its characters are fictional. Any similarities to real life events are just that. No part of this book may be used or reproduced without written permission of the author. All rights reserved by; Etched in Stone Publications

LIFE

Where the piff and cess at?
Where's the next Malcolm X at?
Maybe, he here with life in a box trapped.
He used to tote the nina and the fif in the streets
While bearing the weight of his soul on a Hip-hop beat.
Trying to make sense of a conspiring convolution
They describe Black Beauty as an ongoing infestation...
And the solution?
extermination and/or incarceration.
How can a race be the minority of a sovereignty
Yet, and still be the majority of the penitentiary?
Trying to live with hope
But she's on dope.
Mental genocide knocking at my door, how does she cope?
My ethnicity's life expectancy is amiss
As such, 20's is the new mid-life crisis.
Can't imagine peacefully walking the streets with my son
Not without a kevlar and the latest Smith & Wesson.
Trying to stay ahead by two steps
Listening to the grapevine plan my death.
Are the plans of the devil really deep
Or am I an emotional cripple chewing on concrete?
Mr. Warden - Why are these cells so cold?
Is that asbestos on the wall in the form of mold?

Face/Ash-shabba

Face/ Fetty Boy

DEDICATION

Free, if I could, I would go back in time
and make your heart beat again.
Even if it meant trading yours for mine.
Real niggaz till the end!
I was the brain... you were the heart.

This book is dedicated to my brother/best friend - Curtis Oliver, aka Freedom-Sha. On September 30, 2013, he left this world and went on to the next. Free, I will mourn you until the day I join you. The years are long, but they felt short while you were holding me up. My bid... my life will never be the same. You were the good one. What happened to you should've happened to me. You were supposed to be there when I touched the streets again, bro. Word is bond, if I could control time, I would go back and plead my case to the Creator to change your fate. I will NEVER forget you! Words alone can do no justice to express how much you are going to be missed. Grave yard love!

Easy on'em!
R.I.P. Free

Also, Rest In Peace goes out to: Money Mark, Black Seed, Hubert, Maheem, Dapper Don, Born-E, Cool-C, Country June, Ronnie, Cream Born, G.I., Undo, Noonie, Mugsy, Mont Mont, Mighty Mike, Val Carter, Goose Neck, Tammy Sapp, Lonnetta "Fattie" McCollum, Kevin "Dawg" Bottoms, and Trayvon Martin.

Face/ Fetty Boy

Some Trill Game from the Author
By P. Francis aka Fetty

More or less, if you don't make Fetty, then it don't make sense! That's my conviction- I'm bound by it because belief kills, but it also cures. That's a shout out to whoever's 'bout money over bullshit!

I didn't write this novel trying to kick knowledge or bash anyone for their choices or for their way of life; I respect the game. I crafted it on an avenue of fiction just to show how music-hip hop , Reggae, R&B, Rock & Roll, House, all that shit- can affect an immature mind whether negatively or positively. The output depends on the input… it's all about the Yin & Ying.

But culture, this culture, is more than music, it's a complete lifestyle. What you wear! How you talk! You perception or what's around you, a perception that should be balanced like everything else in the universe.

But many of us don't see it like that. All we see is that our thirteen-year-old child is in love with Lil' Wayne or Snoop Dog. What we don't see is that our children's minds are not yet fully s that are needed, 23,000 more people to fed, 23,000 more people having unprotected sex, spreading disease and populating the earth.

If you were asking to maintain population control, what would you do? You'd do the same thing that's being done all around us- you would use the culture of the people against them. The movies, the media, and the music would be used to trap the minds of our young ones to the point where the parent, who are youngens themselves, can no longer cope with them.

Sometimes, the parents get carted off to the penitentiary, abandoning their children. Now it's up to the grandparents to raise a child that they can't even identify with because they don't understand the culture! The child has to take to the streets; the child damn sure ain't gonna stay in the house. Now his/her favorite rapper becomes a role model.

But, like I said, there's balance in the universe. There's a good to it all and an evil to it all. I came up idolizing Mr. Tupac Shakur. Yeah, his music definitely shaped my brain waves. But his words helped me learn to embrace a simple truth many people "Don't give a fuck about us!" "Born black in a white man's world!" His words showed me "Not to let the evil of the money trap me ever again!" The odds are insurmountable, but "It's still me against the world!"

Pac helped me deal with a lot of adversity I knew was headed my way. His music wasn't solely about flashy shit, gang bangin', or sex like most of what these hip-hop stars spit about today. The media portrayed him to be negative, but when you actually digest what he said, your mind tells you he spoke the truth.

(Shout to Mr. Nasir Jones aka Nas and to Scarface) Yo stayed solid and haven't sold out. It's clear that you were Pac's favorite rappers, which makes you my favorite rapper's favorite rappers. Your words, your examples helped me trudge my way through these fifteen years I've been trapped behind bars-trapped for a crime when the only crime I committed was not following the law of the snitch.

They wanna charge me with Accomplice Liability – What the fuck is Accomplice Liability anyway? I don't hear anybody rappin' about that. I don't hear anybody lacing a track explaining how a person can be charged with a crime just because the bias Prosecutor says he has a theory about what happened, a theory of which he can't prove. Just because you can place a man at the crime scene doesn't make him guilty; he could be a witness… A witness that refuses to snitch. And, since I ain't the type to talk just to be talkin', the Prosecutor named me as a co-defendant to the actual perpetrator of the crime.

You know what came next- minor players in a big league game tried to get us to flip on each other. Hmph- it's a well-

Face/ Fetty Boy

thought-out-money-making system, one that I respect. However, ya'll entertainers, rappers, actors, players of the game...ya'll got to know ya'll roles in this shit. If ya'll turn a blind eye to that, it's just like tellin' me ya'll don't give a fuck! Then it'll be straight F.O.E from here on out- Fetty Over Everything! I could dig it!

Please know that I cast no first stone at anyone. I take responsibility in full for the path I chose to navigate. I've been navigating that pat since the immature age of thirteen. Now I'm thirty seven, mature in the mind and body, still sitting in the penitentiary; the only difference is I now choose to be an author.

Much respect to all the political prisoners and prisoners of Gang (LIE) Wars all across America. Stay solid! Real eyes recognize real lies! For every immature mind out there, be it man, woman, or child, if you know you're not built for navigating...then stay in your lane. Sixty or seventy years in this place is very real (Ask my nigga who brought the wave to the game Max-B)...AIN'T NOTHIN' FICTIONAL ABOUT IT!

Fetty Boy, Peace.
Face.

Face/ Fetty Boy

Chapter 1: Watch All, Trust None

You ever been to Time Square or a championship game and watch confetti fall from the sky? The paper falls from everywhere on everything; it kind'f reminds me of big-ass snow flakes trapped inside a breeze. When you can make money drop like that - like confetti without a motherfuckin' care in the world - that's when you know you done came the fuck up!!! Hmph - rappers talkin' about they makin' it rain, well, make it rain then. Nigga like me makin' it hail... yeah, you need some heat and a much colder heart for that type'f shit. Peep game...They called me Fetty out there. Me and my manz n'em named Freez and Hubby was tighter than two fat bitches stuck in a moose's ass. Hubby and I were two Jamaican born gun slingers ready to let it rip in broad daylight right in front of the precinct if we had to. We were on some classic top shotta badmon ting. The best word to describe us was trouble. And you know what they say in the hood... don't trouble trouble unless you want trouble to trouble you!

Freez was thorough, but he was on some other shit; he wanted to be a rapper. There was a bond between the three of us that was stronger than Afghanistan heroin - just like the dope from Afghanistan was uncut, nothin' or nobody was ever gonna cut our bond. That's just how shit was ever since we were teenagers comin' up in the 4th Ward of Paterson, New Jersey.

The year 1993 blew by us like cars at the Daytona 500. Snoop Dog had niggas on some "Bitches ain't shit but hoes and tricks" type shit, rockin' rugby and hockey jerseys. '94 was all about Wu-Tang - they had all the hoods on some "C.R.E.A.M.

Face/ Fetty Boy

get the money," donnin' in Wallabee Clarks. But '95 was the year that the law caught up with me. A whole bunch'f bullshit that I did, not really thinking before I did it, piled up to a year bid inside the Jamesberg juvenile joint.

Man, that year dragged by like a fat person tryin' to run a marathon. Maybe it was because Miss Pauline's son kept actin' like a fly - always in some shit. The Berg kept puttin' me in the box (detention) for my actions. It was just how Fetty Boy got down, strictly for the niggas from my town, that is; I didn't know anything else.

But that last month of that one-year bid was absolutely the worst; at least, at that time I thought it was.

I called home one day, and my mother was on some other shit. I didn't know exactly what, but I could tell she was upset about somethin'. I tried to ask her about it, but she wouldn't talk over the phone - Mamma-P was no dummy. She told me she would come up for a visit and let me know what the deal was, but that wasn't a good idea at the time. I hated havin' to tell Mamma-P that, even in jail, her only child was still causin' havoc, but it is what it is.

"Nah, Ma. Can't get visits right now," I told her. "I'm in B.M.U.."

"What's that, Frank?" she asked. She was one of the few people I ever let call me Frank. For most people, it was either Franko or Fetty.

"It's the Behavior Modification Unit. It's like lockup, only with a few more privileges."

"Why the fuck you can't stay out'f trouble and come home, Frank? You always fightin' and disrespectin' somebody!"

"Ma, I really need you to just tell me what's goin' on so I won't be in here stressin' and shit. I'm locked in this cell twenty-three hours a day, so all I do is just sit and think. And I don't wanna be in here thinkin' about what you're not tryin' to tell me."

Face/ Fetty Boy

My mom's still put up a fight because she didn't want to upset me. But I'm stubborn like she's stubborn, and I wasn't gonna stop until she spilt the beans, and she knew it.

"Your friend Hubert," she said. I could hear the hurt in her voice. "He got shot up nine times, Frank. He didn't make it."

"What!?! Nah, yo! Nah!"

I didn't even wanna talk after that.

My eyes shed so many tears I caught a headache due to dehydration. I thought about Hubby's mother losing her only son. That could've been me... that could've been my moms.

That's one of the things a gangster knows in the back of his mind, but refuses to think about while doin' wild shit. Here I am in the box, and my number one gunner was out there on his own. The wolves come out when you're separated from the pack. They smell the lion's blood when he's injured; my being in the Berg is what injured Hubby. Now, the wolves done changed the fuckin' game.

Me and Hubby were gonna hustle and shoot our way to stardom. Once we got the paper we wanted, we were gonna use it to back Freez and his rappin' career. Sittin' in that box, all I could do was let the sounds of real niggas like Tupac and MoBB Deep hypnotize my brain waves. Every up-and-coming gangsta kept that sort of music in their hearts and minds. They swore they were gonna be the next Scarface or Pablo Escobar or some shit like that. Me? The music didn't do anything except make me see the game for what it really was - it was changin', and if I didn't wanna end up like Hubby, changin' with the game was a must - fuck bein' stuck in a time capsule. Hubby slept on the game, and sho'nuff, nothing comes to a sleeper except dreams, nightmares, and rude awakenings.

* * * *

When January 16th of the year 1996 rolled through, Franko stepped out the gates of that little punk-ass jail. Because I loved my mother and my freedom, I told myself I was gonna

Face/ Fetty Boy

lay low, walk on eggshells for a little while, makin' giant moves at the same damn time. That would have been easy to do - I had about fifty-six Gs stashed in my attic. But the news about Hubby reminded me that the game changed... new rules, new moves, new players.

The first breath I took outside of the jail filled my lungs with cold air, instantly making me feel alive again. Snow was everywhere. Good thing I was rockin' a fresh pair of three hundred dollar Gortex boots and a yellow and black North Face coat. Before leavin' the streets, three hundred dollars was the cost of most dude's hoopties; but it's a new day, a new hustle... nothin's the same.

Chicks ain't even the same anymore. Only a bullet ago, they were all hoes and tricks, but now Biggie got everyone in the game wifyin' chicks. Dudes buyin' them broads Chanel and Coach-bags, cars, rings n' things... all types of shit.

The block done flipped, too. The 12/12 bags that used to sell for dimes were out there goin' for nickels. It was actually a good thing because the strip I grew up on was steady rockin', while every other block in the neighborhood was on Ramadan - nobody else was eatin'.

My first free morning, I hit the strip early, around nine o'clock. It was the same fake shit goin' on; niggas and bitches actin' like they were happy to see me and what not. The game may have changed, but the strip was the same. The dope fiends were out and about chasin' that smack while the crackheads did the same with that rock - and the hustlers had no problem makin' the chase easy for'em. Even if they were undercover crackheads, you could always tell if someone was a fiend or not. "Always out'f place and in ya face," as my man Hubby used to say.

The winos weren't much better. Thirty to forty degrees out this motherfucka, and there's still five or six of'em out here tippin' bottles like it's happy hour on the block or something. It was like every building on the strip had a designated crackhead, wino, or whore; huh - real fuckin' fixtures in the community.

Face/ Fetty Boy

Some nine-to-five niggas and bitches were still cuttin' across Graham Ave. headin' to the bus stop on their way to work. I even saw a couple'f kids stoppin' to shovel some snow on their way to school. They reminded me of myself when I was in the fourth or fifth grade; I thought pushin' around snow with a shovel used to be the hustle. Ha - now Mr. paper chaser fucks with another kind'f white snow; the kind that'll make you rob, steal or kill for it.

Ms. Wanda's nosey behind was still sittin' in that same window of that fucked up gray house on the corner clockin' people goin' about their business. She probably still thinks nobody peeped her ass because of the big-ass tree in the front of her house. Truth was... the hood was filled with people like Ms. Wanda. She wouldn't dare say shit about the hustlin' that went on out here, but that bitch sees every fuckin' thing - I was almost tempted to ask her if she knew anything about what happened to Hubby.

She waved at me. All I did was flash her a less-than half-quarter smile and a head nod - nosy bitch. I started peepin' some of the other buildings. Not much had changed. The bodega up the block was still pumpin' out egg & cheese bagel sandwiches. The graffiti on the side of it was a little different, though. My man Hubby used to always say, "If you wanna know what's goin' on in the fuckin' hood, read the graffiti on the wall." That's how I know this hood ain't shit - Hubby gets killed and not one person tagged his name on anything.

Amidst all this shit, everybody tried to act like they really loved and missed a nigga. I wasn't beat... A Nigga like me knew what the streets was really hittin' for.

The only real love came from Freez. We were gonna meet up, hit the mall and do some shop-til-we-drop type shit, but Freez hadn't made it to the strip yet. While waitin' for him, I decided to get the 411 on the situation that went down concernin' my man. I knew I'd get Freez's version whenever he and I met up, but there's always three sides to every story in the ghetto - mine, yours, and the truth.

Face/ Fetty Boy

I didn't see any R.I.P. tats. No R.I.P. t-shirts. In fact, nobody mentioned Hubby at all. It was like the nigga never existed out here holdin' the block up for all these suckas. That was like a major sign of disrespect to me; these clowns out here wouldn't understand that.

The lack of respect on the block for Hubby was startin' to get me a little heated - good thing Freez finally showed up. He was late as usual, but he showed up, nonetheless. He came to a stop right in the middle of the street inside a canary yellow Nissan 300Z. The reflection off the white snow made the car appear like it was painted with bright yellow diamonds.

"Damn, my nigga! You ballin' out this bitch, huh?" I said; though I was really thinkin' to myself that this nigga done lost his Goddamn mind drivin' around in this loud-ass car.

Leave it to Freez to respond with some cool slick shit, "You know how it is, my boy. It cost to floss out here, playah."
I had to smile 'cause Freez still thought he was slicker than fish grease.

"What's really hood, though? I see y'all done fucked the strip up with those big-ass 12/12 bags. Y'all ain't even up the price. Y'all dropped that shit instead."

"It's all about quick flips and fat nicks," Freez said. "We got hustlers comin' from all directions lookin' to cop this shit. They buy the nicks from the strip, then go back to their own hoods and sell'em for dimes."

I was only jokin' when I said they fucked the strip up. Truth was... the block was rockin' on all cylinders. Niggas came through with whips like it was a car show; and the bitches were on the sidelines, even this early, tryin' to catch a mark for the day. One chick came up and gave me and Freez two bottles of that Henney. I tossed that shit back straight with no chaser-it's been a minute since I've tasted that Henn-rock. Whew! That Henney made the inside of my chest feel like a grenade went off. My whole insides became warm, which was a good thing; it sort'f gave me an instant shield against the bite of the cold air. At the same time Freez and I were enjoyin' our drink, a few dudes from the strip pulled up. Ron-G pulled up in a black and white Lex Coupe - black paint job, all white leather interior. After him, Wop and Ren rolled through both wheelin' twin three-and-a-quarter Beamers with the hatch in the back so their rides could match. It wouldn't have been much of a car show at all if Lil' Goochie hadn't come through in the candy-apple red RX-7. When those cars hit the strip with the systems knockin' and the engines purring, the bitches started flockin' like it was hunting season. They didn't even give a fuck it was cold outside; those chicks still wore next to nothing.

"Waddup, Fetty Boy?" Ron-G asked.

I decided to boost his ego a little, "Y'all niggas munchin' for real out here, ain'tcha, Ron-Gotti?"

After giving those niggas a fake compliment, I smiled inside my own head. I could sense that my presence was makin' niggas nervous on the block. Though they tried to act like it didn't, but I knew better. Not only was I about that gun-play that'll make a nigga relocate; but at eighteen-years of age and six-foot-three two-hundred-fifty pounds, I was a big young nigga with a knuckle game.

Word traveled quick that Fetty was home. Why else would these niggas roll through so early in the mornin' stylin' and profilin'? Before I left, they were some ashy niggas; now they're actin' like some classy niggas. I'll play along with the charade for now - fake it until I make it with these kats. I mused. Even with all the flossin' they tryin' to do right now, not one of these dudes got paper stacked like me. Before getting locked up, I was the youngest in charge - still am. They didn't know it, but I'm 'bout to shut all of'em down in a minute. Right then, though, all I cared about was findin' out what happened to my nigga Hubby.

"Where y'all comin' from this early?" I asked.

All of them, mainly Lil' Goochie, started tellin' me about some Hackensack bitches they had up in the hotel that night. Usually, after a night of hammerin' some broads, hittin' the I-Hop on Rt. 4 was the thing to do.

Face/ Fetty Boy

"We just left I-Hop, my nigga," Lil' Goochie chimed in. Every couple'f sentences, I kept sayin' shit like, "Word! Oh, yeah! Y'all niggas doin' it like that!?!" I really ain't give a fuck what those jokers were doin'. Like I said, I'd keep up the charade for now.

Lil' Goochie, on the other hand, was my lil' son-son. We went back a long ways, almost as far back as me and Freez. Without me even having to ask, he reached into his glove compartment and pulled out a stack of Franklins. He handed it to me right in front of everyone; that gave me a chance to examine some'f these hatin'-ass niggas' faces. Lil' Goochie knew that, sooner or later, he was gonna have to choose sides. Him hittin' me off told everyone who he would be wit' when the time came.

"Trillz!" I exclaimed. That's just an expression we toss around in the hood. It means a whole bunch'f shit, but right now it means I'm 'bout to go on a shoppin' spree with somebody else's money. "I'm gonna blow all this at Willow Brook Mall later, son."

I shoved the cash in my front pocket, then looked around at the rest of those so-called rich niggas. They all came up with some story about having to go home and pick up some cash. They made promises of meetin' me later on the block so they could hit me off - yeah... like I was gonna wait around for these niggas. Later would turn into tomorrow and tomorrow would be another sob story.

There was no need to worry about what Freez had waitin' for me - he had me covered fo'sho'! With him, I knew he wanted to wait until we were by ourselves. Everything ain't for everybody.

But what I really wanted was some info. on Hubby; something of which I wasn't gettin' from any of these dudes. It was as if the little cream they were makin' caused them to forget all about my boy. The shit had me feelin' some kind'f way, for real. But I kept my composure in check; not wanting to make

Face/ Fetty Boy

myself a suspect by givin' away what I was plannin' on doin'. I decided to just pick Freez's brain on the way to the mall.

    Me and Freez left the strip. I didn't really feel like bein' out there right now anyway. As soon as Freez started the engine, I told him to head over to Hubby's mother's house before we jump on the highway - my tone was callous on purpose. His facial expression gave me just the reaction I was lookin' for... guilt. Freez should've known better. As close as the three of us were, he should've been out here rippin' the ground up tryin' to find out what happened to Hubby. But like I said before, Freez is a thorough dude, but sometimes he just be on some other stuff. He wasn't built for drama, at all. The drama was me and Hubby's lane.

    It was a short ride before we reached 12th and 22nd Ave. Freez never said one word either. I kept the convo quiet, too, just so Freez could marinate in his guilt like some ribs in some good-ass BBQ sauce. Wanting Freez to feel the hurt that I felt. Why? 'Cause if it was him or me that got shot, Hubby would've been Beatin' the streets and killin' everything, including the concrete! Yet, Freez didn't even pour a sip'f liquor in honor of our dead homie.

    When we pulled up in front of the house - Ms. Bev, Hubby's mother, was standin' on the porch. She had some company over. People I didn't really know were leaving; probably some distant relatives stopping by to pay their long-overdue respect. As soon as she laid eyes on me, I saw the tears stream down her face. She raced off the porch and flopped into my arms – the whole time screamin', "Why... why... why!?!"

    I didn't have an answer for her, but damn sure was gonna find one.

    "They took my baby, Frank! They killed him! They took him from me!"

    All I could do was hold her as her sorrows leaked their way onto my jacket. I knew I was like a son to her, and she was like a mother to me. All I did was listen while she vented and released the sadness she was feeling from her only son being

Face/ Fetty Boy

killed. It was as if the sight of me ripped open the scabs from her wounds because me and Hubby were inseparable.

"Nobody comes by here anymore, Frank!" she cried out. "At one point, I couldn't keep those friends of his from over here! They came through here all the time! But, now..."

Hubby was that nigga. People loved him on some real shit. I could understand Ms. Bev's sadness because her son took care of everything around the house. Watchin' the tears stain her cheeks really fucked me up; I couldn't take that shit much longer. I reached inside my pocket and pulled out the stack Lil' Goochie had given me earlier. I offered it to Ms. Bev, but she was just as stubborn as my real mother.

"I don't want your money, Frank! What I need is for you to get out there and find out what happened to my son! I want you to get'em... all of'em, Frank!"

"What's understood don't need to be said, Ms. Bev," I replied.

Ms. Bev didn't even have to ask that. Fetty Boy was gonna tear these streets up if I had to until somebody told me something.

"Yo, Freez, wait for me in the car," I said.

Ms. Bev was ridin' high on emotion; I was too for that matter. And I didn't want anybody, not even Freez, seein' her so hysterical. As Freez headed back to the car, "Ms. Bev, what did the police say?" I questioned.

"You know how those fools do, Frank. They talkin' about it's an ongoing investigation, which means they really don't know shit. Somebody out in them damn streets knows somethin', you hear me? Don't trust none of them boys out there on G.G. Ave. I know my boy was out there late-nights hustlin' wit' them in them streets. Ask that one in the car, Frank. He was out here while you were away!"

Ms. Bev was right about that. Freez was supposed to have Hubby's back while I was down the Berg. It's understandable that shit happens out here in these streets, but whatever

Face/ Fetty Boy

happened got my manz Hubby shit pushed back; and Freez, for some reason, was too shook to speak on it.

    I ain't know what type shit Freez was on, but even the dumbest motherfucka could've figured out what was on my mind... retaliation is a must!

Face/ Fetty Boy

Chapter 2: Veni, Vidi, Vici
(I came, I saw, I conquered)

"Damn, dawg! You've been ridin' around in this loud-ass car, and you ain't been through to see Ms. Bev not one time since my nigga got sent back to the essence?" I found myself borderline screamin' in Freez's ear while he was drivin' us to the mall. I could tell my words were bitin' through his neck like the bitter cold. Freez was my manz, but he still needed to hear this shit. "You ain't help with the funeral! You ain't drop off no scratch for his daughter Bree-Bree! And you ain't got shit to say, Freez! You probably know who did it - don't you? Yeah, you know who killed'm and filled'm with the Lugars from the Ruger."
"Nah, bro. It's just... "
"It's just what, nigga!?! Don't even say shit 'cause your actions done said it all! But you damn sure gonna tell me one thing fo'sho' and two things for certain, though!"
Half my mind was concentratin' on tellin' Freez how much he had fucked up while I was down the Berg. The other half was breathin' in the scenery as we headed down Route 46 preparin' to dip onto Route 23. The drive from P-Town to WillowBrook Mall was only ten minutes if you really knew how to whip it. Being locked up made me forget how I enjoyed seein' all the car dealerships, restaurants, and golf courses along the way.
The car came to a stop. The bass from the system was vibratin' so hard that the windshield was shakin'. I was feelin' energized listenin' to some old Scarface/Ghetto Boyz shit; Face

was goin' in hard on the track. It made me go back in after Freez made a right-hand turn onto the jug handle.

"You gotta have somethin' to tell me, nigga!"

I watched Freez's hands clench the steering wheel tighter. He couldn't even look my way. He knew. Even if I hadn't said a word to him; he knew he had fucked up.

"I think I know who pushed Hubby," he said. He was real apprehensive with his words - almost scared to shit. I think he figured I was gonna black out on him 'cause he knew who killed my manz this whole time and he ain't do shit about it.

"I've just been waitin' for the right time to tell you, yo. Hubby's death is still fresh in the streets. You noticed how, since you've been out, niggas ain't said shit about it."

"Run your mouth, nigga," I said. Freez was definitely my manz, I'd die for that nigga; but my patience was runnin' on E.

Just as the light turned green, and as the car eased around the jug handle, Freez continue, "Word is those papis in the Broadway building did it."

I didn't respond right away 'cause that shit didn't make much sense to me. Those Spanish niggas that ran Broadway were definitely a little territorial, but there was enough flow out there for everybody to eat without havin' to step out'f bounds.

"The papis?" I repeated. "Them overnight thugs? Why the fuck you think they killed him?"

"You know crackhead Anne's building across the street from the papis' building?"

"Yeah... and?"

"Well, Hubby was eatin' hard-body out'f there. He was able to short-stop all'f their sales 'cause he had them big-bag nickels and shit."

I fuckin' knew it!! I thought to myself. Something told me this flow was gonna come with a price. Makin' all those nicks dime-size was a smart move for the block, but Hubby and Freez should've known they were gonna undercut other hustler's business.

Face/ Fetty Boy

"You mean to tell me my nigga got merked out over some big-bag nickels?" Just as soon as I asked the question, my mind was made up. Even though we were practically pulling into the mall parking lot, I already convinced myself that I was gonna deal with those "Mira-Mira" motherfuckas.

Fuck the mall!!
Fuck shoppin'!!
Fuck your mom's if she got a fatty. Retaliation for my nigga will NOT be minimal! I wanted to deal with them niggas, and my mind was formulatin' a plan right there in the car.

"Yo, dig, nigga... fuck this mall shit," I said. "Take me to your crib. All I want from you is a hammer. Keep your money and whatever else you got; I ain't sellin' my nigga out like you did!"

Freez was heated because of the way I was comin' down on him, but he ain't say shit 'cause he knew right was right. He pulled out'f the mall parking lot and began to race back the way we came. He motioned his head toward the glove compartment, and that's when I noticed his eyes were tearin' up. Good for that nigga. Somebody deaded our peeps; some tears and blood needed to be shed. Upon opening the glove compartment, I saw a pretty-ass nineteen-shot .9mm Ruger. The polish on the nozzle told me that shit was fresh out the box.

"Where the bullets at, dawg?" I asked.

"In the trunk. I got you two boxes of bullets, the nine, and I know you said you didn't want any, but I also got some cash for you, big bro."

I told him I ain't want his loot, but I knew he was gonna give it to me anyway. "How much?" I asked.

"Fifteen G's," he said, still sounding as if he wanted to cry.

* * * * *

It took about nine minutes to get back to the hood. Freez

Face/ Fetty Boy

parked the car on the corner of Godwin and Graham Aves right across the street from the little grocery store with the Laundromat next door. I could tell my words were still cuttin' him deep 'cause he was tight-lipped and wasn't sayin' nothin'.

I broke the tension in the air by sayin', "Yo, load the ratchet, nigga. Lemme see how you do that shit."

When I told him to put the bullets in the nine, he looked at me sideways. Freez wasn't one of those stupid clown-ass type'f niggas fakin' jacks out on the block. He knew his limitations, which is probably the reason he ain't do shit when Hubby got killed. But he also knew that a nigga like me knew more about guns than any hustler on the block. He knew something was up, but he loaded the gun anyway.

He was on bullet number six when he said, "I also got a bird for you, and a hundred bricks'f smack, too."

"When were you gonna tell me 'bout that?" I asked.

"Com'n, son, you buggin' now."

"Nah, you was buggin' when you ain't give Hubby his just due, nigga?"

From the way I was shoutin' at Freez, Ray Charles could've seen that he was shook the fuck up. He was so distracted that he loaded the gun with no gloves on. That right there was a big motherfuckin' no-no, especially where we come from.

Right before he slipped the last bullet into place, "Don't fill that clip too high, fool," I said. "Give them bullets room to breathe." When I said that, he finally realized that he had left his finger prints all over the banger. He handed it back to me, but this time, he gripped the gun with a little dust rag that he used to wipe the dashboard. Freez squinted his eyes when he saw me handle the nine with my shirt before I tucked it away. I reached over and hugged his neck to put'm at ease.

After he relaxed a bit, I said, "Look, my nigga, I ain't mad at'chya. I understand that you just not built for this shit- that was me and Hubby's lane. We're the ones who played hard like your mama's nipples." I figured I'd give Freez somethin' to smile at since I came down on him so hard.

Face/ Fetty Boy

"I'm sayin' though, I'm ridin' wit' you on whoever, yo. We've been rollin' mega-thick for years; I ain't havin' you roll on those papis alone, yo."

That's my nigga Freez; he had the roar of a lion, but not the heart. When it comes to violence, real bad-boys move in silence. Under normal circumstances, I wouldn't mind if he rolled with me. But rule number two of the game is never let no one know your next move. Clearly other niggas were disobeyin' the rules. And, without law, there ain't no order. That's exactly why everybody out here frontin', actin' like they big willies and disrespectin' my nigga Hubby.

"You talkin' nonsense now, nigga," I said.

"Nah, Fetty... I wanna roll wit'..."

"You ain't rollin' nowhere, son. Neither am I for that matter. I'd love to push them 'gwat' niggas, but Ms. Bev said the poe-lice know all about how the papis merked our boy. Let the law do their motherfuckin' job for once." I couldn't tell if Freez saw through my lie or not. Then he asked the question I knew he was gonna ask.

"So, what d'you need the ratchet for, then?"

Since I knew he was gonna ask, I already had an answer prepared, "I'm home, nigga. I'm back. Some'f the wolves are gonna run away... some of' em gonna wanna play. Niggas is envious-you feel me? Just let me worry about the wolves and let the poe-lice worry about who killed Hubby. You focus on makin' a better way for us and for Hubby's daughter. You still writin' them rhymes n'shit? 'Cause everybody gotta part to play...rappin' is yours - capice?"

Freez sucked his teeth like he was offended I even asked a question like that. "Man, I keeps a hot sixteen sittin' on deck," he boasted. "In fact, I wrote somethin' for Hubby the other day. Want me to spit it?"

I leaned back in the passenger's seat and looked at him. I thought about the gun with his prints on it tucked away in my waistband. In that brief moment, I thought about a lot'f shit. Freez was my manz... always will be. But niggas like me

and Hubby were wolves... and wolves don't walk with shepherds or sheep.
"Yeah, my nigga," I said with a sly smile, "lemme hear that shit..."

* * * * *

I learned a long time ago that when it comes to murder, you watch all and trust none. If you fuck up and think out loud... that's yo' ass. And, if you even talk to anyone about your intentions... that's all that shit will ever be... a motherfuckin' bad intention. Them homicide detectives will come knockin' before you know it.

The last thing I was gonna do was let Freez in on what I was plannin'; that's why lying to him about Ms. Bev and the jakes was best. Anybody from the hood knows that pressure busts pipes. My man Freez would've definitely folded. If the assumption of him snitchin' ever surfaced, all I would have to do is plant the hammer with his prints on it. Freez better not make any assumptions when word spreads that them niggas in Broadway got hit up.

* * * * *

I let a month shoot by without makin' any moves. I played the block. Played the clubs. Played a few bitches while still on my lay-low. During the course of all that, my moms talked me into goin' back to school. She said that was the only way she was gonna put a car in her name for me - that, and I had to get a license.

While jugglin' all that, I took the work Freez had given me, then snatched up two young-boys from around the way. It took less than a week to turn them lil' niggas into Jordan and Pippin, while I sat back and coached like Phil Jackson.

I was out chillin' on the block when one of the young-boys

Face/ Fetty Boy

named Dead Eye rolled through. He was a perfect soldier. All I had to do was give him the playbook; that lil' nigga was hungry enough to eat the block up. Only thing was, I had to put him onto the strategy of how to do this shit. A nigga can't just show up on the strip runnin' full-speed out the gate. This ain't a motherfuckin' sprint, it's a marathon. That's the problem with most hustlers - those niggas thinkin' "right now" instead of just thinkin' "right". Dead Eye was a quick study. He did exactly what I told him to do, him and his other manz Jazz-O.

"Break all that shit down," I told' em. "I don't care how y'all do it. When y'all finish, take half."

"Half?"

I knew that was gonna fuck'em up. "Yeah, half, my niggas. This here is real trill nigga shit. Later for all that leech & stunt dummy shit. You feel me?"

While those young boys were eatin' up the idea of workin' for me, I smiled to myself. Encouragement sweetens labor, I thought. And down the line, I knew I was gonna need some loyal niggas like these two - believe that!

* * * * *

I was never much of a team player, so I kept my game and business completely separated - money and blood don't mix. I don't like nobody in my game or coke lane, especially bitches. But Crackhead Anne was a bitch that was down for whatever...whenever... however. I never could figure out how that bitch could get higher than the stratosphere and still keep her shit together. There wasn't much that Fetty didn't know about in the hood. But that bitch was a mystery - real talk.

I was sittin' in her living room watchin' music videos (Channel Live's song "Smokin' Mad Izzm" was on) while Anne was in her bedroom smokin' some base. This hood-rat chick named Tiffany was in the kitchen hookin' up some tender vittles for me - a little curry chicken, rice & peas, with some fried, ripe plantains on the side. Niggas ain't know, but I liked

Face/ Fetty Boy

chillin' over at Anne's; shit was mad clean with cable TV. She would be in her bedroom busy doin' whatever a crackhead does. I'd be in her living room while some other chick, usually Tiffany, would be gettin' ready to put some good food in my mouth, and I'd put that long dick in hers after I was done eatin'.

As the island aroma tickled the fuck out'f my nostrils, I picked up the phone book and flipped through the yellow pages. When I found the number to the specialty shop I wanted, I hit the remote to the TV so the sound could add to the noise Tiff was makin' with those pots and pans. I placed my order over the phone, then gave the service clerk Anne's address and credit card number.

A few minutes later, the food was ready. Before eating, Anne came out the bedroom, and I told her that I ordered a little somethin'-somethin' and not to fuck with the package when it arrived. She acted just like a bitch and tried to talk slick... that was until I flashed an 8-ball in front of her face. I thought to myself, "Bitch, you may not be like the rest of these skanky-ass crackheads out here, but you still a crackhead."

She snatched the 8-ball, then went back in the bedroom and did what she do. I ate the food that Tiffany cooked like I was a hostage or some shit. After the stomach was tight, I beat the back of Tiff's tonsils up, then spun off.

* * * * *

It took a week for that package to touch ground. The shit had me heated 'cause the ad in the yellow pages said three day delivery. Fuck it, at least the shit came.

Anne paged me 911 to let me know to come through. I gave Freez some excuse about studyin' for the written test for my license. Then I dipped off before anybody else could ask any questions.

The night air was warmer than usual, and the rain was smackin' the concrete so hard, I could barely hear the thunder.

Face/ Fetty Boy

I was rockin' my Columbia rain suit with the boots to match. The snow was meltin' and that made movin' silently and swiftly easier 'cause not many people were out on the block.

Anne opened the door to her rest and I dipped inside. While closing the door and stomping my wet boots on the mat, Anne just stood there in front of me with her arms folded over her pointy-ass titties and her lips poked the fuck out. I knew what she wanted. Every time I came to her spot, I'd hit her off with an 8-ball. But, this time, I purposefully didn't bring anything with me.

"It's stormin' out that motherfucka, Anne. I shut shop down hours ago; I ain't got nothin' on me. But I got two bills for you though, ma." When I said that shit, her face lit up like a movie sign outside the theater.

Ha - just like I knew she would, Anne snatched up the bills and stormed across the street to the Broadway building so she could cop from the papis. I watched her up until she dipped into the stairwell. Usually, five or six hustlers would be inside takin' turns on sales. I noticed two other fiends go in ahead of Anne. That would give me plenty of time to grab the package and handle my handle.

* * * * *

Only three or four minutes ticked off the clock. Anne was pacing in front of Hector gettin' ready to get her hands on that base when this nigga named June Bug started complainin' that Hector was cuttin' in on his sale.

"Hector, lemme get twelve for fifty," Anne said.

"Yo, Hec! It's my turn, man!" June Bug shouted.

"June Bug, you know I don't like fuckin' wit' you," Anne shouted back. "Your shit be burnin' like gasoline or some shit. On top'f that, them nicks you be sellin' are just like your shitty-ass dick... too goddam small!"

"Bitch, fuck you! Why don't you trek your bony ass over to G.G. Ave. and cop your shit in the rain, then?"

Face/ Fetty Boy

While June Bug and Anne were hollerin' on some nut shit, some lady stumbled into the building's hallway. She was a big-ass bitch, but you could tell, back in the day, her shit was right and she used to be somethin' special for someone. Her titties stuck out so far, they turned the corner a few seconds before she did. She was older, all the hustlers could tell because she had gray hair, but she still looked like she had a donkey stickin' out her back! She closed her umbrella after shakin' it off; then stepped further into the hallway and pinched her nose together 'cause the spot smelled just like the color of the walls... piss yellow. Even though the lighting was dim, Anne noticed that the lady was rockin' a dark-blue floral dress. The lady also had a big-ass pocketbook, about the size a grandmother would carry.

"You still here, Anne?" June Bug shouted. "Take yo' ass out in the rain and get your shit, bitch!"

Of course, Anne had somethin' slick to say, and of course, Hector was about to slap the shit out'f June Bug for fuckin' up his paper. The rest of the crackheads and hustlers were busy doin' what they do. What happened next fucked everybody up...

Out came the Ruger. The lady with the donkey for an ass pulled the hammer right out of her purse, then started lettin' that shit rip! Each time the gun went off, it sounded just like the thunder that was rumblin' through the night sky.

Bock!

The woman whacked one nigga who was leanin' up against the pissy-ass wall. When that nigga fell down, you could see the bloody silhouette of his face splashed right on the goddamn wall!

Bock! Bock!

Two other dudes tried to dip inside one of the apartments, but got their backs torn instead.

No one ever understood how crackheads could run so fast after gettin' high out'f their fuckin' minds, but two of'em jetted toward the lady with the Ruger, ran up the side of the

Face/ Fetty Boy

wall, then bolted through the door. That shit looked like somethin' straight out'f The Matrix.

Bock! Bock!

Two more shots echoed off the walls of the hallway and, when it was all said and done, the last hustler and crackhead was sprawled on the dingy floor leakin' like two punctured pig bellies.

The woman kicked over every dead body in the hall. Hector... dead than a motherfucka. June Bug... even deader. Crackhead Anne defied all odds that said she would die from an overdose. Instead, the bitch ended up gettin' sent on her way to meet her maker because of a bullet up in her wig piece. "Oh, well... sometimes you bite the bear... sometimes the bear bites you. That's just how the game go," the grandma shooter thought with no remorse about what just popped off.

* * * * *

Inside my own head, I was laughin' like a motherfucka. But I had to carry out every detail of my plan to make sure nobody was gonna dime me out. When I stepped back out into the stormy night, I adjusted the fake butt pad I was wearin' - that shit was startin' to make my ass itch.

A few suspect niggas started gatherin' around after hearin' the shots pop off. I made sure they saw me, or saw the old lady with the donkey and the big-ass titties, by bustin' a couple'f shots in the air. I even screamed out like a bitch as I made my way to the whip that I bought from a well-known car thief from Newark I had met down The Berg.

I jetted straight over to Bunker's Hill. That was a deserted part of town not too many cats were up on. I parked the car next to the train tracks, then changed out'f my costume quicker than Clark Kent in a phone booth. Doused the ride with gasoline, then stood back and watched the flames dance to life. Torching the dress, wig, butt pad and fake tits.. all that shit. The only thing I kept was the hammer.

The shit went like clockwork. I already had Tiffany's car

Face/ Fetty Boy

waitin' for me by the tracks. I told her I'd have that shit back to her by midnight, but I was outside her mom's apartment by 11:35.

I honked the horn a few times.

"Damn, Fetty!" Tiff shouted. "You mad early! I thought you said midnight and shit?"

"Expect the unexpected," I said. "You know what I'm sayin'?"

That bitch loved it when I spit that street life pimp shit at her - I could see that pussy creamin' through her tight-ass nylon stretch pants.

Hmph - by one A.M., I had already splashed the back of Tiff's throat two or three times. That bitch definitely mastered the art of givin' brain. Don't let nobody tell you nothin' different. I ain't a selfish nigga; I banged her back loose until she nutted all over my dick. Ha! That bitch is a real freak 'cause, after she creamed my dick, she turned around and sucked that motherfucka clean, again.

While she was goin' in on the cockasaurus, my Mobile Motorola flip phone rang. It snapped me out'f my thoughts 'cause I was really runnin' the events of the past few hours through my mind. Did I get all 'dem niggas? Did I get the nigga that shot Hubby? Mother had'em... mother made'em... motherfuck'em!

My phone rang for the third and fourth time.

"Who 'dis?" I said.

"It's me, Freez, nigga!" he sounded shook daddy.

I felt myself gettin' ready to bust off in Tiff's mouth again, so I rushed the convo. "Waddup, nigga? It's late, run your mouth."

"Yo, mad niggas just got pushed over in the Broadway building, big bro!"

In my best surprised voice, "Word?" I said. "Get the fuck out'f here!"

"Real talk, nigga. Yo, where you at, though?" Freez questioned.

I laughed. "I'm at your ol' lady crib... oh shit..." I

Face/ Fetty Boy

was definitely on my way to givin' Tiff another milk shake.
"My ol' lady?" Freez retorted.
"Yeah, dun." I said. I handed the phone to Tiff," Here, say wassup to my nigga, bitch." My dick was steady taking up all the room in her mouth.
"Hmm... hey, Freez," Tiff mumbled into the phone, then went back to her part-time job.
"Yo, you's a nasty nigga for real, son," Freez said. "Y'all been there all night?"
"Oh, shit.. yeah, nigga! I'm on nut number five! And you fuckin' my shit up!" I said.
"My bad, son. I'll see you on the block."
I ain't really hear that nigga. I had already flipped the phone shut. What I wanted to do was done; I needed to plant the seed for my alibi. Freez thought that me and Tiffany had been in this motherfucka all night. And, speakin' of plantin' seeds... goddamn, this bitch just slurped my balls in her mouth! God don't like ugly, but He sure loves the hungry... 'cause Tiff had a mouthful! And, like Pac said, revenge is the sweetest thing next to gettin' some pussy or your dick sucked.
The jakes talkin' about my potnah's death is an ongoing investigation. Oh, yeah? Well, now the shootin' in the Broadway building is an ongoing investigation. Case cold, game cold, niggas! No leads! Investigate that shit!

Face/ Fetty Boy

Chapter 3: Illy-Ill

I let a couple'f months roll off the calendar. I had my faculties on some get money, but lay low type shit 'cause the streets was watchin' - and soon to be talkin', too. As far as everyone knew, wasn't shit happenin' on the block. But just because I was stationary didn't mean my black ass wasn't makin' major moves.

Blendin' in meant I had to act like the rest of these thespian-ass niggas, which was makin' me sick to my stomach. All I heard was everybody givin' their spiel about what they thought went down at the Broadway building. And, just like everyone on the block, I acted surprised like I didn't know shit. I heard one lil' nigga jokin' around talkin' about, "Fetty did it!" That's that bullshit right there, I thought to myself. I ain't never met a nigga who would tell on himself and not tell on another nigga.

The streets ain't nothin' but a wealth of paper and information. Usually, the gossip that spread in the hood was on point than a motherfucka. But the way I laid my game down flat had the entire hood fucked up. Not only did I use misdirection on all these lames by makin' people think a crazy bitch pulled this off, but I pushed anybody who could've possibly put the pieces together. Let other niggas tell it, everybody and their

Face/ Fetty Boy

mama knew what went down. But it ain't what they know, people...it's what they can prove. It's all or nothin' from here on out.

The first thing on my agenda after comin' home was done; I wanted to avenge my nigga's death, and that was done. Nobody else stepped up to the fuckin' plate. My next goal was to shut all these flossin'-ass niggas down on the strip. I didn't want them niggas gettin' nothin'! Why? 'Cause when Hubby got pushed, that's what all these fake-ass clowns did... nothin'! We all know the mathematics to the game; nothin' plus nothin' equals nothin'!

After a while, the buzz about Broadway quieted down for good. The summer seemed to be approachin' quicker than expected, and it was nights like this that everybody couldn't help being posted up on the block.

Niggas and bitches came through showing off their new toys with candy colored paint jobs. I saw this one dude with one'f those bikes that had the twin-headlights fresh off the Kawasaki manufacturer line - just like the one Puff featured in "The Benjamins" video. That shit roared down the strip in a loud-ass shiny blur; I couldn't even see who was ridin' it.

Other kats sported through in whips with the systems pumpin' Mob Deep, Nas, Bad Boyz... without doubt, Pac was rippin' up the airwaves with his new shit "I Hit'em Up". A lot'f people opened up their windows and let their stereo systems shake the whole block to life. That night, G.G. Ave. was like 125th Street in front of the Apollo.

Hustlers were on the grind. Damn near all of'em were rockin' army fatigues. A real playah in the game knows to keep their antennas up when you see everybody rockin' the same shit – if somethin' pops off, it's hard to identify a person if everybody looks alike. That's especially true for a jury. It's mad easy to create doubt in a square's mind if there were a hundred people on the block wearin' the same shit as the person on trial.

Crackheads and fiends were out in droves.

Bitches were chasin' paper and dick - like flies on shit

Face/ Fetty Boy

they were all over the niggas that was getting money on the block.

Then there was the common crowd - people who played the block only because they lived there - gathering on the corners with their favorite liquor in hand wrapped in brown paper bags.

10:30 at night didn't mean shit, even the kids were still out jumpin' Double Dutch under the street lights.

The scene was electric from top to bottom. The Mom & Pop stores sold their little specialty foods - They usually stayed open late because, durin' the day, they would get the honest money, and at night, they stacked that not-so-honest money.

Some project niggas tried to roll through, as well; but they gassed up as soon as they hit the strip... they knew what it was hittin' for. Soldiers stayed posted up everywhere out here - in the alleyways, people's porches, storefronts, even on the rooftops. The shit looked like a scene parallel to Vietnam.

Amid the organized chaos, I heard somebody shoutin' my name out on some rah-rah shit. I ain't turn around or nothin'. I kept my ass posted up against a car owned by some red-bone chick named Kimberly that was tryin' to get my number. I kept sippin' my Henn-rock and countin' loot, at the same time, my eyes were scannin' the entire block tryin' to stay on point like a sniper.

"Where that nigga Fetty at!?!" the voice shouted again.

By this time, Dead Eye came from makin' a sale out this alleyway we called "the cut". The cut was a good spot to post up at 'cause, once you dashed through, you would end up several blocks over from the strip. That was good to know in case a raid jumped off. Dead Eye leaned up against the car next to me with a spliff in his mouth while I started spittin' some game to him about how we was gonna shut all these so-called money-getters down. "First the block, then other nigga's blocks one at a time, then the world, nigga," I told him. "All you

Face/ Fetty Boy

gotta do is play your part." All the while, the voice callin' my name was gettin' closer and closer.

"Yo, where that nigga Fetty at? All y'all niggas out here and ain't nobody seen Fetty?"

The person hollerin' my name didn't know it at the time, but all my lil' dudes started gatherin' around with their hands beneath their army jackets grippin' their bangers.

Shit was about to get thick. But just that quick, I started playin' the voice over in my head. There was only one nigga I knew whose loud-behind slick-soundin' voice could cut through all the noise on the strip.

I told my team to breathe easy, then turned around. Just like I thought. It was my boy-boy... motherfuckin' Illy-Ill. One of my ace-boon-coons.

A few weeks back, I heard some talk about Illy-Ill gettin' out'f Bordentown, another one of New Jersey's young adult facilities, aka Buck Town. All the young niggas on the block called Bordentown gladiator school. Dudes came out'f there with their fight game up to the ceiling. Not only were those lil' niggas knucklin' up all the time, but they came out spittin' rhymes by some dude they called Jay-Z. Older niggas on the strip was like, "Who the fuck is that?"

Illy-Ill was just like them young boys. He was a classic live wire fo'sho'! He had been locked up for four years after catchin' a bad break ridin' the bus back from coppin' smack in Harlem. "One Time", meaning the poe-poe, ran down on him as he got off at the bus stop on Broadway & Graham; he got knocked with a half'f bird. It was his first case, but still... the courts sent my nigga down shit's creek.

Niggas in the hood was happy about that. Not only was Illy-Ill comin' up in the dope game, but he was also a beast with that boxin' shit. Most niggas came out'f Bordentown ready to toss somebody's grill piece; Ill went in that motherfucka takin' titles to add to the ones he already had on the streets! He was a six footer, but a skinny, witty muscular type dude. Nobody knew for sure, but word was he was on his way to

Face/ Fetty Boy

the Olympics before he got knocked. He always said that little bid fucked his life up. But Ill loved the streets and he respected the game.

I motioned with a slight head nod, then everyone peeped across the street to see Ill standin' there wearin' an army jacket and a pair'f black jeans. He still looked to be every bit of the live wire that he was as he hustled his way over to give me a hug. Illy-Ill was a dynamite stick that could blow over and over again at any time. He could go from zero to a hundred in less than a second! The way he is now is the way he was the day I first met him - a straight thoroughbred. And for that reason alone, he had my respect.

"Oh, shit! That's my nigga Fetty!" he shouted. "Wassup, doggie!?!" I don't know where Illy-Ill got this "doggie" shit from. I never said anything about it 'cause it was funny as hell every time he said it.

"Wassup, my nigga?" I responded after embracin' him in a gangster's hug. "When yo' ass get out, Ill?"

"Today, nigga. How you see me right now is how I walked out them motherfuckin' prison doors."

"I'm sayin' though, son, what happen to your eye and shit?" I asked. As soon as the question left my lips, I remembered that Bordentown had a boxing team that was a force to be reckoned with. Ill probably let a punch slip through while he was knock-in' somebody the fuck out.

"Pht! This ain't nothin' but cataracts from bein' in the ring, doggie, feel me? You know Illy-Ill go stupid hard when the gloves are on... or off. It's the same ol' thing to Illy-Ill, doggie."

While me and Ill chopped it up, everybody else just sat back and peeped the scenery. Most of these dudes on the block weren't even around when Ill was last out here. Shit – on the real, most of'em were babies.

I could see some people were mad jealous 'cause I was treatin' Illy-Ill like he was my brother from another mother. Even some of the stray bitches on the strip started hawkin'.

Face/ Fetty Boy

"A, yo," Ill said, "lemme holla at you alone for a minute." nodding my head at Dead Eye; that was just to tell him to keep his eyes - or eye - sharp while I kicked it with my nigga for a bit. Me and Illy-Ill decided to walk up Godwin Ave. We crossed the street and played the sidewalk heavy just to avoid all the hustle and bustle away from the rest of the hungry-ass hooligans.

"What's on your mind, my nigga?" I asked.

"Dig, right... you know that herb-ass nigga Piggy over on Hamilton Ave, doggie?"

Piggy. I never let any thoughts about a nigga like Piggy rent any space in my head. How the fuck he gonna be a gangster and his ass is named after the fuckin' jakes? This nigga is named after an animal that will eat it's own doo-doo 'cause he can't control his own fuckin' appetite.

"Yeah, I know that scumbag," I answered. "Why?"

Ill started goin' in on how this nigga Piggy was tossin' my name around on some foul shit to'm. He was tryin' to put batteries in Ill's back tellin' him not to fuck with me 'cause I was bad dope. Ill said that Piggy was tellin' motherfuckas that I was havin' the young niggas on my team go around killin' people.

"And peep this shit, doggie," Illy-Ill continued, "That fag-ass nigga is tryin' to fuck your rep up with all the connects. He tellin' them that you be makin' deals, then beatin' niggas n'shit. He kicked your back in to my face, doggie!"

"Yo, Ill, that's just 'cause that nigga got no choice but to play the sidelines like a cheerleader. We done ran his old ass up off of G.G. Ave.. He could eat a dick. Fuck'm, nawmean? He's just playin' movie scripts in his head. He is right about one thing though, Ill. I do have goons and guns on deck. But I'm too happy to see you to be payin' that big-dumb-country nigga any mind. Let him keep wet dreamin', fuck around and get wet. Fifty shots out the tech will soak his ass, that's a bet."

Me and Ill chopped it up for a minute. I was happy to

Face/ Fetty Boy

see that nigga for real. We dipped into the liquor store and copped some more of that Henney. We tossed that shit back. Fucked with a few bitches. Other niggas kept tryin' to get in our company like we was all Good Fellas n'shit. We told them whack-ass niggas to beat it.

This other dude named Born with the gold in his grill rolled through with his little car-stealin' clique, drinkin' Jack Daniels. Born was this karate nigga from down on Union Ave. Him and his team had a little rep n'shit. They came through on some rah-rah shit, just wantin' to be seen. That's when I really knew that Illy-Ill hadn't changed a bit. He turned around and cracked Born right in his mug... blood rushin'...split his shit to the white meat. I ain't even look at the few niggas that were mobbin' with Born. Once they saw me, they gassed the fuck up in the other direction. I knew all that karate shit wasn't about nothin'.

Ill ran the nigga's pockets, then stepped off. I looked at my henchman like he was crazy.

"What, doggie?" he said. "That nigga's lil' brother Prince ass betted Illy-Ill on the Giants game when we were down Bee Tee. Nigga went home and never paid me - nawmean?"

"Same ol' Illy-Ill," I said. Always refering to himself in the third person. "Yo, look... I got this money n'shit for you at the spot. I'm gonna roll through tomorrow and hit you off." I offered the cash, but I should've known that Ill wouldn't have accepted it. He never did like takin' handouts. Everything he got, he hustled hard for it. You gotta keep a nigga like this on the team 'cause that type'f hunger is unexplainable.

"Man, later for that money shit," Ill said. "Illy-Ill ready to start grindin' tonight, doggie - ASAP! I ain't waitin' and I ain't bullshittin'. Them crackers done maxed me out, doggie. I ain't home on no furlough. I ain't got no parole. No programs. No ankle bracelet. None of that shit. I'm freer than Nelson Mandela, my nigga."

Ill was a slick talkin' nigga for real. But he meant what-

Face/ Fetty Boy

ever came out of his mouth. His talk was real. I remember back in the day he used to have this silver coin. He'd flip that shit high in the air. If it landed on heads... niggas would know Illy-Ill was in the area 'cause he was gonna come through and rob everything! If it came up tails... he kept it moving on some chill shit. He must've flipped the coin right before he came to see me 'cause this nigga was ready to just jump right back in the game like it ain't nothin'.

"You sure that's what you wanna do, Ill? You just came home today n'shit."

"My nigga, why you think I came straight to you? You think the streets is talkin', nigga, you should hear the jails! Niggas talkin' 'bout you got that work, money, and a fuckin' cemetery under your belt. I'm off my Jay-Z shit, doggie. Can a nigga live?"

Illy-Ill was always a funny nigga. Sometimes he said shit and I ain't know what the fuck he was talkin' about, but I would laugh anyway 'cause he was an animated nigga. Like right now, I didn't have a reasonable clue, much less a reasonable doubt about who this Jay-Z nigga was he kept talkin' about. The one thing I did know was that I loved how Illy-Ill was comin' right now. You gotta feel his drive. First night out and he wants to get right back in the game? Most niggas would expect dudes on the strip to pamper them for a month or two. Either that or they would be milkin' some broad for her paycheck or welfare money. Not my nigga Ill. Like I said, he hustled hard for his. We made our way back to where Dead Eye was hustlin'.

"Yo, Dead Eye. Come here, lil' bro. Dig, give Illy-Ill those fifty grams I just gave you to bag up." As he ran off to hit the stash, "Yo, Ill, I got a hundred more for you, too. I'll hit you off when we come outside tomorrow. But do me a favor for tonight, my nigga."

"You say it, then it is what it is, doggie."

"Let's just chill for tonight. Get drunk. When you ready to take it down, I'll give you the work we talked about so you can bag it up yourself."

Face/ Fetty Boy

"Yo, that's wassup. It's a bet, Fetty. For real. I'm gonna get drunk off some of that Absolute, ya feel me?"

I laughed to myself. Illy-Ill been locked up for too long talkin' that Absolute shit. And this is right after we just got finished sippin' on some Henn-rock.

"You's a funny-ass nigga, man," I said. "Shyiiit, don't nobody fuck with that Absolute no more; that shit done with. We does the Hennessey thing out here. That Absolute and Christian Brothers shit is for them broke niggas who ain't gettin' no paper.

We hit the liquor store up again and copped another fifth. Ill was on his Martin Lawrence shit; he had everybody crackin' the fuck up. It was a little past 11:00 and I kept peepin' my watch 'cause we had been out there for a few hours and hadn't seen Freez all night.

Then, here come Freez late as usual. At least he ain't drivin' that fucked up loud-ass car no more. His new purple M3 looked almost invisible under the dark sky.

"They finally let that crazy nigga Illy-Ill back out here?" Freez shouted after he rolled down the passenger's side window.

"We heard you was in the system wilin' out, yo."

Illy-Ill didn't hear nothin' Freez was sayin'. His eyes were glued to the whip and his head wouldn't stop boppin' because the car's sound system was bumpin' Mobb Deep's "Shook Ones" all the way up and down the strip.

"Aaaah shit!" Illy-Ill shouted. "Yo, 'freez', nigga! Hands in the air!" Ill always liked to make fun of nigga's names. "This ride is meltin' Hot! Lemme drive that over to 10th Ave right quick so I can go see my cousin."

"You know how to handle a stick, nigga?" Freez asked.

"Oh, shit! That's a stick, doggie?. Yo, Fetty, man... you gonna have to drive this shit, nigga. The only time Illy-Ill work the stick is when I'm fuckin' them bitches - nawmean?"

"Yo, Ill," Freez said with a smile, "you is still a funny-ass nigga, yo."

Face/ Fetty Boy

"That's how I do, doggie. I'll break a nigga jaw while laughin' at his ass, ya feel me? Later for that, though. Get out, nigga. Let Fetty drive this motherfucka! I wanna ride shotgun with the king of the town."

Ha - this nigga Ill just called me the king of the town n'shit. He wasn't too far off. I ain't even execute my entire plan yet and niggas was already bowin' down ready to kiss the ring. Plus my nigga Illy-Ill is home, too. Man, we gonna be sellin' more white powder out this bitch than Johnson & Johnson ever could imagine!

Ill is already gettin' in right where he fit in, too. Before he left the slum, he had a reputation for pushin' up on niggas... sonnin' them out for their shit. In a way, that's what he was doin' to Freez right now by makin'm get out'f his own car. I could tell Freez felt some kind'f way. I just gave him a head nod tellin' him to breathe easy and let me and Ill cruise for a bit. Freez hopped in the back.

Illy-Ill jumped right in the passenger's seat not wasting no time. As soon as he got in the car, he took the Mobb Deep tape out and put in this nigga Jay-Z. Me and Freez looked at him like, "How the fuck you gonna be walkin' around with the nigga's album in your pocket?"

The dude could spit; he said some slick shit on the tape. But me and Freez was still on our raw shit - Mobb Deep, Lox, Pac.

Ill had me cruise through damn near every drug spot in P-Town. And every time Ill saw somebody he knew, he pushed up on them niggas. The nigga would yell, "Pull over, doggie!" at lest ten times. Every kat we saw, Ill would be like, "Yo, that's my cousin right there!"

I was like, "Damn, nigga, how many cousins you got?"

By the time we reached 12th Ave, we saw a bunch'f niggas gathered around smokin', drinkin', and hustlin'. Ill hopped out the car and walked right into the middle of these nigga's cipher. Ill hit them niggas up for damn near everything. I saw one dude give up his chain and watch.

Face/ Fetty Boy

"Yo, Freez, you see this shit right here?" I said. "This is why this nigga wanted us to ride wit'm. He knew once niggas seen us wit'm, his intimidation factor would swell up like the Hulk, feel me? Ain't nobody gonna front on him with us sittin' right here."

Freez ain't really say much. I think he was still on tilt about Ill wantin' to floss around in his car. In my mind, I'm thinkin', "Man, the nigga just came home, Freez... lighten the fuck up." But I ain't say shit. What's understood don't need to be said, ya' dig?

After we hit about six or seven spots, Ill came off with over five Gs, a bunch'f jewelry, a few bitches numbers – nigga had a good night. Fuck it, he deserved more than that... Ill was that motherfuckin' nigga.

I maneuvered the V back toward the strip. Once we hit G.G. Ave, we noticed that the block was deader than the morgue out that motherfucka'. Nobody was around, except a flock of crackheads chasin' after them big-bag nicks.

We pulled up in front of the cut and Dead Eye appeared out'f nowhere like a fuckin' ninja.

"Yo, Dead Eye, what the fuck happened out here, lil' bro?" I said. "Where everybody go?"

"Man, them Task Force niggas came through. Motherfuckas scattered like a bunch'f roaches when you turn the lights on n'shit."

"Word up?" Niggas always looked to me to make the decisions, so I had to ask, "They get anybody I give a fuck about?"

"Just Lil'-Goochie n'them for loiterin', yo. Gooch wasn't dirty, though. But they did find a bunch'f shit. Niggas tossed their hammers while they were runnin', but the Task Force found most'f them shits. They even went in the cut and got your manz fifty grams."

Sometimes I amaze my fuckin' self - on the real - 'cause I swear to God, I knew this lil' nigga was gonna say that shit.

Face/ Fetty Boy

"Them niggas came through deep - fifteen boats and a paddy wagon deep! Ya' feel me?"

"Yeah, I heard, lil' bro. Listen, peep game; take it in for the night, son. I don't want you out here unless you got lookouts spotted up on the rooftops - you dig?"

"But money gonna be out this motherfucka, Fetty! You know how this shit be."

"Fuck that; take it in. Better safe than sorry, lil' nigga. This team got plans. And plans only work if you got soldiers to carry'em out. I don't need none'f y'all gettin' popped on some dumb shit."

"True 'dat."

After I convinced Dead Eye to bounce for the night, we started to head down the hill toward The Towers where Illy-Ill's grandmother lived. That's where Ill liked to post up at to get away from the drama in the streets. But as I rounded the corner, Ill told me to head over to C.C.P. project buildings. He wanted to check in on his cousin named "Word Is Bond" or some shit like that. This nigga and his motherfuckin' cousins! "Aight, yo," I said. "Just make sure you meet me and Freez on the strip by 1:00 tomorrow afternoon. We gotta make up for those fifty that them jakes took. I still got some more shit to hit you off wit', though. You good?" Ill got out the car, then Freez hopped in the front seat. Ill just stood outside the whip starin' in at us like he had hell-a-shit on his mind.

Finally, "Yeah, I'm good," he said. "Oh, yeah... one more thing, doggie..." Ill stared right into my eyes. The nigga didn't blink. And his mouth was fixed like he was about to go in on a nigga in the ring. He told me some shit that reminded me the game is mad real, "...Watch them niggas that's close to you, dawg. It be the ones who smoke blunts witcha' that wanna getcha'. One..."

Face/ Fetty Boy

Chapter 4: Can't Go Wrong

Murphy's Law - what can go wrong... will! You hear all those country boys in the game down in the dirty South say that shit. Them country niggas spoke the truth.

My first three and a half months back on the streets seemed like nothin' could go wrong. I had a plan. The shit fell into place perfectly. I knew Freez was gonna have some work waitin' on me. I took the bird and the hundred sleeves of smack that he gave me, then put the young boys on. Dead Eye and his little team sold all of it in no time. What they didn't know was that I had already found a connect to re-up with.

I was fuckin' wit' this kat named Jose Louis on 146th & Amsterdam Up-town Harlem - a little spot right in the cut. I never liked travelin' that far just to get some drugs, But, it was necessary 'cause I didn't want niggas fuckin' wit' my protocol.

One thing about me, fo'sho', Fetty Boy respects the game. When I came home, power moves was made, but I laid back and peeped the scene out at the same time. Just two years ago, niggas were runnin' up in other nigga's spots robbin' the connects. Since Mayor Gulianni took over NYC and added more cops to the streets, the fuzz response time got quicker – niggas were forced to run game on the connects. The street-rules have always been a nigga is only allowed to keep what he can hold onto. Now, niggas was beatin' the connects like that shit wasn't about nothin' - straight gettin' butter from the duck whenever they could. The trick was to spend big. Cop enough raw from the connect so they would fuck with you again and again. The thing was, you had to do that shit for a little while, but don't let them learn shit about you - your real name, where you're from, shit like that. The connects started gettin' smarter, though; they stopped lettin' the hustlers go inside their buildings. Instead, niggas had to wait outside in a designated vehicle to place an order. It was like bein' at a motherfuckin' drive-through.

    I told Jose my name was Born-E and that I had a quiet little operation down in Asbury Park. I gave him some story about not liking to take long trips back and forth on the NJ Turnpike. I told him about the State Troopers bein' on some racial profilin' type shit - the best lie to tell is the one that got a little truth in it. I told him for that reason, and that reason alone, I liked to cop big - real big - just every once in a while, though. It was a provocative plan to get this nigga's cocaine in my hand!

    Jose ate that story up like it was filet mignon. The first time, I just copped one bird. Next, it was two. The two turned into three, then four - which made Jose smile every time he saw my face.

    At seventeen-five ($17,500) a pop, in order to keep my order big with the connect, I had to start coppin' for other niggas, too. I'd throw him thirty-five grand for two. Freez would get one for himself. Ron Gotti would go in with us, also. Basically, any nigga on the strip that wanted to get their hands on this bangin'-ass coke had to go through me. I had to play that shit smart, though; I didn't beat none of my friends; I needed them just as much as they needed me. What they paid for is what they got. The only thing I charged extra for was for me havin' to take the risk back and forth across the George Washington Bridge with mad paper and the bomb. Shiiiit, I came up off of that alone. It had to be done that way;

Face/ Fetty Boy

I couldn't put other niggas onto the connect. Movin' like that gave me complete control over the strip. I knew when niggas had coke and how much.

It was about 10:30 on a Tuesday mornin' when I arrived at the coke spot early just to make sure Jose had enough product to cover my order. Man, if niggas thought 4th Ward was jumpin', then they needed to take a trip up to Harlem.

I never saw so many fiends, prostitutes, and hustlers all in one spot before. They were some brazen and bold motherfuckas, right out in the broad daylight, coppin', smokin', shootin' up... trickin'. The shit was fucked up for real. The buildings were missin' windows and doors. The streets were potholed. Motherfuckas ain't have no teeth. Goddamn, even the fuckin' mailman was a crackhead. Even with all this goin' on, it was still like a regular neighborhood. People were makin' food deliveries on peddle bikes. Business suit wearin' dudes came through to catch the bus over on Amsterdam. People hollered out the windows back and forth askin' to borrow some sugar or some shit like that. It fucked me up, at first, how two worlds could just coexist right next to each other like it wasn't nothin'. It was the same shit back in the 4th Ward. The only difference was Harlem was bigger and way more wide the fuck open.

I brought myself back to reality after peepin' the scenery for a few minutes. I was comin' to see Jose so I could cop big... real fuckin' big. But for that nigga, today was also gonna be the day that Murphy's Law went into effect!

Jose's top soldier - this Gwat named Tito - came out from the building. I acted like I didn't see him at first; niggas do strange shit when they think nobody's watchin'.

Tito decided to peep me standin' there for almost a minute before he said, "Wassup, poppa? My main mang Boon. Wassup with you, mang?"

This nigga's accent had him talkin' crazier than a motherfucka. Every time he tried to say "Born", that shit came out sounding like "Boon" instead. Actin' surprised, "Oh, shit, Tito.

Face/ Fetty Boy

How you, yo?" I asked.

"I cool, mang. Ju'know?"

"Yo, where's Jose?" I asked. "I need to holla at him before I put my order in."

He looked at me sideways, while puffin' on a Newport at the same time. One of his eyebrows was raised higher than the other and his upper lip was curled in a snarl like he was on some tough nigga shit. If I didn't need all'f this coke, I would have smacked the nigga so hard, he would've forgot how to speak Spanish.

He nodded his head toward the light-blue astro-van that they usually had me sit in whenever I came to cop.

"He comeeng soon, mang. Sit in van. I go get heem for you." Tito disappeared into the building.

I looked around through the van's slightly tinted windows and watched the electricity of the block shock the world. I wasn't sure, but I think I peeped a few gwat niggas on the rooftops clockin' my position. A few papis strolled by the van, duckin' their bandanna-covered heads to have a look inside, basically mindin' my business instead'f their own.

Before I knew it, five minutes had passed. As soon as the bandanna bitches went on their way, Jose popped up out'f nowhere. He pulled open the van door, then sat in the seat opposite mine. without giving him a chance to hit me with his usual greeting. I went straight in... hard...

"Yo, Jose, listen, bro. I came up here mad early so I could beat the traffic and duck them State Trooper boys over in Jersey. My manz let me hold the car with the stash spot n'shit..." Jose kept tappin' my knee tryin' to stop me from runnin' my game. He was shakin' his head up and down as if he knew already what I was goin' to ask him. But I'm an A to the Z type person; once I start somethin', I goes all the way in. "...Now, I told you a couple'f months back when we first started doin' business that I just came home. I ain't tryin' to find my way back to prison for traffickin' all this work back and forth, poppa. I've been spendin' hell-a-paper with you. I ain't come up here

Face/ Fetty Boy

with no shorts, the money matched the product every single time. Now listen, your coke is the best shit from Miami to Maine; shiiiit, it might even be the best from Maine to Spain, Bro! Who the fuck knows? What I wanna know is what you think about this shit?"

I unzipped the book-bag sittin' in my lap and let the smell of the paper fuck with Jose's nose for a lil' bit. Even the richest cartel would allow itself to be hypnotized by money; how the fuck you think them niggas got so rich?

"This right here is a hundred and five large, Poppa. But, before I throw this shit at you, I'm gonna need some consignment from you, dawg..."

Jose started breathin' in the sight and the smell off all the stacks in my book-bag. I had'm; his mind wasn't on nothin' but the money. "...I can't keep running back and forth up here coppin', yo. It would be better for me if I just came up here with the loot while I still had product movin' in South Jersey. If that ain't swift enough for you, then you gonna have to meet me halfway with the coke. We'll make the deal in Newark somewhere 'cause this travelin' shit is gettin' mad dangerous for me. Dig, Poppa? If not, I'm gonna have to take this paper to somebody who do dig what I'm sayin'."

Jose didn't say shit. He just sat there lookin' at the cash. I knew what was goin' through his mind; there ain't a connect on the East Coast that liked givin' out consignments. But every connect liked that motherfuckin' bread.

I zipped my book-bag shut just to make Jose think that the hundred and five large was slippin' through his fingers. He patted me on the back of my hand tryin' to tell me to relax a bit. Yeah... I got this nigga.

"How much..." Jose paused to place emphasis on his next words "...consignment you talkeeng about, my mang?"

"Like I said, I got a hundred-five right here. I'm coppin' six of them things with my own money, feel me? At least you could spot me six to match what I'm spendin' - unless you tryin' to throw a nigga more than that?" Butter from the duck,

Face/ Fetty Boy

nigga, I thought to myself. Ha, ha... butter from the motherfuckin' duck. "Them bricks go quick down in South Jersey, and I could be your man down there. But I need more product so I don't have to keep comin' up here. You see the news n'shit, Jose. You know what's goin' on with them Jersey State Troopers and all that racial profilin' shit, right?"

I was spittin' the game from my hip at him like a true playah would spit it. I already knew that Jose wasn't feelin' that meet me halfway shit. These niggas Up-town were relaxed and extra greedy. Ain't no way in hell a connect like this is gonna be travelin' with some work; especially not across state lines.

* * * * *

"Consignment, huh?" Jose said. He kept his upper lip curved and repeatedly ran his tongue across his teeth as if he had some candy stuck in his gums. I could tell by the look in his eyes that he was buyin' my story. "Ju'know, we get big shipment last night. I trust you, poppa. You want four kilos on top'f kilos you want to buy? This, I can do. If this go right, me an'ju, we do big tings - comprende?"

"Got one!" I screamed to myself after I saw Jose give a head nod to one of his runners.

That's what my mind was sayin', but my mouth had to keep strokin' this gwat nigga's ego, "That's what's up," I said with a smile. "Jose, my brotha, you will not regret this."

When I handed Jose the bag with the stacks, his eyes grew wide like somebody was holdin' them open with two fingers. I swore I saw a tear of joy roll down his face; money must really get this nigga's dick hard. Too bad, 'cause this is the last time Jose is ever gonna see my ass. And it's definitely the last time I'm gonna be handing over my loot. "You gonna have to take yo' ass down to Asbury Park and look for 'Boon', nigga," I joked to myself, as Jose got out the van and disappeared with my money.

While clownin' this nigga inside my head, Tito bopped his frail ass up to the Astro-Van and hopped in. He had a plastic bag in his hand; it was like one'f those bags you get at the grocery market for fifteen items or less. Inside were a bunch'f old shirts, but the shirts were really there to hide the ten keys.

"You pay for six Kilos," Tito said, "but thee boss throw to you four more. Ju'know what that is, poppa?"

After a pause and a smirk at this dumb-ass nigga, "Yeah, yo," I said. "I know how much that is. It's seventy."

"Seven... and... four zeroes." When Tito repeated the price back to me, he mimicked the numbers with his hand as if he was doin' sign language. The more time spent with this nigga, the more and more I felt like crackin' him in his shit - this ol' missin' tooth-ass spick. "seven and four zeroes, this is important number, Poppa. Ju'know what other number is important? Hmph? Ju don't know? Thirty. Thirty also important number, poppa. It is how much days you have to pay back the seven and four zeroes. Rain. Sleet. Snow. Tu comprende?"

Sittin' in that van and lookin' at that nigga, I was never more happy to beat a motherfucka in my life! Word!

"Jose no want to come look for you, mang. If you no come in thirty days-"

I had to cut that nigga off before he said somethin' that was gonna make me have to blast my way out'f Harlem, "Just tell Jose "Boon" said good lookin' out, aight? And fuck thirty days, nigga. Y'all will see me in three weeks - God willing. It's a good deal for the both'f us; ain't nothin' gonna go wrong. Now, lemme get the fuck out'f here wit' all this work before one'f these dumb-ass niggas around here gets antsy."

* * * * *

Ha - ain't nothin' gonna go wrong except for y'all niggas. Those next few weeks, shit on the strip was out'f fuckin' con-

Face/ Fetty Boy

trol! Once I gave everybody their work, then put a few other niggas on, the dollars started rollin' in like pizza dough. I was on some floss 'cause I'm the boss type shit for real. I was blowin' twenty to thirty stacks a week at the gamblin' hole - in - the - wall spots alone. On top of that, I was buyin' all kinds'f whips - foreign cars, SUVs, hoopties... all that shit. I'd cruise for a while, then crash them shits up; I'd end up givin' most of the cars away to my lil' manz n'em.

Sometimes, if I crashed a ride, I'd have to hop out and haul ass. Nigga like me ain't have no driver's license; plus I stayed bent with a fiff on me - jakes ain't gettin' me for no fuckin' DUI or for carryin' a concealed weapon. I was buyin' all the stock on the shelves at the bars in the club and the liquor stores. One week, I had a tab so high that shit cost more than my last ride - a Q-45 Infinity!

When I get that liquor up in me, it ain't nothin' nice. My heart gets cold - colder than a whore's heart in the 1950's. And my speech is slicker than that whore's pimp.

Talk about a nigga losin' his grip. I was straight wildin' after that come up from them Up-town gwats. I needed to get a handle on my shit and quick! My lavish habits was takin' a toll. Money was gettin' low. I was rippin' and runnin' without rest. I couldn't drive around any longer without a license if I wanted to continue duckin' Paterson Police.

Get a license.
Get moms to put a new whip in her name.
Get on my grind and find a new connect to beat.
Not necessarily in that order, but that was my new plan. 'Cause I learned earlier in the game that if you don't have nothin' goin', you ain't got shit comin'.

* * * * *

Who would've thought passin' the written DMV test was gonna be such a headache? The test wasn't hard, it was just

Face/ Fetty Boy

tricky. I thought I could just roll through there and pass it with common sense and street smarts. I failed that shit three fuckin' times before realizing that I needed to study the handbook.

It was a Friday, Memorial Day weekend, and we had run into my homegirl Sha-Sha. She used to live on the strip before I got locked up. Her and her family must've moved 'cause I ain't seen them since I've been back. But, on Memorial Day, everybody makes a cameo through the strip. Niggas roll through flossin' their new whips and rockin' gear they got from one of the spots over in NewYork. Females weren't any different. Their hair was done. The big-hoop earrings and ill extensions came out. Most'f them rocked their little mall outfits - skirts that fit like a second layer of skin and raised mid-drift tops that were just as tight so they could show off their pierced belly buttons.

Me and Freez were on the block chillin' while the strip was buzzin' like a 5,000 volt live wire. We were coolin' in front of Auel's Grocery Store. Auel was this six-foot-six three hundred pound Puerto Rican-ass nigga. He had to be that big if he wanted to keep his store in the hood. While sittin' inside Freez's freshly painted candy-apple red 325-i convertible, just killin' time before we headed to Bernini's East inside Garden State Mall; we had already ordered our outfits custom made to fit, we just needed to pick'em up.

Memorial Day wasn't the only reason why niggas were about to get their floss on. One of my dudes was throwin' a boogie-ass (bourgeois) party at this lil' spot called Brokers over in East Orange. The spot used to be called Club-88, until they fixed it up and renamed it.

As I sat in Freez's ride, "Fetty?" I heard this high-pitched but sexy voice call out. I turned around and saw my homegirl Sha-Sha standing on the sidewalk lookin' like a doggie style just waitin' to happen.

"Oh, shit!" I smiled and said. "Sha-Sha, what's good wit' you, yo?"

Face/ Fetty Boy

Sha stepped closer to the whip and leaned in to kiss me. "Damn, Fetty, when you came home?" she asked with a smile that was almost too big for her face.

"Sha, I've been out here since January, tryin' to eat a meal or two."

"And how is it I'm just runnin' into you? I walk through here all the time on my way home."

"I thought this strip was your home; where you stayin' at now?"

Sha-Sha told me that her family had moved down on the Boulevard. For somebody who used to live in the ghetto, that was a huge come up. We kicked it for a bit while waitin' on Freez to come out'f the bodega. She asked me what my plans were now that I was back on the streets. When she asked the question, she batted her eyelashes and flashed me a naughty smile. Sha-Sha knew what the fuck it was... I bleed and breathe this shit out here.

Instead of tellin' her my business in the streets, I put her D to how I was attendin' Essex County Community College. She was impressed by that shit; most bitches are when they find out that a thoroughbred know how to think, fuck, and smack the shit out'f them at the same time.

"Now, that's what's up, Fetty! What you studyin' over there?" she asked.

"Ain't nothin' major, ma. Just this little drafting degree I'm workin' on. I'm only doin' it 'cause my moms said that if I keep up this college shit and get my license, she would put a brand new ride in her name for me. Only problem is I can't pass that fuckin' written test, Sha."

"I know, right? That shit is kind'f hard. That's why I skipped all that shit and bought one'f them score-cards from my cousin."

Score-card? I thought to myself. What the fuck is that shit? Sha noticed I ain't know what the fuck she was talkin' about so she leaned further into the car to get all my attention.

Face/ Fetty Boy

Her big-ass chocolate titties poked out at me like I was in a 3-D theater. Sha-Sha done came the fuck up - for real!

"A score-card," she began to explain, "is this little card they give to high school students as a permit whenever they pass Driver's Ed. in school. My cousin got her hands on a bunch'f them shits."

"Word? What she sellin' them for?" I asked.

"Fifteen dollars."

Did she just say fifteen dollars? That's the problem with people nowadays; motherfuckas just don't know how to hustle. Her cousin could be out here sellin' them shits for a hundred bald eagles a pop! Probably more than that. It's easy to do the science to this here - niggas got money to buy all types of whips, but no license to drive' em. Dudes out here will come out their pocket for one of them score-cards... if they get hip to the game.

"Hey, yo, where your cousin at right now?" I asked.

"Probably home. We can call and see."

I told Sha-Sha to go inside Auel's Grocery so we could use the pay phone. I was souped up like Oodles & Noodles! This written test was kickin' my ass. I was so excited about cheatin' the system that I got change for a dollar and gave Sha all four quarters to make a twenty-five cent phone call.

After a few seconds, "Nina, wassup girl?" Sha-Sha said into the pay phone. "What you doin'? I hear that. Hey listen... I got my homeboy right here and he need one'f them score-cards."

Her cousin Nina must've started runnin' her mouth on some slick shit 'cause Sha wanted me to talk to her directly. "Hold on, Nina, lemme put Fetty on the phone."

A little jokey-joke should get this chick wide open. Plus, ladies don't know what to do with themselves once they hear my Barry White voice over the phone. "Yo, what's the deal, Ms. DMV," I asked. "When can we do this road test and all that?"

I got a little chuckle out'f her. Then she got right down

Face/ Fetty Boy

to business like she wasn't even beat.

"I go to school," she said, "and I don't get home until after three."

Pht! I know this bitch don't think she the only motherfucka that goes to school. "What a co-inkie-dink, I go to school too, yo. I don't make it back to the city til around the same time."

"What school you got to?" Nina asked.

"Essex County, but later for that shit. Whatchu doin' right now?"

"Now? Like, right now?"

What is this chick, a fuckin' owl? "Yeah, right now. 'Cause me and my manz is on our way to the mall. It's a little after six, we could swing by and do this thing right now."

After she sucked her teeth, "That's cool with me," Nina said. "I live in Building-1 of the Towers, apartment 8-M. Tell my cousin to give you my phone number in case you forget my address."

"As bad as I need my permit... believe me... I ain't gonna forget. You said Towers Building-1, apartment 8-N."

"No! I said-"

"I'm just fuckin' witchu. I know, it's 8-M, as in me and my manz will be there in fifteen minutes."

"If you say y'all comin', don't have me waitin' 'cause I got shit to do!"

Ha! I liked this chick already. I didn't even respond to her slick shit. I gave the phone back to Sha-Sha, then gave a head nod to my nigga Freez. "Yo, Sha, tell your smart-mouth cousin I'ma roll through in about fifteen."

After we walked out the store, me and Sha joked around a bit, while Freez started the engine to his car.

"Fetty, you look damn good," Sha-Sha said as she ran her hand down the center of my chest. "You got taller, too. You all big n'shit."

"Hmph - thanks, Sha." I pulled her to the sidewalk and handed her a fifty spot. "You don't know how bad I needed that permit."

She pulled me close to her and kissed me on my cheek, then whispered into my ear. "You was always one of the good ones," she said. "You and Hubert. That shit was real fucked up what happened to him."

Finally! I shouted inside my own head. Somebody showin' some real love for my nigga Hubby besides me. "Yo, good lookin', Sha... real talk."

I got in the car with Freez and we sped off. Just in time too. When Sha mentioned Hubby's name, my eyes almost became too weak to hold back my tears.

Face/ Fetty Boy

Chapter 5: Puppy Love at First Sight

Nobody in the Towers knew how to act when they saw us roll through. It only took eight minutes to get there; and as soon as Freez doubled parked the Beamer in the fire lane, everybody outside started marvelin' over the sound system and the BBS rims. I told Freez to park in the fire lane - all in a gesture of showin' off, of course - 'cause I knew all these dames out here would be on our dicks, and all these crab-ass niggas would be jealous as hell. Sometimes a gesture will go a lot farther than words. And, right now, Freez's whip was tellin' all these people in the Towers that the only language me and Freez talked... was bucks!

It didn't matter what these money-hungry bitches were doin', immediately, they had eyes on us.

People flooded their balconies; old folks, little kids, everybody was lookin' down from those tall-ass buildings. Those who didn't come outside stood in front of their building, just to see who was rollin' through the spot on some superstar shit.

Everybody was actin' like we were Suge & Dre or Big & Puff. I ain't gonna stunt, it sure did feel like it. And the whole time I was wonderin' if ol' girl Nina was peepin' us or not. Shawty kind'f turned me on the way she was talkin' slick on the phone.

I quickly pushed the thought from my mind 'cause the fact

Face/ Fetty Boy

of the matter was... the car wasn't mine, nor was I dressed to impress. I was still rockin' the same shit I wore to school earlier - a plain ol' pair of blue dockers, a casual button down, and a pair of fresh swamp Gortex Timberlands. Shit, if anything, Freez had a better shot at baggin' this chick than I did, especially if the bitch look like somethin'. He was the one actually four-wheelin' out this motherfucka. Not only was his car talkin' money, but his clothes were sayin' the same thing - dark-blue Ecko Unlimited jeans, Mecca t-shirt, and he was rockin' a brand new pair of Gortex's that didn't even hit the stores yet. My nigga had the chain danglin' with his pinkie-ring & things to match. That was his norm. That nigga dressed like that 'cause he had hella hustle and muscle - that's just how he does it.

As we got out the ride, I noticed Freez had left the top down and the system still thumpin'. He did right. We weren't plannin' on stayin' long, plus these soft-ass project niggas knew we were 4th Ward niggas. They couldn't stand the type'f drama me and Freez would bring if these niggas fucked with our shit.

When we made it inside the freshly painted vestibule, I pressed the button for apartment 8-M.

"Who is it?" that voice I liked called out.

You know I had to holla back with some slick shit, "Fetty Montana, that's who. And the sick Arabic Scarface with me."

She repeated, "Who?" like I was speakin' Russian or some shit.

"Yo, is Nina there? This Fetty."

Me and Freez snickered at each other after we heard Nina buzz us in. We took the elevator up to the eighth floor, and I was a little surprised when we stepped off. This spot was a little luxurious to be a project building. No wonder why they call this shit the Towers. There were no broken lights in the hallway, which was painted like a bright tennis ball yellow, and the place was so clean I could actually hear my Tims squeak across the floor with every step.

Face/ Fetty Boy

We didn't know whether to go left or right when we stepped into the hallway; this down the hill shit was foreign to us up-the-hill niggas. Then it hit me - the C.C.P. projects across the street was identical to this one. I used to fuck this chicken head over there back in the day. If my memory serves me correctly, I'm supposed to make a right out'f the elevator.

Freez followed me down the hall, and just like I thought, 8-M was in the far corner.

I knocked on the door two times, and before I even reached the third knock, the door flew open. I kind'f lost myself after seein' this chick for the first time. I can't really describe what happened, it was definitely a what-the-fuck moment, though! Lemme find out Cleopatra had been hidin' out all these centuries in the motherfuckin' Towers!

She was shorter than the average chick - petite, but that ass was type phat. How'd Biggie say that shit, "Make a nigga wanna eat dat!" I tried to get a sense of how long her hair was, but it was like a jet-black waterfall that just kept on flowin' downward. Her hair spilled over her hips, then I lost sight for a bit 'cause I noticed that Nina was bowlegged. You know them bowlegged bitches know how to throw it back like a female quarterback! Her face looked like delicate curves of chocolate. You know what they say... the blacker the berry, the sweeter the juice! She was a sexy lil' motherfucka with the swagger to match.

She was on her feminine shit right then, too. Rockin' this brightly colored floral spring dress with a matchin' silk scarf tied around her neck. And her pretty-ass feet... WOW! Wearin' a pair of sandals, which allowed me to see all of her pretty airbrushed toenails. She even sported a toe-ring, and after further inspection, I noticed she had a thumb-ring to match. Who does that?

It don't even matter 'cause this chick was makin' that shit work. I didn't know that this breed of bitch existed anymore; it was all new to me. She was wifey material fo'sho', but I couldn't let her know that. I did how Fetty always do,

Face/ Fetty Boy

kept the composure cooler than the central air. It was hard, though. I don't toss the "wifey" word around often, and I done fucked with many'a bad ducks in my time. I usually fuck'em, don't love'em, then leave'em; but shorty here was type special. Don't ask me why. Don't ask me what made her so different. Maybe it was because she appeared so self-confident in her dress code. Just know this bitch was official doe! I always kept my guard up when dealin' with broads, but this chick was bad enough to catch me slippin' in the first round and put me out for the count.

"Hey, how you doin'?" she asked after stretchin' her arm out for a handshake.

Soft just like I thought it was.

"Yo, waddup? I'm Fetty. And this is my potnah Freez right here."

"I already know Freez," Nina said. "I met him over Sha-Sha's house one time." I watched her look Freez up and down, peepin' out his gear n'shit. This bitch jockin' my nigga's swag already. After she closed the door, "Y'all could sit on the couch," she said. "Y'all want somethin' to drink?"

Now, that's what I'm talkin' about right there; she got good home trainin', too! I was even impressed by the neatness of her apartment. It was a complete opposite of the outside of the building. New furniture, not that cheap shit, either. The place had a little class 'cause she had some artwork and family photos posted on the walls. On top of that, the only thing that smelled better than the apartment was her. Her living arrangements were plush to say the least.

"We good on the drinks," I said. I laughed to myself 'cause she noticed that Freez was waitin' on me to make all the decisions.

"Okay, since y'all don't want no drinks, lemme go and get your score-card."

She left the room only for a couple'f seconds. When she came back, she had this smirk on her face 'cause she saw that my eyes were still followin' her cute little ass. She stared

Face/ Fetty Boy

right at me, actually, it was like she stared through me. She had that woman's intuition shit goin' on. It wasn't hard to tell that she knew a nigga was feelin' her.

I played it cool as she sat next to me on the couch. She had this little blue card in her hand, must be the score-card, I thought to myself. Truth be told, this chick was so hot, I almost forgot that I came here 'bout somethin' other than her.

"So, how does this work, again?" I asked.

She smiled and said, "Just take your butt over to the DMV and give this card and your ID to whoever is in window number four. Simple. Easy. No sweat. Just tell'em that you're about to graduate from Kennedy High School, and they will give you your permit. You think you can handle that, or d'you need me to draw you a blue print?"

I was too busy smilin' inside my own head to respond with my usual slick shit. My nigga Freez, on the other hand, couldn't refrain himself. "Oh, nah, dawg. I know she ain't say that shit to my nigga Fetty Montana?" Freez called himself puttin' Nina in check, but he was really clownin' me on the low.

"Nah, Freez," I said while starin' Nina in her eyes. "That ain't about nothin', son. I like a chick who can speak her mind - throw it back at a brotha. Feel me?" Before Nina or Freez could say anything. "So, that's it, huh? Just show up at the DMV and show'em this here card?"

"That's it," Nina repeated. "It's like I said, simple... easy... no sweat. Now, where's my money."

This Nina chick was talkin' slicker than a jar of hair grease. I flashed my whites at her again, then shook my head at her like I was impressed. The look on her face told me that she could tell I was strokin' her ego. This chick was feelin' herself, as she should have, 'cause she was a straight dime. But that confident swagger she was showin' me disappeared the very second I pulled the monster knot from my pocket. I peeled the bills back slowly so she could see that the stack was all Jacksons and Franko Faces. I put a Franko (hundred dollar bill) in her hand, then looked her in her eyes the same way she

Face/ Fetty Boy

had been lookin' at me since I stepped foot inside her apartment. I don't give a fuck how confident or good lookin' a chick is; money will drop the panties on the baddest bitch - or, at least, get it wet!

"So, what d'you go to school for?" Nina asked.

One look at my cash flow, and the bitch changed up her whole convo.

"Drafting," I said, straight to the point and not offerin' any more info. Usually, whenever I meet chicks for the first time, I'd be on some super Casanova shit. But this chick had me on some insecure bullshit. Even after I wowed her with the knot, her spell was still workin' on me.

"So, who's car is that outside?" she asked.

I answered by noddin' my head toward Freez. Then, to take the attention away from the fact the car wasn't mine, I asked her, "So, where you from, Nigeria or somewhere?"

"No, nigga!" All'f her attitude came out when she said that. "How you gonna ask me somethin' like that? Where are you from with that accent of yours?"

"I'm Jamaican," I answered, "and for the second time, where are you from?"

"I'm American, boy. That's where I'm from!"

One minute, this Nina chick was classy, another minute, she was ghetto. Her little back and forth shit was kind'f sexy.

"So, you not scared livin' in this big-ass building by yourself?" I asked.

"Scared of what?" When I asked that question, all the ghetto came right out'f her again. "I grew up next door in C.C.P.! And those projects are, by far, worse than these."

We enjoyed her company for a little while longer. If me and Freez didn't have to get to the mall before it closed, We would have stayed their just so I could soak up some more of this chick. It ain't everyday you meet a girl from C.C.P. who could go from classy to sassy in the blink of an eye. But too much of a good thing could be bad for you. I decided to roll out before this chick had me wide the hell open.

Face/ Fetty Boy

We said our good-byes; I kept'em short on purpose. As me and Freez left her apartment, I didn't even look back while we were walking away. I looked down and checked my beeper like I had other shit to do. I'd be damned if I was gonna let that chick know that she had some kind'f power over me. That shit wouldn't have been smart at all.

From the elevator ride all the way to the car, Freez went in on me with his shit.

"My nigga, that chick is on your dick, dawg! Bag dat! Quick, nigga! You gotta wife that pretty lil' motherfucka! Please do that shit for me, dawg!"

"Nigga, you the one with the bangin'-ass whip with the pinkie-ring and things on."

"Fuck all that, nigga. She want you, kid. You ain't see how that bitch was lookin' at you?"

Freez was on some straight sucka shit. He was actin' like if I fucked Nina, it would be like he fucked her, too. I never understood why some niggas thought like that. Freez was right about one thing, though, it did seem like Nina was feelin' me. I told Freez that I still had her number and, on top of that, now I knew where she lived. I can bag & tag that some other time in the near future. My main concern now was gettin' my permit, then my license. A week ago, I saw this money green G.S. 300 Lexus at this dealership over on Route 46. I wanna snap for the summer in that shit.

"After I cop the whip, I gotta find a new connect so I can gank his ass like the last mira-mira motherfucka. Feel me?"

"Yeah, yo. Do that," Freez said. "I'm tired of Vic and the rest of them punk-ass niggas over-pricing me for that garbage they got. Twenty-three large for a pie? fuck them niggas."

We laughed about that shit all the way until we reached Route 4 headin' to the Garden State Mall. We put the top down and puffed on the hydro while listenin' to some beats at the same time. A song was playin' by these young niggas called L.O.X. that had just signed with Bad Boys under that nigga Puff Daddy. I told Freez that's how I wanted his ass to be

Face/ Fetty Boy

— straight ballin' like them Bad Boy niggas. Freez's flow was nicer than most'f them rap kats anyway. I told him we were gonna push this coke until we got him into the hip-hop arena. After that, we'd pop off Fetti Mobb Entertainment. Then, Fetti Boy's Record Label. Get Freez into the rap game, get my mama a house... the shit's gonna happen - believe that!

"Yeah, yeah," Freez said while turnin' up the volume. "Them Bad Boy niggas eatin' the streets up with this L.O.X. mixed tape!"

He wasn't lyin'. Murdah Ma$e... Junior Mafia... and of course, the Notorious B.I.G. - them niggas had the hood on smash. They even changed the way hood niggas started to dress. I guess the sayin' is true - art imitates life, and life imitates art. Either that, or Biggie changed the dress code so niggas like me wouldn't be whylin' out at any of his shows; nobody liked shootin' shit up while stylin' in their fresh clothes.

Puff had niggas rockin' $2,500 alligator Bloodline shoes. $4,500 reptile suits. And B.I.G. bought back the pinkie-ring and things.

That's why me and Freez were headed to the mall; our outfits were gonna be dapper just like them kats. The rings alone would cost us $12,000 a piece, and that's after we talked the jeweler Muhammad down from $18,000. Hagglin' a better price was always gonna be easy. Me and Freez were regulars at Bernini's, plus we always grabbed two of everything. Boy, them snooty niggas loved it whenever we walked into the mall; whoever took care of us was gonna have a huge commission check by the end of the week. That's just how we did; fresh to death out this bitch. That was our dress code for Brokers later on tonight. It's gonna be super sick. Bitches and niggas from Bergen County, Passaic, Union, and Essex County would be comin' through to stunt a little harder than the next nigga. And that right there is the difference between these other niggas and the 4th Ward niggas; these other niggas stuntin'. Me and Freez does this stuntin' shit even when we not tryin'... shittin' for real.

Face/ Fetty Boy

On the road to the riches and diamond rings, niggas! We was real niggas... doin' real things.

* * * * *

When we got to Brokers, all the so-called heavy hitters found out just how hard us P-Town niggas really ball. It was around 12:15 AM and the lines were so long it looked like the party was on the outside of the club. Long lines weren't ever really a problem for us, though. It didn't matter where we were at - the movies, the mall, the skatin' rink, the bowlin' alley, restaurants... we didn't wait in line for nothing. We knew everybody; actually, it was more like everybody knew us. Plus, we knew the guy that was throwin' the party tonight; gettin' in through the VIP line wasn't 'bout nothin' but showin' our faces or snappin' our fingers.

We didn't park the car right away. We pulled up right in front of the main entrance, peepin' out the scenery. There were so many high-price whores out there, the sidewalks and building walls looked like they were painted with nothin' but tits, ass, and extensions. I could tell Freez was keepin' count of how many dime pieces he was gonna bag tonight. I called myself doin' the same thing; but my mind was still stuck on Cleopatra.

Even with the nipple and ass show that was goin' on, we still saw a lot'f suspect niggas rollin' through. Me and Freez had decided to go party over in NY instead. That changed quickly once I spotted one'f my cronies I hadn't seen in a while.

My nigga Pretty New was from the 4th Ward, but not our strip. He stomped up and down Governor Street pumpin' his krills; he had been munchin' up there on the solo tip for over a year now. He used to rip the block up with his cousin and their little crew, but the rest of them niggas fell off or got knocked. Just how much Pretty New was munchin' was obvious judgin' by the car this nigga just pulled up in. He was four-wheelin' a freshly painted candy-yellow Lex Coupe with

Face/ Fetty Boy

the top custom chopped. Man, that shit hit the eyesight harder than a Tyson punch.

New was one of them fast talkin' funny niggas; everybody loved this nigga, even niggas who loved to hate'm. I was glad as shit when we saw him pull up. He can play a big part in the things I had planned. He was thorough. Trusted. You gotta use niggas like that. But never misuse' em - 'cause teamwork always makes the dream work.

"Wassup, my niggas?" Pretty New said, smilin' because he saw how people were starin' at his whip.

"What's really good wit' you, New?" I asked.

"Ain't shit, my nigga, just E-Classing and profilin'."

"You profilin' a little hard out this bitch, ain'tcha?" Freez asked. He was commentin' on how dope New's ride was.

"Nah," Pretty New said with a nonchalant smile. "Just chillin' regular, Freez. Just chillin' regular, ya dig? Look at you, though. Them B.B.S. rims look cute on your lil' Beamer. You got the little paint job. The rims shinin'... that shit lookin' like HELLO!" There New go with that funny shit again, I thought to myself. He was complimentin' Freez's car even though he knew he had the better lookin' whip. "But fuck all that; y'all not goin' in the club?" New asked.

"Yeah," I said, "now that you done upped the real nigga count out this bitch, we gonna go in and toss a few drinks back wit' ya."

"Yeah, yeah. I hear that hot shit. Go park that cute shit y'all drivin' and let's do this, man."

Pretty New fucked me up; that nigga was funny for no reason at all. I don't even think he knew he was funny, it's just how he was. Anytime somebody said somethin' that got him excited, he'd be like, "Yeah, yeah!" Plus, that nigga talked so fast, he could have hit you with ten jokes before you could think of one.

"We tryin' to find a good parkin' spot, New," Freez said.

"Shiiiit, y'all niggas better hurry up. You know these niggas over here will steal yo' shit, strip yo' shit, then sell

Face/ Fetty Boy

yo' own shit back to you 'fore you even get out the car. Don't let that shit happen 'cause Im'a talk 'bout y'all niggas."

After we all busted out laughin', "Goddamn, New! You is a funny-ass nigga, yo," I exclaimed. "But you know ain't nobody gonna jack no cars from us G.G. Ave. niggas. I'll have Freez leave this shit right here still running in the middle of the street and it'll still be here when we come back out."

"Yeah, yeah! Ha - if y'all niggas park that shit there, I'm jackin' that motherfucka myself!"

"Hey, yo, New man... cut that shit out! You comedian-ass nigga. We gonna go n'park. I'm glad I ran into you, for real, son. I gotta holla at you 'bout somethin'."

"Yeah, yeah. That's what it is, Fetty boyeee. I hope you ain't tryin' to come up with no sob story or excuses n'shit; you sent word that we were supposed to do breakfast last week, nigga. What happened? You my whoadie, but you know G. Street niggas don't beg or buy friends."

I had to admit... Pretty New was right about that shit. "New, I hear that fly, funky shit you spittin', but you know how it is out here. I've simply been caught up. That's my bad I ain't get wit' you since I've been home, and I apologize for missin' our appointment at I-Hop last week. I got graveyard love for you, and you know this, man."

"Aight then, my nigga, you get the Presidential pardon. But the bar is on you tonight," New claimed with a Koolade smile."

"That's without sayin'," I said. But you gonna be spendin' some of that G. Street loochie up in there, too."

"Yeah, yeah! You already know! Let's get to that Bourbon & Bubbly!"

* * * * *

Meanwhile, on the strip, Illy-Ill, Dead Eye, and Lil' Goochie hugged the block like three Broad Street bullies rakin' in the dough; the late-night/early-mornin' hustle of the summer time was a must. The dark blanket of the sky reminded me of somethin' this old head told me one time, "When it comes to doin' dirt, the night time is the right time."

Dead Eye was in the cut where they trap from with about five thousand big-bag nickels in a huge Zip-lock bag. Illy-Ill was at the entrance of the alleyway guarding Dead Eye and the package.

Even though it was summer time, Ill was hooded down with the mac tied to a Timberland bootstring strapped over his shoulder underneath a spring jacket. Goochie, on the other hand, was out and about on the strip running sales and looking out for the poe-lice.

"Build-Build!" he would yell if he spotted a cop car or a vehicle that could possibly belong to some undercovers. Build-Build was 5 Percenter talk for eighty-eighty. None of us really remembered where the term eighty-eighty came from; I just know it was from some old cop show.

Once the coast was clear, Gooch shouted, "Twelve for 49!" as he approached the cut with some frail-lookin' dude.

The shout was for Dead Eye to bring out twelve of them things. The same routine would repeat itself until all five thousand jums were gone.

But shit goes wrong even in the smoothest of operations when money is involved. How'd Biggie say that shit? "Mo' money, mo' problems." That's real talk for yo' ass, but you gotta respect it if you're in the game I'm in.

Ron Gotti and some of his crew had came out on the strip and positioned themselves down the block. There was nothin' strange about that; it was somethin' he always did. But, this time, he was tryin' to intentionally short stop the sales that were goin' to Illy-Illy and company.

"Yo, lil' nigga!" Ron Gotti yelled at Lil' Goochie. "That's my custie!"

The little raggedy lady Gooch was tryin' to sell to turned and told Gotti, "I like what neph got. I've been smokin' it all night, and that's what I want."

Face/ Fetty Boy

    Gotti tried to show his ass after he heard that shit. He yelled some stupid nonsense, then grabbed the crackhead by her arm so she couldn't walk back up the street with Gooch. I don't know what be on nigga's mind sometimes; Gotti probably figured he could be the bully for the night since I wasn't out there. Ha, ha... wrong.

    Ron Gotti put his hand on his waist like he was gonna pull his burner. He yanked the crackhead toward him, then hollered at one'f his runners. "Bring out fiftteen'f them things!" he commanded. Just as soon as his runner took the first step- Bloom!

    The gunshot echoed off the buildings on the strip like a thunder bolt falling from the sky. The bullet ricocheted off the concrete right by Gotti's feet and left a spark that looked as if a fire cracker had just been lit. Every hustler, every fiend, every nondescript turned into mannequins as Illy-Ill stepped from the shadows in the cut with both hands grippin' the semi.

    "That there was the warnin' shot, pussy!" Ill said. "The next one's gonna find a home in ya dome, chump." Before Ron Gotti could even run his mouth, Ill went straight in on him and laid the law down. "What the fuck is you doin' out here anyway, nigga? You ain't from 'round here - DON'T SAY SHIT, NIGGA!" Illy-Ill shouted when one of Gotti's boys slowly raised his hands in an attempt to calm Ill down. "Fetty and Freez may put up with yo' shit, but I'm zero tolerance, nigga. It's a new day dawnin' out this motherfucka. Get wit' the program or get the fuck from 'round here."

    I told y'all, Illy-Ill was a straight live wire; you gotta love a nigga like that, but you also gotta control him. The way he just shined on Ron Gotti and his clique was gonna be good for business. Them niggas had the puppy-dog face on when they were forced to tuck tail. They spun off without makin' a single sale. But like I said, it was good for business... but bad for war.

Face/ Fetty Boy

Chapter 6: In the Club

Security was deeper than the abyss at Broker's tonight. It didn't matter, though; most'f the dudes workin' the door were from P-Town - they already knew what it was whenever me and Freez hit the scene. The head bouncer lifted the heavy, red velvet rope, then us Ward niggas strolled straight through lookin' like diplomats walkin' out the courtroom scott-free.

    I snapped my wrist back to check the time. Freez flashed his "I'm-a-cool-nigga smile" when he saw me peek at the watch- he knew I was only profilin', lettin' everybody peep the wine- face Rolex. Me, him, and Pretty New kept our stride and headed in intendin' to go straight for the bar; not looking at anyone. But, if you ain't never believe nothin' in your life, please believe damn near everybody was lookin' at what they thought were three, young, black tycoons.

    Me and Freez both had on Armani suits. Freez's suit was like a baby powder blue - he liked them bright colors n'shit. Mine was more of an off-white or a cream color - "C.R.E.A.M. Get the money... Dollar dollar bill y'all."

    I snapped the lapel to my suit jacket so my diamond-dipped Jesus piece could dangle, swingin' left to right on the Cuban link. We hadn't even made it inside yet, and one of the bouncers told me that he cleared an entire section for us upstairs, then waved us through. I nodded my head at him, then made a B-line toward the picture man off to the right.

    Without words or a second thought, people in the V.I.P. line cleared a space for me and my niggas to walk through.

Face/ Fetty Boy

Our swagger was straight-up extra! Some other nigga was gettin' the V.I.P. treatment, too, until he accidentally stepped on one'f my Mauri Gators. I ain't even look at'm. I ain't say shit to'm. I just waved my hand like, "Move, nigga... get the fuck out my way." If I didn't tell Pretty New to come on and forget about it, he would've peeled the homie shit back.

The clown who stepped on my $875 shoes had this chick with him who was a'ight lookin'; I'd get up in them guts if I was drunk enough. "Heeeyy! Can a Sista roll wit' you?" she shouted. New turned and smiled at her. The bitch started fixin' her hair and perkin' her titties up n'shit - you know how them high-priced hookers do.

"You wanna roll wit' us?" New asked.

"I'll do more than roll wit' you!" the hooker shouted.

"You hot enough to roll wit' us?"

"Yeah!" she answered.

"You on fire n'shit?"

"Yeah, I'm meltin', daddy!"

"Well, stop, drop, and roll then, bitch!"

Hey, yo, motherfuckas in the line couldn't hold back. Even above the music, all we heard was everybody laughin' at this chick. Freez had to grab New before he started really goin' in on her.

"Come'n, New. Leave that bitch alone, man, so we can go and flick it up, nigga."

"Yeah, yeah! True 'dat, nigga. Yo, Fetty, this is our first flick together since they let yo' black ass out from 'round them dirty White Boys and Ricans. I hope they ain't have my nigga down there washin' nobody's draws n'shit."

"Come'n, New," I said. "Go 'head wit' that shit, you silly-ass nigga."

Once we were all the way inside, I held up three fingers toward the picture man to let him know that me and my niggas were next.

"A'ight, Fetty! You got it!" the picture man said. I remember thinkin' to myself, "Damn, how the fuck this nigga know my name?" It wasn't nothin' major. It was just a reminder for me and my dudes to stay on point - in other words... floss with caution. You never know who might be watchin' up in this spot.

We took so many pictures, the nigga ran out'f film. Freez hit the dude off with a Franco for his time, then the three of us headed toward the bar upstairs.

"Time to hit that bar!" Freez eagerly shouted.

"Now, you know you can't drink, nigga," said New. "Fuck around and ball that pretty red Black Man's Wagon up that you just copped!"

When we got upstairs, I had to keep tellin' myself purse first, ass last. There were enough bitches in here to keep a nigga thoroughly distracted. I wasn't about to let one'f these chicks hypnotize me like Nina's ass did; besides, right now, I really needed to holla at my nigga New about his connect.

"Yo, yo, bartender, what y'all got up in this motherfucka?" New shouted.

The bartender, an average lookin' redbone chick, with red hair to match responded with every bit of her attitude, "What you want?"

"Bitch!" New shouted back. I knew I shouldn't have let him order the drinks. That nigga don't hold his tongue for nothing; that's one'f the reasons why I love this nigga. "Watch ya tone before I get that ass tossed out'f my man's party. You see these two niggas I'm sittin' wit'? We'll buy the bar up in this bitch - you included!"

The bartender sucked her teeth. "Do it then, nigga!" she said. "Ain't nobody impressed with all that shit!"

She rolled her eyes, then went to serve a Heineken to another customer.

"Yo, New, chill the fuck out, man. Let's talk, nigga," I said. "Hey, miss, you got that Hennessy XO Cognac back there?"

"Mm-hm," she mouthed. "But it's a hundred dollars a pop."

Rolling her eyes as she served another customer. It was

Face/ Fetty Boy

almost like she was tryin' to ignore us.
"You see?" Pretty New shouted. "You see that shit, my nigga? You thinkin' it's always me. It's this bitch!"
"I know, brah. The bitch back there askin' for it, but chill out, dawg. Let's enjoy ourselves over here." Turning my attention to the bartender, "Excuse me, miss. This here is ten dead green Franklins... a G... a thousand dollars. It's for me and my peoples here. If you would be so kind, please let me know when that runs out. Better yet, bitch, here's another $1,500. Put some Crystal with that shit. The word for the night is 'keep'. As in 'keep' the ice in our glasses, 'keep' pourin', 'keep' your mouth shut, and I might let you 'keep' the change."

A bitch will keep on bein' a bitch if a nigga allow it. I ain't that type'f nigga, though. Redhead's eyes almost fell out'f her face when she peeped the knots me, Freez, and New were holdin'. It's true what they say, money talks, and bullshit walks. And right now, it was tellin' this bitch to shut the fuck up and do her goddam job.

She glanced over the counter and looked us up and down. Her whole demeanor changed. She saw the rings n'things, the gators, the big mother fuckin' Jesus piece medallion swingin' on the Cuban link. She damn near did a back flip after seein' New rockin' his Ostrich suit with the three quarter Ostrich shoes to match. His watch and chain was platinum, and the rest of his jewelry was all white gold.

"What, y'all rappers or somethin'?" Redhead asked. Our paper moistened this bitch's panties with the quickness.

I pointed at Freez, "He's the rapper. Other than that, we're just some ghetto celebrities - hood movie stars. Feel me?"

The redheaded bartender stayed jockin' our style after that. She kept tryin' to talk to me and Freez, but the only words we had for her ass was pour the fuckin' drinks. I wasn't bein' rude to her by being on some bullshit; I was just lettin' her know her place in the world for the way she tried to shine on my nigga Pretty New. Another reason why I kept iggin' her is because I wanted to keep her out'f me and New's conversation.

"Yo, New, I heard when your cousin got knocked, he hooked you up with a bangin' dope and coke connect. I need to get in on that. I did some bullshit and ganked my last connect for four punk-ass birds. I'm regrettin' that shit like a mother- fucka now..."

"Listen here, whoadie," New interupted. "I know you think I'm this jokin'-ass nigga n'shit, smackin' niggas and fuckin' all sorts of bitches, but I think shit through before I do it. 'Cause in my eyes, it's better for people to hate me or laugh at me than it is to have'em feel sorry for me. I ain't tellin' you nothin' new, Fetty, 'cause you think the same fuckin' way, but you should've came and found me when you first got out, yo. I would've talked you out that sucka shit the rest'f these petty-grind-petty-crime-ass niggas be on out here. The game done flipped; you can't be out here beatin' connects, brah - especially mine. That nigga charge $28,000 a key; non-negotiable. Plus the nigga won't deal with nobody but me."

"New, you can't be serious right now, dawg. This is me you talkin' to, nigga. Remember who was the only nigga wit' you in the Youth House when them Dog Pound project niggas tried to stomp yo' ass out, yo."

I didn't like pullin' trump cards on niggas, especially niggas I fuck with heavy; but I had to call a spade a spade. I always thought that was some sucka shit when a nigga reminded another nigga what he did for him n'shit. In my book, if you wanted to show somebody some love, show'em some love for no fuckin' reason at all. That's why mad niggas was loyal to me. But truth be told, that same loyalty can, AND WILL, get me killed! That or a hundred years if I'm not careful. But, right now, I need to get in on this motherfuckin' connect.

New figured out I was feelin' some kind'f way about his response to my question. He knew there is nothin' but brotherly love for him. He said it himself, I was a thinker. He also

Face/ Fetty Boy

knew Fetty could be a sneaky motherfucka when he wanna be; that shit right there make a nigga dangerous. Ask anybody on the strip - fuck the strip - the whole town, they'll tell you quicker than you can ask'em... Fetty Boy is a motherfuckin' problem!

"A'ight, look here, whoadie. I'ma see if I can get you the same price I'm gettin'-"

Before New could finish his sentence I broke in, "And how much is that, New?"

"Two five a brick, my nigga. If you cop ten or more, Jose will let'em go for 23."

Whoa! I said to myself. The music was loud as hell, the bitches was everywhere and doin' everything. The decibels in the club were louder than the stands at a sold out football game. But, when Pretty New said the name Jose, it was as if all that shit went silent inside my head.

"Did you say Jose, New? As in Jose from 146th & Amsterdam?"

"Yeah, nigga. How the fuck you know my connect?"

Oh, shit. I didn't wanna tell my homie that I beat his connect for four of them things. It's best I keep that shit to myself for right now.

"Huh? Oh, nah. I used to fuck with him before I got knocked off," I told him. "I ain't think he would still be up and runnin' this long. What I'm gonna do is shoot over there and holla at'm next week. You ain't even gotta mention my name; let me surprise him. A'ight, my nigga?"

The world is a fuckin' conundrum; big as hell, but small as shit. How the hell is New gonna have the same connect I just beat? When I heard that shit it almost fucked my buzz up.

I let the bad news roll off my chest while me and New stayed kickin' it at the bar. We gave a few bitches the time of day and, at the same time, Freez was on the dance floor doin' his one-two thing. The news about Jose kind'f flat-lined all my energy, but then somethin' happened that shocked my ass right back to life.

Face/ Fetty Boy

This chick named Eve walked up next to me rockin' this sexy-ass, all white Versace dress, that hugged her curves like a latex glove. There were plenty bad-ass bitches on the dance floor - titties talkin', asses bouncin'. But Evey-Eve's shit was bouncin' all over the place and she was standin' still! That ass was straight spreadin' like a rumor! I wanted to get up and give her a hug 'cause I hadn't seen her since I'd been home, but my dick was under the bar counter salutin' the entire room. Eve looked like a tall glass of milk standin' there in that tight-ass white dress; all she needed was for me to dip the chocolate in and stir that shit up.

"Hey, Fetty," she said. From the door, the drawn out slur in her voice let me know she was tipsy than a motherfucka.

"Waddup, Evey-Eve? You lookin' like money that ain't never been touched before, waitin' on me to spend it-"

Less than a second, no exaggeration, after I gave her the compliment, Eve's tongue dove in my mouth like it was the Olympics or something. That shit took a nigga by surprise. Without even thinkin', my hands reached around her and grabbed them ass cheeks while we tongue wrestled at the same time. Man, her ass felt and looked like two big, soft Milk-Duds on a Barbie Doll. Nigga like me got some big-ass hands and could barely squeeze that shit.

Normally, this type'f shit wasn't nothin'. But this is Eve we talkin' about. She was older than me and lived in the hood all her life. I knew her whole family - all'f her siblings; all them bitches were hot. But Evey-Eve was on some extra shit. She kept a job at the hospital, I think she was a nurse or some shit. Independent. Sexy as hell. She was the type'f female everybody respected. I know mad niggas who used to run their mouth talkin' 'bout they had hit that. Truth be told, you had to be that nigga to even look at Eve.

The kiss lasted for mere seconds, but to me, it was an eternity. You know that fresh to def feelin' you get when you're rockin' the smoothest gear and the shiniest jewels? Eve had me feelin' like I just hit the Mega-Million-Dollar lottery!

Face/ Fetty Boy

Our tongues broke free, then she whispered somethin' in my ear and walked off. Don't ask me what she said 'cause I couldn't tell you. Maybe the music was too loud. Maybe I was in shock... I don't know.

I looked at Pretty New and the nigga looked happier than me. He did the same shit Freez did when I met Nina.

"Godayyum! Fuck her, my boy! Eat 'dat pussy! Lick that shit three times for Freez and four times for me, nigga! You gotta wife that ass!"

New was drunk as hell, which only made him more funny. I couldn't leave him by himself 'cause he would've definitely gotten into something. We stayed at the bar; New with his buzz on and me in my daze. I listened to this crazy nigga go on and on all night. But the whole time, I was thinkin' about how to approach Eve to get her to let me spend the night.

It was closin' time. By law, all night clubs in Jersey had to be closed by two AM, but like I said before, we knew the host of the party, and we convinced him to keep rockin' until close to three.

I wanted to be outside ahead of the rest of the crowd so I could catch Eve, so I grabbed Freez and New, and we rolled out about ten minutes early.

As soon as we stepped out into the open air, this broke-ass nigga named Ant, AKA Cold Cheeks, drove by in his fucked up Mazda. He was the male diva type; a straight terricloth-ass nigga... soft. And guess who the fuck was sittin' in the passenger's seat. Man, when I saw Eve ridin' wit' that nigga, I felt like shootin' his car up. She decided to leave with this pennyless-ass geek? This clown was a wanna-be baller from a broke-ass side block off Market Street. Watchin' this shit made me feel like I jumped off the moon and landed on earth flat on my back. The alcohol must've made her kiss me like that. Fuck it... I felt like that 7 Up commercial - "Never had it, never will."

As more people poured out of the closing club, we saw

Face/ Fetty Boy

the same chicks that was sweatin' us on the way in. Even after Pretty New dissed the main chick, them hookers still wanted to roll with us. I wasn't even in the mood. Truth was, you could've added all these bitches up and they wouldn't have equaled a fraction of what Eve was. I just wanted to go home and sleep it off. My ego wouldn't allow me to accept what just happened, so I took Freez's Beamer while him and New spun off with the same bitches that were ball huggin' and dick lickin' outside earlier. One broad had some smudges on the back of her dress. Lemme find out New actually made her get on the ground and roll!

    They headed over to The Loop Motel on 1 & 9. I went home and went str-8 to sleep. I dreamed. It ain't too hard to figure out what I dreamt about, either. Damn! Since when did it become so hard being a realist?

Face/ Fetty Boy

Chapter 7: Reminiscin'

I was so tired and upset about the previous night's events that I went to sleep with the radio on. It woke me up at around quarter after nine. When I looked at my alarm clock, and seen the score-card I had copped from Nina on top'f the night stand. That just reminded me I had mad shit to do.

Gettin' up was my intention, but my thoughts were swimmin' in my brain like the planets swimmin' in the cosmos. My mind was everywhere; plus, the song on the radio had me on some nostalgic shit - Pete Rock & C.L. Smoothe's "Reminiscin'" came on. You know those lyrics made me lay there even longer...my thoughts took over...

Ms. DMV aka Cleopatra is a bad bitch... I gotta get over to the Division of Motor Vehicles and handle this permit situation... my operation was runnin' smoothly, but I still needed to find a new connect like yesterday! Coppin' a half'f bird at a time, then rockin' that shit down myself had me goin' hand-to-hand wit' Dead Eye n'them... at least for now, I ain't gotta touch that eighty large that's put up, I thought to myself.

Nina... I should call her... nah, I don't know what Freez talkin' about, she ain't feelin' me like that.

I need to stack some more chips...

Illy-Ill is a funny nigga... when I got home from Brokers, Dead Eye called me and told me about the way Ill dealt with Ron-G last night... I need to stack some more chips... I should get Ill to rob Freez's ass... I know his chips are up-

Man, what the fuck am I talkin' about? Freez is my brotha... that's the sleep deprivation talkin' right there...

Face/ Fetty Boy

    I need a new connect... Lot'f niggas fucked up in the game, so they playin' it foul... My mama told me love and hate travel in the same boat...
    I need a new connect...
    Damn! Evey-Eve still got my dick hard! "When I reminisce over you, my God!"
    I need a new connect... I wonder if I should tell Jose I got knocked 'fore I had a chance to pay him for the work he gave me? Would he buy that shit? Would he try to get at me up there? Fuck it... in the bible, Paul said try'em all and the weak ones twice...
    My nigga Hubby would've loved to be chillin' at Broker's with us last night... he's probably havin' his own party down in hell or up in heaven right now.
    I finally come home from prison, and my nigga is dead... and I'm still out here fuckin' wit' the same niggas who ain't send me shit when I was down the Berg.
    Yo, Nina, Nina, Nina... that's a bad bitch... I wonder if she's home this early? I wonder if she's up?
    Chick like that gotta have a man... so what... fuck'm.
    Would she understand if I told her how I was livin' out here? How would she handle the idea of me out here playin' chicken with my life while duckin' all these see-somethin'-say-somethin'-ass niggas? Will she accept me for me? I think she would... She's different... I'ma call her...
    Yeah, I'ma do that...
    But I need a connect...
    If Nina gives me that pussy, I'm runnin' up in her poody bald headed... yeah... lemme call this chick...
    I left her phone number next to the score-card on my night stand. I reached out for it, but my hand changed directions almost instinctively, and wound up under my bed searchin' for the plate of cook-up I had waitin' to be bagged up.
    After grabbin' the plate, I took out a Gem Star razor and about a thousand 12/12 little baggies. I gotta drop somethin off

Face/ Fetty Boy

to Dead Eye and them young boys in a few hours; might as well start choppin' this shit up while I'm on the phone with shawty.

Ever since them fuckin' jakes found the guns and the fifty grams, they've been blitzin' the strip. Shit is still a little hectic out there; Dead Eye ain't gonna have time to bag this and push it. Illy-Ill is too busy bein' a cowboy enforcin' the law. I'll bag it myself; better safe than sorry. Besides, I bag better than all them dudes anyway. Their shit is always light. I've been payin' Dead Eye and his crew out my own pocket; Illy-Ill was down by law just on the strength, but I still hit him off lovely. As soon as I get this new connect, though, it's goin' back to half'n half.

I sat up and put the plate on my lap. In one motion, I grabbed Nina's number, dialed, and trapped the phone between my ear and shoulder. After listenin' to the other end ring for the third time, I decided to be on my polite shit just in case I was disturbin' her by callin' this early. She picked up.

"Hello. Good morning," I said. I can't even remember the last time I told anyone good morning. "Can I please speak to Nina?"

"Speakin' - who dis?"

Yeah, there go that ghetto fabulous mess she was on the other day, still classy and sassy. "Oh, this Fetty. How you doin', ma?"

"I'm alright. You got your score-card, what you callin' here for, boy?"

Yo, this chick fucks me up, for real. "Well, like I told you yesterday, I just came home and I don't have any female friends to, you know, kick it wit'. I ain't the type to be hangin' around dudes all the time; the world is full'f snakes and fakes, feel me? I woke up hungry for a female's perspective. That, and I'm a bit sexually frustrated...." I wonder what's goin' through her mind right now... "I was type impressed with

Face/ Fetty Boy

what I saw. So, I was wonderin' if your boyfriend wouldn't mind you havin' a male friend?" That was probably the corniest shit I had ever said to a female... but it worked.

"Who said I got a boyfriend?" Nina responded. By the tone of her voice, I could tell she was smirkin' those sexy-ass lips into the other end of the phone.

"Well, do you?"

"No, and I ain't lookin' for one, either. I'm too busy with school and all that to be focusing on the bullshit."

"You never had a man in your life?"

"Yeah, my father... until he passed away a few months ago."

When she told me her pops had died, I felt a deep hurt all up in my rib cage. I know all about love and loss. I also know that a girl won't tell a nigga no shit like that unless she's really feelin' him.

"Sorry to hear that, ma."

Before realizing it, it was damn near ten o'clock. I had ol' girl gigglin', tellin' me about her dreams in life. Nina was definitely a go-getter. I respected her style. That trance she had me in when we first met was just as strong as ever.

She was startin' to tell me about the rest of her family when I realized that I hadn't started choppin' at the cookie yet. I picked up the blade and started hackin' away. That shit sounded like a machete hittin' a butcher's cuttin' board over and over. It didn't dawn on me that ol' girl would be able to hear the shit, or even have a clue about what I was doin' on the other end.

"Boy, tell me you are not doin' what it sounds like you doin'!" she yelled into the phone. She sounded a bit more excited than angry. I still didn't know how to read it, though.

"What you talkin' about, ma?"

"You think I don't got ears? I know that sound 'cause my father used to do the same thing."

Change the subject, Fetty... change the subject, I thought to myself.

"Then you already know what it's hittin' for. So, when

Face/ Fetty Boy

can I take you out?"

"Boy, I don't even know you that well to be goin' somewhere wit' you."

"Well, I'm gonna have to stalk you some more so you can get to know me, then. You ain't the type of chick a dude just calls one time - feel me? Who knows, we might even end up bein' the dynamic duo."

Nina laughed into the phone for a good twenty seconds. I ain't talkin' about a chick's sexy little giggle, either. This girl was laughin' her ass off. It kind'f had me feelin' some kind'f way until I realized what she was gettin' at.

"Oh, now you on some Batman and Robin shit, huh?" she asked, while still laughin'.

"Yo, Batman was that dude!" I said. "He's the only super hero who handled his handle wit' no super powers. He learned his enemy so he could burn his enemy, ya dig? And you know he had stacks on top'f stacks, right?"

After suckin' her teeth, "Listen to you," Nina said. "You think you the only one who know about the Dark Night n'shit? I wasn't laughin' at Batman, I was laughin' because I was picturin' your ass wearin' them tight-ass black tights - ha, ha!"

Oh, now this chick got jokes. "Whoa, ma... what Fetty Boy look like wearin' some Batman tights?"

"Ha, ha... ain't nobody say nothin' about you dressin' like Batman. If we're gonna be the dynamic duo, I'm Batgirl, and you're ass is Robin... ha, ha..."

I got this chick wide open. If you make a bitch cry, that's when you know she love you. You make a bitch laugh, that's when you know she wanna fuck you.

"Forget you and your 'fagtastic' jokes," I said as she kept on laughin; "And how you gonna be Batgirl when I'ma have that ass purrin' under the sheets like Catwoman all night?"

She sucked her teeth again, "Whateva!" she said. But I could still hear her laughin' softly to herself.

"Nah, but listen, ma... on a serious note, I don't want you gettin' the wrong idea thinkin' I go around sweatin' females

Face/ Fetty Boy

all day. That ain't me, it never was. And don't get no big head n'shit just because a brotha wanna take you out. It really ain't even about you. I just like the way I feel when I'm around you. And when I talk with you. I ain't one'f these niggas who don't know their place out here. I know exactly what it is. Now, I don't know what day and I don't know what time, but believe what I say when I tell ya... we goin' out..."

* * * * *

When I got off the phone with Nina, I finished choppin' the cook-up and, bagged all that shit up in record speed.

I damn near ran to the shower 'cause my breath and body odor was a little tart. A fresh bar of Irish Spring was waitin' for me on the soap shelf - Irish Spring was a white boy's soap, but it smelled good as hell.

As the hot water penetrated my flesh, I started reflectin' on my phone call with Nina-

"Did I just spend an hour talkin' to this bitch about cartoons and fairy tales?" I asked myself.

Don't matter, though... I think she feelin' me.

* * * * *

The morning and afternoon flew by quickly. I was so excited about kickin' it with Nina that I almost forgot it was Saturday. I didn't really feel like goin', but I had told Freez that I would chill with him at the Bergenfield Rink. That's where we had spent most Saturday nights since I had been home. Tonight was a little different 'cause Flex was gonna be deejayin' and he always brings that live New York club scene with him.

Another reason I decided to go was because Freez was supposed to be havin' a rap battle in the parkin' lot after the rink lets out. I figured I'd go and watch him embarrass another kat on the mic.

Me and Freez met up on the strip, then we drove out to

Face/ Fetty Boy

Bergenfield to the skatin' rink. It was nothin' but another show of, "it cost to floss," when we got there.

Just like any other large hip-hop venue, the car and fashion show in the parkin' lot was serious.

We looked the part - walked it, and talked it. Our gear was almost identical, only thing was we were rockin' different colors. We both rocked a pair of Enyce Velour bottom sweatpants - Freez's were a bluish color, mine were like an almond-brown. We had on Esco t-shirts to match, along with a pair of Timberland construction boots with the eight-inch brown cushion around the ankle.

I had the Jesus piece danglin' again, and Freez had the Lexus sign pendant with crushed diamonds swingin'. Because Freez was wearin' blue, he had on a Yankee's fitted cap. And very rarely did you see either one of us go out without rockin' pinkie rings n'things. Our style was jiggy like two pro ball players instead of the hoodstahs we were. Just like the other night at Brokers, we were superstars all over again.

Queens kats, Bronx niggas... Harlem; bitches from Jersey City, Newport, Paterson... even niggas and bitches from as far as Connecticut flooded the rink.

Like usual, Funk Master Flex didn't start Deejayin' until around eleven o'clock. The skatin' rink turned into a dance floor, while everybody wearin' roller skates cruised around us formin' the shape of a race track.

Flex hit everybody with a little M.O.B.B. Deep - some joints off the "Hell on Earth" album. We went ballistic!

He popped off some Biggie after that, and that's when all the dudes and broads really went in with the dancin' - more like havin' vertical sex standin' up. Once Flex spun the last Biggie joint, "One More Chance", he stopped the music altogether.

I don't know how it got so quiet in the spot with all the people that were there, but all I heard around me was shawties

Face/ Fetty Boy

breathin' hard from gettin' air-fucked.

Flex broke the silence, "Yo, Yo!" he said. His voice echoed over the mic and through the speakers givin' life to the entire skatin' rink. "Hold up, New York and New Jersey! I got some new shit for you hip-hop virgins out there! Check out my man Jay-Z!"

He put his head phones to his ear and scratched the record back and forth a few times, then let his finger slip. When Foxy Brown's first line of the track penetrated everybody's ears, it was like we were all under a musical spell - "Ain't no nigga like the one I got... Then Jay-Z's voice came in, No one can fuck you better... Then back to Foxy Brown, Sleeps around but he gives me a lot..." Yo, you think bitches was gettin' air-fucked before? Yo, the skirts went up. Kats fingers was in chicks ass cracks and the whole nine. If a female wasn't gettin' fingered, she had her ass up against somebody's dick gyratin' like a motherfucka! It was like one huge Tri-state Area dance-orgy out that motherfucka.

"Yo, Freez, that's that rapper Ill let us listen to the other night," I said.

Flex hit us with a few more joints, "This is serious, people!" he kept on yellin'. The place went bonkers - straight bananas!

"Freez, brah, I gotta get that Jay-Z tape, dawg."

"Man, fuck that nigga," Freez said playfully, "I'm still 2-pac'ed out my mind. Thug life, baaabaaay!"

Pht - thug life... you wasn't screamin' that shit when them Puerto Rican dudes hit up my manz Hubby, I thought to myself.

I still wanted to put Freez on blast, but decided against it 'cause we were havin' a good time, and I ain't want my mood gettin' twisted. "All I know, kat daddy, is you betta not blow our money battlin' them N.Y. niggas out in the parkin' lot."

"I got this, brah! I got some serious bars I've been workin' on. And I gotta a new flow!"

I swear to God, for ten G's... this nigga better do what

he do...

When we went back outside, it seemed like more people had come to the rink just to see the rap battle. Word-of-mouth is a motherfucka; me and Freez didn't tell nobody about the battle, yet everybody was waitin' in the lot like it was an after party.

It was the first time Freez had ever battled Billy Hoffa from the Bronx. Hoffa had a little spit game - dude was kinda nice. Most of them Bronx niggas played the hip-hop game heavy. But, just like Freez had never gone up against Hoffa... Hoffa had never gone against Freez. Hoffa was from out'f town; the rule was that out'f towners had to spit first...

"Yo, I'm realla 'den this nigga, he fakin'... Fuck'm, he hatin', gotta fry'm like bacon... I don't got no patience, fuck'm I ain't waitin'... I'm the son of Satan, his soul is for the takin'... They say this nigga hot (sucked his teeth), but he don't spit bars, he spit dicks... Bronx nigga reppin' my strip, I'm straight sick... Ain't none'f you niggas flyer, ya whole clique is liars... niggas know 'bout my hood, we these niggas suppliers... New York, New York nigga, we so ill... Y'all so fake nigga, we so fo'real... We ain't gotta talk, you want war? What the drill?"

The lot exploded.

With a huge NY crowd out there, I found myself wishin' that Illy-Ill or Dead Eye was in the crowd somewhere with a strap in their waistband.

It took almost two minutes for niggas to stop howlin' n'shit. Hoffa's whole crew was jumpin' around and hollerin' at the top of their lungs. They covered their mouths with one hand and pointed fingers at me and Freez like we were some suckas or somethin'.

Like I said, this was the first time Freez had ever battled Billy Hoffa. It was also the first time I had ever saw Hoffa's little brother - grimy-ass Blanco Jermaine. He was the loudest out'f all those Bronx niggas; a movie was playin' in his head and a sound track was comin' out'f his mouth. I heard about'm;

Face/ Fetty Boy

nine times out'f ten, you end up meetin' a nigga's reputation before you even meet the nigga. And, judgin' by the way he was laughin' and lookin' at me, I could tell he heard about me, too. This was the first time our paths had crossed... but it wouldn't be the last...

"Yo! When I say Fetty, y'all say mob - Fetty-"
"Mob!", the crowd chanted.
"Fetty!"
"Mob!"
"Fetty, Fetty!"
"Mob, Mob!"
"Fetty, Fetty!"
"Mob, Mob!"

I was wonderin' how Freez was gonna get one up on this nigga. Hoffa may have had a lot'f niggas with him, but the truth of the matter was we were in Jersey, homefield advantage. Freez did the one thing he could do that would out-match the illest emcee - he played the crowd. After hittin' them off with the chorus again, Freez went in on ol' boy...

"I told'm I ain't playin', we get it, we got fetti... Been had fetti, eatin' lobsters and spaghetti... Nigga ain't ready, we gettin' cake like Little Debby... Oh yeah, did I tell y'all niggas we got fetti? Shout out to them haters, fuck'em we stay winnin', my car is ugly, straight black like a gremlin... I went from sleepin' in the studio, rockin' the same clothes for weeks... huggin' the streets... Mama said, boy you's a beast, So, all I did was go hard 'cause I'm a beast wit' it... Look at me now, nigga, I'm on a beat wit' it... Goin' hard, peep skills, we Fetty mobbin'... And look at my enemies, these niggas they steady starvin'... When I say Fetty, y'all say mob, Fetty-"

"Mob!"
"Fetty!"
"Mob!"

Face/ Fetty Boy

Freez had the crowd goin' again. Hoffa and all them niggas were straight ice grillin'. I wasn't even sure if Freez's spit game was slicker than Hoffa's. What did it was the way Freez delivered his shit. He was an animated nigga; he played the part... looked the part. He ain't even give Hoffa a chance to spit again. The crowd wanted to hear more of Freez anyway...

"I told'm he wasn't ready, I'm here wit' my nigga Fetty... We go hard on'em, yeah I told you he wasn't ready... I ain't playin' wit' this nigga, I'm sick dude... Chain 'round my neck, my wrist look like fish food... What? And your bitch dude... She wanna suck and fuck a nigga, I'm the shit dude... You wanted to bust me, you can't even touch me... Son, you disgust me, I ate ya rhymes like they was lunch meat... You fag-ass nigga, wait, (turning to the crowd) he ain't no bad-ass nigga... He bait, he fake, look at this sad-ass nigga's face... Y'all betta come and get'm, before I dead'm... Matter fact, sit back and watch how I nail'm... Bdddaat! Oh, shit, now his fuckin' family done lost'm... Run y'all asses back to the Bronx and don't say shit... But before you go, drop the ten grand on the pavement... Comin' over here to New Jeruz, you lose... rockin' ya bitch's shoes... what's those, Jimmy Choo's?"

Face/ Fetty Boy

Chapter 8: Clientele

Listenin' to Freez duffin' Billy Hoffa in that rap battle had made me more focused than ever. Me and my team are gonna push this coke until we hit millionaire status. Then, when we get Fetti Mobb Ent. up and runnin', Freez will have his own record label n'shit. He ain't gonna have to showcase his shit to some non-descript niggas in the parkin' lot of some fuckin' skatin' rink no more. My plans were comin' together; the one thing I really needed to do, though, was find a new connect. But no matter how well you plan or how well you execute, there's always gonna be some hatin'-ass niggas prayin' for your downfall. That ain't gonna be my future, though. I learned a long time ago - the best way to predict the future is to create your own.

    That's how all these other niggas made it out here - in the game or otherwise. New music artists were poppin' up all over the place. The group hittin' hard then was the Fugees. Consisting of two Haitian dudes along with this one chick from Newark. Jersey hadn't had a big hip-hop act like that since the homie Treach and Naughty By Nature came out with O.P.P. in '92. It was '96, and these Fugee kats were eatin' up the airwaves. Every bumpin' system was pumpin' out some Fugee beats.

"Fu La La La..." or "Ready or not, here I come, you can't hide... I'm gonna fiiind you..." The Fugees stayed rockin'.

    Everybody was makin' their own future. It was time for me to make mine.

Face/ Fetty Boy

It was like I blinked my eyes and the month of June just zoomed right by. It was still hot outside. The strip was an electric scenery as usual - gold diggers, hustlers, fiends, hookers, winos and pimps... money was everywhere and it was definitely changin' hands. But, every time I turned around, the money seemed to be landin' in the same person's hand. E-Rick.

E-Rick was slightly older than the niggas in my crew. He was a sho'nuff slickstah. But he had respect; people idolized him. You could never tell by lookin' at him, but this nigga done seen more and been through more than a little bit in the drug game. I thought I was a pure example of a nigga growin' up fast, but E-Rick had me beat by a mile. He had everybody beat - the hustlers, the addicts... even the cops. The jakes had no idea that E-Rick was hustlin' because every time you saw him, on the strip or anywhere else, he looked like he just got finished workin' in some office cubicle or something.

Even if he was out hustlin', he would do stuff just to throw people off. He wore reading glasses that he didn't even need. He didn't care if it was hot out, he'd still rocked a pair'f casual slacks and some expensive dress shoes. A few times, this nigga came on the block to trap wearin' a suit and tie.

The dude was so soft spoken, I could barely hear him. He talked one way to everybody. Every word he used was proper English, and he had respect even for the foulest person. The crackheads loved'm 'cause he treated them like fuckin' royalty. If the fiends were short on cash or if they were on E (empty), E-Rick still hit'em off. I never understood why he did that shit. I was always taught never to trust no fuckin' basehead. Not only did this nigga trust'em, he would give'em free shit on the strength. I sat back and thought about that shit one day - the crackheads are the cornerstone of the business. If you hustlin', you gotta treat'em right.

And, because of that, every time E-Rick hit the block,

Face/ Fetty Boy

all the crackheads flocked to him. And, like I said, he treated everybody with respect. So, anybody lookin' to cop would flock right to him - and so would all the money. The nigga had supreme clientele out this world.

At first I thought one'f the rowdy kats on the block was gonna push him, but E-Rick was the exact opposite of a dummy. He only hit the strip for forty minutes to an hour, tops. After that, you wouldn't see that nigga for days, weeks even. But every time us hustlers saw his 850i Beamer roll up, we knew to put our shit back in the stash and send our runners home. It was like every crackhead in North Jersey had instant message, facebook or twitter back then; they knew exactly when E-Rick was hittin' the strip.

E-Rick on the strip was somethin' to see. He'd come out, by himself, with a thousand dimes, and that shit would be gone in forty fuckin' minutes. Mind you, other niggas sold five-dollar bags in the 4th Ward. But E-Rick would come back three days later with about seven hundred twenty-bags, and he'd sell that shit quicker than other dudes sellin' nicks.

He'd disappear for a week, maybe a month, then come right back and do the same thing all over again. G.G. Ave had gotten used to the likes of E-Rick since the mid-eighties. That's just how it was... epic!

* * * * *

Tonight on the strip, though, I was in a fucked up mood. I didn't want nobody around me; not even Freez or Illy-Ill. I just sat my ass in the cut atop a milk crate, straight dolo, bubble gum chewin' and eye screwin' any nigga that walked by...including E-Rick.

It took every bit of common sense not to smack this nigga when he invaded my personal space and tried to give me some rap
"Talk about it, young G," E-Rick said. There he go wit' 'dat proper English shit. "You look like you have something

heavy on your mind." He pointed at me with one hand and at some crackheads with the other, "You are the baller," he said, "they are the crawlers. No baller should ever let any crawlers see him looking how you're looking right now."

    I didn't even look at E while he was talkin'. He probably thought my mood was all fucked up 'cause he was makin' all the money while everybody else was on the sideline. I mean, that had a little somethin' to do with it, but I munch plenty when E-Rick ain't around. That dumb-ass move I pulled with the connect up in the Bronx was weighin' heavy on my mind, though. If anybody knew what to say to get that shit out my head... it was E-Rick.

    "Yeah E, man, shit kind'f fucked up right now. I fucked up a good thing with my last supplier. And now I'm not sure if I'm comin' or goin'. Don't get me wrong, I'm gettin' plenty'f chips out this motherfucka, but them Dominican dudes uptown is somethin' else. I refuse to spend all my money with them, while they treatin' us like slaves - feel me?"

    I sat out there on that milk crate in the warmth of the night just spillin' my thoughts to E-Rick like a patient and he was my therapist. I told him everything about how I ganked Jose for four bricks. I told him how Hubby's death was weighin' on me when I had first come home. That nigga E was a good listener. I got thorough niggas in my camp, but for the most part, most'f them ain't nothin' but yes men. Whatever I said... them niggas was gonna do it. It was like that the first day I walked into the game. But E-Rick had been around; I knew if nothin' else, he was gonna put it to me straight.

    "My brother," E-Rick began, "I don't have to tell you because you already know... you shouldn't have done that. You have got to stay on point in this game; it's the natural order out here. I don't care if you have a crew with you or not, it's every man for himself out here. Looking over both shoulders is already a twenty-four hour job. Why on earth would you do something that forces you to look over your shoulders and behind you more than you already have to?"

Face/ Fetty Boy

"But that's how it was when I hit the streets again, E. When I came home from prison, everybody was beatin' connects."

"So, how come you haven't jumped off the George Washington Bridge yet, because it's plenty of fools doing that, too? Don't try to answer that, just listen. A vicious death or a long prison sentence is awaiting you, my brother. I'll say it again, they are going to put you behind bars forever or someone is going to kill you. What you need to do is take a page out of your man Hubby's book and read it thoroughly - word for word, young G."

Damn! E-Rick hit me with some shit my mother used to say. The truth was... he was right. Like he said before, I ain't the crawler, I'm the baller. Why the fuck am I out here doin' what these crawlers out here doin'?

The next couple of minutes silently ticked past us. I ain't say shit and neither did E. We just sat there watchin' the ebb and flow of the game unfold right before our eyes. I don't know why it had us in such a trance; it wasn't like we hadn't seen this shit before. Niggas duckin' in and out between the buildings tryin' to hide from the jakes. Crackheads actin' like they're your best friend, knowin' they'll stab you in your fuckin' face if someone else got cheaper or better product. Stick up boys layin' in the cut, waitin' for the wolves to take it in for the night. Another pimp slappin' the shit out'f another five-dollar whore. Chips just stayed gettin' flipped from pocket to pocket out this motherfucka. The game of hustlin' was immortal; it was us playahs that died off. And sittin' here with E-Rick made me realize that I had to make better decisions while I'm still alive in this game. That's what makes life so difficult; life forces us to make decisions. If you don't make a choice or make the wrong choice, life will make the choice for ya.

The same thing applies to the street game - take ya shot, or the shot will take you.

E-Rick finally broke the silence. "It's a hard knock life,

young G," he said. "So, next time, don't take your knock so hard. And don't sweat this connect thing so much, either. I like to see without looking, you understand what I'm saying? And I see how you move out here, and because of that, I'm going to hook you up. Tomorrow. Two o'clock. Meet me right at this very spot, and I'll put you onto one of my connects." I tried to interrupt E-Rick just so I could thank him for the hook up, but he held his finger in the air tellin' me not to speak and just kept on schoolin' me. "Two o'clock, Fetty. One fifty-nine is no good and two-zero-one is worst than that. I deal with prime time, Fetty Boy. Prime time and T-I-M-E. time - as in time is man's enemy. So, don't be late."

E-Rick left me sittin' on my milk crate.

He went right back to burnin' up the block, and everybody else went right back to hatin' on him. The niggas on my team tried askin' me what we had spent the past ten minutes talkin' about. I ain't tell'em shit though.

"Just Choppin' it up," I lied. I told the runners to get ready so they could get that paper once E-Rick was done stackin' his. Tomorrow's gonna be a new day. 'Bout time, too. I'm tired of coppin' that overpriced garbage from Vic and the rest'f them niggas on 135th and Broadway. Thanks to E, it's about to be on again.

Face/ Fetty Boy

Chapter 9: Game Recognize Game & Hoes Do Too

The way E-Rick spit that game to me, you best believe I was on time the next day. Hookin' up with the new connect was like eatin' dessert at Friendly's - sweeter than a motherfucka! I didn't tell anyone in my clique a word, either. Gotta be tight-grill with ya situations sometimes; dudes are like hoes... love to run their mouth. As far as they knew, I had peaced things up with my old connect. I flooded the hood with so much white, it was like winter time in August on the block. With the connect problem out the way, I had time to do other things.

For example, a few weeks later, I finally carried my ass up to the DMV in White Man's Land also known as Wayne New Jersey. That shit didn't go at all as planned. Some old-ass nosy-behind white lady fucked the whole scheme up.

I had stopped by my Mom's crib and snatched up all my necessary ID's - social security card, birth certificate... the whole nine. I gets up to the DMV, fills out the paperwork, then jumps in line. By the time I got to the window, I could read the vibe comin' off the old grumpy bitch. She was past her prime, nobody was tossin' her any cock, she hated her job, and the look on her face said she hated black people even more. You

Face/ Fetty Boy

know I was ass-out 'cause I'm blacker than the blackest black motherfucka.

This bitch looked me right in my face and asked, "How old are you again?"

"I'm sixteen, miss."

As soon as I answered the lady, I wanted to kick myself in the ass 'cause my ID said I was eighteen. And the most important thing about the score-card is that you gotta use it while you're still enrolled in high school and while you're still sixteen.

"Your ID says your eighteen," she said with her old raspy voice.

"Huh? Oh, yeah, I... uh... had the score-card for a while because I had dropped out. Now that I'm back in school, I just wanted to see if my score-card was still..."

"No, it ain't good anymore," the old bitch interrupted. "You want your permit, you have to re-take the written test."

The squint in her eye and the smirk of her lips told me that she knew I was tryin' to game her old-wrinkled ass. She probably done already snagged a bunch'f niggas comin' up here with these fuckin' score-cards. I quickly snatched up all my ID's and hauled ass up out'f there before this white bitch called the man on me.

It was a small setback; coppin' the new whip that I wanted was gonna have to wait until the summer was almost over. The shit was kind'f funny actually. I was still in a good mood, though. Things were goin' smooth with the connect, and almost gettin' caught at the DMV had given me another reason to call Nina's sexy ass.

"Hello," the voice said. Out the gate, I knew it wasn't Nina's.

So I asked, "Yes, can I speak with Nina, please?" The woman on the phone sounded a little older than the average chick, so I had to be on my polite shit.

"And, may I ask who's calling?" the woman said.

"Oh, um... just tell her it's Franco."

Face/ Fetty Boy

After a few seconds, "Hello," Nina said, "who is this?"

"It's me, Fetty. I had to use my real name 'cause I didn't know if that was your mother or not."

"Well, it was. So, what d'you want, boy... I'm studyin'?"

"Yo, breathe easy, ma. I was just chillin' over my mom's house and I decided to give you a call. I just figured you would like to know that Fetty Boy almost went to jail today messin' wit' you and your little score-card."

She sucked her teeth into the phone. And, judging by the brief silence, I could tell that she rolled her eyes, too. "You almost go to jail everyday doin' the crap that you do. You don't need no score-card for that," she said. Her little slick vernacular made me smile. "So, what happened, anyway?" she asked, at the same time, laughin' as if she knew I would get caught.

I told her about the old white lady callin' my bluff. Nina just started laughin' harder and harder. She had a cute lil' giggle.

"That's what you get for lookin' so old," she said. You look like you twenty instead of seventeen."

"That's all you got to say for yourself?"

"What you want me to say? You tryin' to get a refund or somethin'?"

"You bein' real corny right now," I told her. "That little hundred dollars ain't about nothin'. What I need is for you to help me study for that written test whenever we go out on that date that you owe me."

The phone went silent.

I leaned back on my mother's couch and kicked my feet up on the coffee table, while smokin' a bogey, even though my mother would've slapped me in the back of my head if she ever saw me doin' that. I could hear Nina smilin' into the phone. She was tryin' not to act like it, but I knew I was growin' on her.

After suckin' her teeth again, "Aight, boy," she said. "But call me back later, though. I really need to study for

Face/ Fetty Boy

these tests that's comin' up."

Got her! I thought to myself. Then I asked, "What time?"

"Holler at me around ten tonight. I should be free by then."

"You got that, shawty." Before we even hung up the phone, I had this song playin' in my head that reminded me of how bad Nina's body was - "Face down, ass up... That's the way I like to fuck!" And couldn't wait to hit Cleo with the diznick.

* * * * *

Weeks flew by like lambos on a raceway. Me and Nina stayed kickin' it every night, that's even with her hittin' me with that "Oh, I gotta study" shit. I re- spected her game. She was serious about educatin' herself; who am I to come between that? But I was serious about diggin' in them guts. Not only that, but ol' girl was bonafided wifey material... I was puttin' my bid in for real, by fakin' it to make it. We even went on a few dates.

Nina took me to spots all over my area that I didn't even know existed. We hit up T.G.I. Friday on Hamburg Turnpike a number of times. There was this place called Fudrucker's on the easthbound side of Route 4 that sold these huge-ass hamburgers. When the waitress brought one of them shits to our table I was like, "What the fuck?!"

This famous white dude named Kenny Rogers - I think he was a country singer - had a restaurant in Engelwood; we hit that up three or four times. The most expensive place we went to, though, was probably 6 Brothers' Restaurant on Route 46 in Wayne. The swordfish in that spot was bangin' better than the Crips & Bloods!

I took her bowlin', to the movies and even Roller Skatin'.

I ain't see no parts of the pussy and niggas were already callin' her my girl. It was whatever, though. I'm young. I'm a shot caller. Not to mention Hood rich. I don't care how you slice it, that right there ain't nothin' but the mathematical formula for pussy.

Face/ Fetty Boy

And, as bad as I wanted to be balls deep in that ass, it didn't really bother me that Nina was playin' keep away with the pussy. We were still having a good time. The girl even went with me to the DMV so I could take the written test - of course, with Nina's help, I passed that shit with flying colors.

The thing that really blew my mind is that Nina insisted that she go with me whenever I went up to Spanish Harlem to cop from the new connect E-Rick had put me on to. I wanted to keep my life in the streets away from her. But the chick was feelin' me... I was feelin' her. She wanted to be around me, so I took her wherever I went.

Before we would hit the coke spot in Spanish Harlem, Nina would take me to 145th and St. Nicholas. She liked to eat the shrimp at this little fish and chips spot located on the corner next to the subway. After gettin' our shrimp on, we would go cop them bricks. She would even open and burn the tips of the bags whenever I bagged up in front of her.

It was little shit like that she would always do that made me fall in love with the girl all over again every time I'd pick her up in the morning. Yeah, you heard it right - a nigga fell in love and ain't even taste the pussy yet.

I told myself I wouldn't wife none'f these bitches from around my way. But ol' girl was a keeper. She wasn't like the rest'f these 4th Ward hookers. I used to fuck'em, don't love'em, then leave'em. I ain't even get around to the fuckin' part yet, and was already loving her. So, you know I ain't gonna leave her.

* * * * *

We were posted up one night in front of my mom's brownstone condominium-style apartment. We had just gotten back from a 7 o'clock movie at the Clifton theater.

Whenever we would get back from a date, Nina liked to sit in the car and talk while gazin' up at the stars. Which was cool with me. Like I said, I respected her game. She had

Face/ Fetty Boy

direction. She wasn't tryin' to change'em, but she damn sure was tryin' to make a nigga a part of her life.

And you know what happens when a chick is thinkin' about a kat like that. Eventually, the "where are we goin' with this relationship" talk comes up. "So, when are you going to officially make me your girlfriend?" Nina asked. That fucked me up right there 'cause I kind'f already thought she was. "Because you got way too many female friends," she continued,

"for me to be callin' myself your girl."

I smiled at her.

"Kick all your male friends to the curb and we can do this," I said. "If I can't have no females in my camp, you can't have no other niggas sniffin' around the bushes. Feel me?"

"Who have I been spendin' all my time with, Fetty? All of my precious time... twenty-four-seven?"

"True 'dat," I jokingly said. To get the fruit, I guess I gotta climb the tree first. "If that's the case, you can consider all of my so-called female friends voted off the island. And, if you think you can handle it, I'm ready to turn this friendship into a relationship, and the relationship into a partnership. You think you can handle that... potnah?"

A chick doesn't really know what to do when a nigga asks her to be his partner. Callin' a girl a girlfriend is givin' her too much power. Now she's gonna expect shit all the time. She'll want you to wear certain clothes. Be available at a certain time. Talk a certain way. Fuck all that. If you call her a fuck friend, she's already gonna know what it's hittin' for. Only problem with that is she's gonna have a real boyfriend on the side who's gonna be fuckin' her, too. But if you call her your partner, that means she's all in. She's gonna know what to do before you even ask. She's gonna know that she needs to suck on your balls, nibble on your balls, then hum while your nuts are deep in her mouth. She's gonna know what to cook and how to cook it. She's gonna know what to say and how to say it. She's gonna know what to give and know what to take.

Face/ Fetty Boy

You gotta teach her that what effects one effects the other. If you can teach a bitch all that, then you gotta make her your partner... potnah.

"I can handle bein' your partner," she said with those thick-ass lips.

"Nah, yo. You can't say it like that. It's potnah. Lemme hear you say it."

"Potnah."

Oh, shit, yo. She sounded cuter than a motherfucka when she said that shit. She looked in my face and started starin' at my lips like she wanted to tongue me down.

"Potnah," she repeated.

I leaned over and let her give me a little tongue action. She started hand-jobbin' me, then stared me in my eyes as she sucked on my bottom lip. She must've gotten that tingly feeling that chicks get whenever they get horny 'cause all of a sudden, ol' girl had to use the bathroom.

"I gotta pee," she said. "Can we go upstairs?"

"That's cool. But we gotta be quiet 'cause my moms is restin' up so she can go to work tomorrow."

She gave me that look. You know the look, the glance that can say a thousand fuckin' things. But all she said was, "We ain't gonna be up there long enough to make any noise; all I gotta do is pee."

I could hear Nina upstairs; a loose floor board was right outside the bathroom. Every time somebody walked on it, the floor would make a sound as if my mom's crib was a old haunted house or somethin'.

I hit up the fridge for some apple juice - quietly dropped some ice into two glasses. After flippin' the switch off in the kitchen, I tip-toed upstairs tryin' not to wake my moms. By the time I reached my bedroom, Nina was already bein' nosy, snoopin' around n'shit. She had that innocent look on her face when I caught her.

My closet door was slightly opened. She must've been checkin' my gear. The kicks were lined up on the floor of the closet, whatever could fit. I had brand new boxes of Tims and Nikes stacked in the corner by my stereo that hadn't even been worn yet.

    I watched Nina stroll her sexy ass over to my dresser. She picked up one of my watches and slipped it over her wrist. The Movado slid all the way down to her elbow. Next, she took my twenty inch Cuban link. When she slung it around her neck, the diamond encrusted crucifix hung low on her; next to her coochie. She smiled at me, then took the apple juice from my hand. She took a sip. Another sip. Every time she tasted some, she licked her lips like she wanted somethin' else in her mouth. Man, my PePe jeans looked like I pitched a tent under them motherfuckas. She keep talkin' this no sex shit, but she keep on teasin' me.

    I can't even remember how we ended up on the bed. One minute I'm standin' there holdin' apple juice and turnin' on the TV, the next minute both of us got our shirts off, rollin' around in a lip lock. All this time we had been goin' out, I was hornier than a teenager at a porno shoot. I wasn't sure, but I think Nina was fiendin' for the dick just as much as I was chasin' after the pussy. We were like an overheated engine of a Lamborghini, and somebody just opened the hood so we could let out the steam.

    Shit was real heated. But, according to Nina a few weeks ago, she made it perfectly clear that sex was out the question- talkin' 'bout she wasn't ready for all that; her school, her career and all that. Plus, she had on these tight-ass Blue Levi's jeans; I already told myself them shits wasn't comin' off.

    While we got lost in the kiss, my hand found its way to her full-sized Breasts. I palmed the shit out of one of them big motherfuckas, gave the pinch stroke to the nipple and everything.

    "You smell sooo fuckin' good, girl," I told her. Then worked my tongue into her ear hole and breathed on her neck hard and heavy. Fuck it - might as well go all in now, I told myself. While my one hand was still teasin' her titty, I used the other hand to undo the buttons of her jeans. I remembered she told me once that she never wore panties; my dick damn near jumped out my pants.

I found her clit with ease and got well acquainted with it for a while. Her hands started roamin' my chest and back; I took that as a sign to keep on keepin' on. I left the clit alone and started finger fuckin' her. That went on for about two minutes, then what happened next was like somethin' straight out'f a Poltergeist movie. It was as if Nina was possessed all of a sudden, like a spirit took her body over.

She couldn't resist a nigga any longer. All that no pussy shit went right out the window. She practically shoved me off her so she could wriggle out of her jeans. She yanked them shits down to her ankles, then kicked both her shoes off. Once she got her jeans all the way off, she started tuggin' at my zipper like a hostage on a king-sized candy bar.

"I want it!" she screamed. "Gimme that dick!"

"Shh." I had to remind her that my moms was still in the other room asleep, but it was like Nina didn't even give a fuck about that. A nigga was so excited, I almost forgot what to do!

I shook that shit off quick, though. Then put two ice cubes from the juice glass into my mouth. I ain't know much about suckin' on some pussy, but tonight I was feelin' a little spontaneous. After I numbed up her clit, I spit the cubes into her hot pussy so they could melt; probably could've boiled an egg up in there. Yo, I sucked on the lips of her pussy like it was guava juice. Talk about goin' crazy. Shawty grabbed the back of my head and wouldn't let go. My moms had to hear that shit in the next room 'cause, every time my tongue flicked that clit, Nina moaned like a nympho.

"Ooh, shit! I want it! Come on, Fetty! Please! Give that shit to me! I need that big-black-cock in my pussy!"

I heard! Ha, ha... all that good girl shit went out the door. Cleopatra is a motherfuckin' freak!

I put her legs up and pounded that juicy pussy like a porn star. It got to the point where I ain't give a fuck about the noise. I went in straight for ten minutes, long dickin' from the tip to the balls like a jack hammer!

Oh, I'm 'bout to flip this over, I said to myself. Nina had a confused look on her face when I tossed her legs to the side and turned that ass over. She knew what to do, though. Like I said, a good potnah knows what to do before you ask. She automatically arched that ass in the air. I grabbed her hips and used my thumbs to spread her chocolate mounds. We were both facin' toward the mirror on my dresser, so I was able to see the look in her eyes. She gritted her teeth as I popped the cockasaurus in that tight, but wet pussy. Man, her fuck-face was tellin' me that I was turning corners on her spine that she didn't even know she had.

Barely able to breathe, "Oh, my god, Fetty!" Nina shouted. "This is your pussy! This is your pussy from now on! Fuck it! Fuck it harder!"

It got to the point where her screams of pleasure sounded almost like she was cryin'. I looked into the mirror and saw her eyes disappear into her head. That shit turned me on even more. I exploded so hard in the pussy that a lot'f the jizz spilled right back out. At that moment, I thought back about a month ago when I told myself I was gonna run up in Nina bald headed. Her pussy was so good, my dick forgot that it already spit up in her; my shit was back to rock hard in no time. The pussy-pound dance lasted for almost two and a half hours. A nigga caught two charlie-horses. I busted off five times up in that cum canal. Ol' girl shot back three orgasms herself. The same way she begged me to fuck her, she had to beg me to stop. As soon as I pulled out, Nina fell to the bed like someone punched her in the back of her head or somethin'. She ain't move out'f that position until mornin'.

* * * * *

The next day after school, Nina was waitin' on my doorstep when I got home. She didn't have to say anything; the look on her face told me she wanted me to beat the skins up some

Face/ Fetty Boy

more. That Capone-N-Noreaga song came to mind, "You work all day, Come home for foreplay..." Instead of work, Nina ran home from school for the dick. It became our regular routine. One day, she was ridin' the pole and, right before she was about to cum, she said, "All we do is fuck, Fetty!" I ain't pay that shit no mind 'cause, truth be told, Nina was the first chick to ever make me cum multiple times. Normally it was a nut, maybe two, then I was Outty-5,000. But this shit here had to be love in its purest form. I told her no other girl could keep my shit hard like she could. I told her the reason why I stay up in the pussy is because I loved her.

After she heard that, she couldn't control herself anymore, neither of us could. We fucked like a couple'f runaway slaves. The park... we fucked in it. If it was rainin'... we still fucked outside. I crept in the shower on her, she crept in the shower on me. While shoppin' at the mall, we would dip into the bathroom and pop each other off in the stall. Everybody probably did the fuckin' in the movie theater thing. But when we went to see the movie Love Jones, seein' Lorenz Tate fuck the shit out'f Nia Long sent me and Nina over the top. We hauled ass straight to the parkin' lot. I bent her over the passenger's seat while I stood outside the car and pounded that pussy. We stayed in that position for almost twenty minutes!

Nina had the illest pussy on the planet. Dammit! It stayed wetter than an aquarium. How did Method Man say it? "I gotta love jones for her body and her skin tone..."

Word had gotten out that I had wifed her pretty ass, and all the hatin'-ass bitches started throwin' free pussy at a nigga just for fun. All the chicks hated on Nina, but couldn't none of them top her. Shit worked out for me, though; I was gettin' more butts than an ashtray!

Face/ Fetty Boy

10 The Drought

E-Rick's connect was the truth. The hood stayed flooded the entire summer, which meant I was off the block and up in Nina most of the time. The only time my team needed to see me was when the Narcos ran down on the block. I'd come through and make sure everybody made bail. I kept this bail bondsman named Scottie on retainer to handle that type'f shit. The strip didn't need to see no parts of Fetty for the rest of the summer. Just like that new Jay-Z song go, I was "Feelin' It!" Jay-Z's "Reasonable Doubt" album was official tissue - and "Feelin' It" was my absolute favorite rap song ever! The game had me "feelin' it like a high you can only get from the lye."

    The hood don't stop for nobody - the jakes, the hustlers, crackheads... nobody. One monkey don't stop no show. If you kill one, ten more are waitin' to take his place. The game was like an immortal monster - you can't kill it no matter how hard you try. But, you know what they say, if you wanna take a beast down, you gotta cut off it's head. And the head of the strip, the very thing that kept the block breathin', was the coke. When the drought came, the beast got his motherfuckin' head cut off.

    Word was some Mexican dude, comin' from the West Coast on Route 80 headin' to N.Y.C., fell asleep at the wheel in a truck carryin' 2,500 kilos. That shit can only mean one

Face/ Fetty Boy

thing- kats who were already holdin' onto a little somethin' were gonna jack their prices sky-fuckin'-high - especially them fuckin' Dominicans. The Wet Back was carryin' their shit when the truck overturned; of course they were gonna shoot the price up to cover the loss. That's just how the drug game go.

Ain't no tellin' how long a drought will last. I was heated about that 'cause I was plannin' to cop my new whip by my September 3rd b-day - right around Labor Day. Another thing that had me concerned about the drought was I had been trickin' heavy with most of my paper. The salespersons at the mall were happy as shit whenever me and Nina rolled through. We was coppin' this outfit, that outfit. These shoes, those coach bags. Nina's college tuition... her mama's bills... I was takin' care of all that shit. Not to mention Nina's high maintenance habits- hair done... nails done... everyting did!

Coke was so scarce in all of Jersey that the strip went back to sellin' them small-ass 38/38 size bags that were hard as fuck to open. The only thing was we had to push'em for dimes and fifteens instead of nicks; me and my team were definitely feelin' the hunger pains of the game. Anybody with leftover product would always take advantage of a drought.

A week or two shot by. The new connect was on some funny shit, tellin' me there wasn't any work; come to find out, he was still sellin' to E-Rick and all the other old-heads who fit that category.

Shit had me vexed. But, what the fuck was I gonna do? It's not like I can force the nigga to sell me his product. The truth of the matter was I had to take the L, at least for now. Whenever the new connect did decided to throw me a bone, he sold the birds for forty G's instead of the usual twenty-five. That shit just made me wanna gank his punk ass just like I did the last connect. I kept tellin' Freez that we should rob the new connect, and surprisingly he was all for it. Freez was reduced to sellin' half of a nick for fifteen; he probably wanted to rob the connect more than I did. He even had his mind fixed on headin' down South when he heard those tiny-ass nicks were goin' for

Face/ Fetty Boy

twenties down there. I wasn't tryin' to hear that leavin' the hood shit just to go and take over another nigga's turf. Especially not after what happened to my man Nayshawn. When he went that route, them country bamma niggas sent him back to his mama in a pine box. If I let my niggas start goin' down there, it would turn out to be more trouble than it's worth. I understand that the murder game is part of the drug game; but it ain't wise to go lookin' for that shit. Besides, me and my niggas are 4th Ward for life; ain't no need to go scramble somewhere else.

Three weeks to a month was the max for a drought. Yet, here it was six weeks later, and these stinkin'-ass Goya bean eatin' niggas were still taxin' us... just because they could. That's how the game go. Fuck it!

* * * * *

In the meantime in between time, me and Illy-Ill came up with a way to supplement our income. The drought was just about over, but the strip was still feelin' its effects. The new plan was to go across the bridge into Harlem to scope out niggas with out'f state plates - CT, DE, NJ, PA, MASS, VI. We were gonna catch'em before or after they went into Spanish Harlem to cop their drugs. Illy-Ill liked to call it jooks; that's when we would take a nigga for all his shit. Only problem was we had to move swift and slick because of what was known as TNT days.

TNT days was when the cops would be raidin' the Harlem blocks in full force. They would just come around shakin' shit up. So, when shit got hot, we had this chick named Tiff posted up at the rendezvous - a high maintenance hair salon. Not just any old beauty parlor; it had to be a place that catered to high price whores, gold diggers, and rich mistresses. A spot Tiff liked to use was known as Sasha's. It was located around the corner from the Polo Grounds on 151st Street. Anybody who was somebody's girlfriend hit this spot up to get their

Face/ Fetty Boy

hair and nails done. Drug dealers' chicks. Pro ball players' chicks. Bitches that owned their own companies. If they were a so-called somebody, that meant they went to Sasha's.

A beauty salon ain't no different from a barber shop. The way males talk about all types of shit while gettin' their hair cut, females do the same ol 'thing. And Tiff would just be sittin' in the salon soakin' in all the gossip.

Tiff would blend in and partake in all the chatter about nothin'. But, on the low, she'd be scopin' the place out for some rich nigga who was droppin' his bitch off; either she would beep me 911 or call on the flip-phone after finding the marks. Then me and Illy-Ill would follow their ass home and gank'em.

Tiff was inside Sasha's gettin' her do did, at the same time, readin' the latest issue of Ebony mag, when this chick named Crystal came ridin' in on her high horse. As soon as Crystal hit the shop, all the whispers started; it seemed like everybody knew who she was, except Tiff.

"Damn, girl!" Crystal's hairdresser shouted. "Whose white Benz truck you just pulled up in?"

Crystal sucked her teeth as if to say the truck was small pennies to somebody of her status, as she sat down in the rotating leather chair. "That's just a little somethin' Marcus bought me for my birthday last week."

"A little somethin'?" the hairdresser repeated. "Well, that little somethin' looks like it cost a pretty penny."

"Ha! A pretty penny is worth every bit of a pretty piece'f ass, don't you think?" Crystal responded.

All of the high-priced hookers laughed it up as Crystal was gettin' her hair done. The laughter turned into gossip, and the gossip turned into braggin'. All the bitches were sayin' how their man bought them this or their man bought them that. Eventually, the braggin' turned into talkin' too goddamn much.

Crystal let it slip out how her man Marcus had shit on lock, moving birds from Spring Valley to Mount Vernon. She said somethin' about how they recently purchased a 20,000 square foot house up in Rockland County. Then the bitch did

Face/ Fetty Boy

the ultimate no-no; she bragged about which Catholic school her two kids went to. She gave up the name of the school, where it was at, her kids names; the bitch didn't have any idea that she handed me some leverage to rob her and her markass bustah of a boyfriend.

Tiff went right to the pay phone and beeped a nigga.

* * * * *

It wasn't always automatic. Sometimes, we'd be ridin' around Harlem for hours tryin' to find the perfect mark - especially when them TNT boys were out and about.

Most of the time, we stayed blunted, just chillin'. Of course, that left room for funny niggas like Illy-Ill to entertain us n'shit.

Gooch was drivin' a little slower than usual because it was drizzlin' out when he decided to ask, "Yo, Ill? Why do niggas always say, 'happier than a fag down Bordentown'?"

I just shook my head and laughed 'cause I knew the car ride was about to turn into Def Jam Comedy Hour.

"That ain't about nothin', doggie. A lot'f niggas down Buck Town be havin' fuck-boys; they don't even be hidin' that shit either. Thorough dudes, killas, boxing niggas, fake gangsta niggas with reps... all them niggas packin' fudge. They be caterin' to them fags, makin' their bids easy n'shit. That's where that dumb-ass sayin' comes from. At least, that's how it used to be down Buck Town, doggie. Niggas your age comin' in there now, Gooch. They ain't tryin' to hear that shit."

We sat there and listened as Gooch decided to ask the silliest question in history, "Did any of them fags ever come onto you, Ill?"

"Think that if you want to, doggie. All them fag niggas got a gay radar - gaydar, nigga. They know who wit' it and who ain't from the door. If you's a menace like me, the motherfuckin' jakes don't even wanna talk to you, so you know them fags ain't gonna say shit; much less, look at a nigga. Besides,

Face/ Fetty Boy

motherfucka, the only ass I ever ran up in down there was your mom's when she came down to visit me!"

Just like I thought. It wasn't gonna be long before Ill went in on the jokes. I was the only one in the crew that could really shoot back whenever Ill started firin'.

"Yo, Ill, since you got all the gay answers, answer this shit here. What's the difference between a batty boy parade and a bisexual pride parade?" I knew I fucked him and Gooch up with that, so I just answered for him. "The difference is...the bisexual parade goes both ways... like you, nigga!"

There was so much laughter after that, I couldn't even hear the music playin' anymore. And Ill ain't the type to be clowned unless he clowns back harder.

"Oh, yeah! You tryin' to get funny on Illy-Ill, doggie? I got one for you, doggie. You in the joint right, and some fag nigga on your unit writes you a letter. Would you write him back or tear it up, nigga?"

I ain't even have to think about that one, "I'd tear that shit up, nigga. What the fuck?"

As soon as I answered, both Gooch and Illy-Ill started gyratin' like they were fuckin a bitch doggie style or somethin'. They started singin', "Tear it uuup! Tear it uuup! Fetty gonna tear that aaass uuup!"

"Oh, hell no!" I shouted. "I meant the letter, nigga! I'd beat the punk ass and stuff the letter down his throat!"

"Nah.. too late, doggie! Tear it uuup! Don't try to clean that shit up now; you better clean that shit off your dick, nigga!"

I knew I shouldn't have tried to clown Illy-Ill. That's a funny motherfucka right there. Him and Gooch laughed at a nigga for eight more blocks. I was happy as hell when I got that page from Tiff.

* * * * *

Face/ Fetty Boy

It took all of two minutes for me, Ill, and Gooch to arrive at Sasha's. Freez was supposed to be the driver whenever we went on our robbin' sprees, but nobody knew where to find him earlier. Didn't matter; Lil' Goochie was just as good with the wheel.

I got out the whip and headed toward the salon, but Tiff was waitin' for me out front. She gave me a head nod tellin' me not to get too close - she didn't want nobody to see her talkin' to me. She got in the car with Robin Hood and the rest of the bandits, then started goin' in on the chick Crystal.

"Yo, Fetty! This bitch is paid up for motherfuckin' real, yo!" Tiff hollered. "She's in there runnin' her mouth about how her man got this and got that. He's supposed to be some kingpin nigga from Yonkers. The bitch drivin' that white truck wit' the temporary plates in the back window parked right over there."

I looked at the white Benz truck Tiff was pointin' at; it was worth an easy fifty G's.

"Aight, Tiff. Say no more, we on it." I leaned back from the passenger's seat and gave Tiff a little kiss just to make her feel like she was important.

"If it's on like you say it's on," Illy-Ill joined in, "then we gonna follow this bitch all night 'til she take her ass home. We can catch her and her man slippin'... I ain't above robbin' no bitch, doggie. I'll jack a leprechaun for his pot of gold, so you know I'll do the same thing to a gold diggin' broad!"

After we finished laughin' at Illy-Ill's funny ass for the third time, Tiff continued with the rundown, "Crystal told the whole salon how her and Marcus just bought a house up in Rockland County close to Bear Mountain," she said.

"Cool, Tiff," I said. "Go back in there and get your hair done; you lookin' like a hot mess." I smacked her on the ass as she got out the ride. "When you're done, go home. I'll stop by your mom's house as soon as we pull this jooks off. I'll have a little somethin' for you."

Face/ Fetty Boy

We thought we were gonna have to be on some real live stake-out type shit. However, Crystal's fine, black ass came strollin' out the shop about a half hour later with her Baywatch body and Toni Braxton hair style.

Before getting into her vehicle, she checked her hair in the mirror on the driver's side. Whoever this guy Marcus was, he sure knew how to pick'em; his lady's shit was tight. She hopped in her truck, then dipped right onto the Palisades Parkway, after crossin' the George Washington bridge. If the girl wasn't so caught up into her vanity, she might've I doubt it - but she might've noticed that we were followin' her at a three car distance.

She got off the Palisades at exit 56.

We got off at the same exit eight seconds behind her.

Less than a two-minute drive later, Crystal pulled up in front of this huge country-style home.

The house had a three-car garage. Tennis court. Basketball court. We couldn't tell from our position, but I know there was a pool, too. The grass was cut. In fact, every house on this street looked like somethin' straight out'f Better Homes & Gardens.

We watched Crystal press the button on her garage door opener; the garage on the far-right opened up.

Illy-Ill was already out the car with the chrome Smith & Wesson .38 hidden behind his back. He crept up slowly; the shit had to be timed perfectly. Most expensive garage doors automatically close once the car is safely in its spot. As soon as the door began to come down, Ill ducked under it and grabbed the bitch from behind with one hand around her mouth and the other holdin' the banger to her throat.

He licked the bitch's ear, then whispered to her on some creepy stalker shit, "Open the garage door back up, bitch."

As soon as the door slid back open, me and Gooch dipped inside, then drew our pistols. Next to Crystal's ride was a pearl white CLK Benz convertible.

After pointing toward the car, "Bitch, whose shit is this?" I asked. Crystal was almost too frightened to answer me. Ill

Face/ Fetty Boy

still had his hand around her mouth while tears still streamed from her eyes. Her fear almost caused her to hyperventilate "I'ma tell my manz to let go," I said. "If you scream, I'm lettin' go of one'f these bullets - ya dig?"

Crystal squeezed her eyes shut and shook her head up and down. I told Illy-Ill to let her breathe so she could answer my question.

"Th-th-the car... belongs... to my b-boyfriend Marcus," she said.

"That nigga inside?"

Crystal's tears fell a little heavier as she shook her head in the affirmative. I think what really made her cry was the sight of Lil' Gooch standin' next to me holdin' his glock and a fresh roll of duct tape.

"Gooch... Ill, y'all go 'head and tape this bitch up right here. Leave her ass in the back of the truck."

The inside of the crib spoke dollar signs just as much as the outside. This nigga actually had crystal chandeliers hangin' everywhere. I could tell this Marcus kat wasn't the ordinary street dealer. Porcelain vases, self portraits on the wall, white-swirl marble floors... shyiit, I was tempted to dump this nigga and his bitch in the river, then move the fuck in.

"What the fuck," Illy-Ill loudly whispered after he and Lil' Gooch entered from the garage. They must've been out there playin' with that whore's pussy after they duct taped her ass; I can only assume 'cause I'd been waitin' for almost ten minutes for them to come inside. "Yo, if this nigga ballin' like this, then niggas in Jersey is hustlin' the fuck backwards, doggie. Do you see this motherfucka's house?"

I ignored Ill and Gooch marvelin' over this nigga's spot; it ain't easy to impress me. I never was the type to give a fuck 'bout what another nigga had... unless, of course, I was plannin' on takin' it. I wasn't no playa hater either. Shiiit, Fetty congratulates if anything. There are only two types of people I've ever hated - that's a lyin'-ass bitch and a cryin'-ass nigga.

"Y'all finish ridin' this nigga's dick, yo?" I asked. Before my menz had a chance to say somethin' slick, I kept on with the questions. "Is that bitch tied up good out there?"

Lil' Gooch smiled at me like a pervert waitin' outside of an all-girls Catholic school. He reached inside his pocket and pulled out what looked like a pair of panties.

"Man, y'all niggas took the bitch's underwear?" I asked.

"Whoa! 'Y'all' ain't do shit, doggie," Illy-Ill quickly replied. "This freak-booty-nigga did that shit all by himself." Then Ill tilted his head to the side and smiled at me, too. "I'm glad he did though... that bitch shit tight than a motherfucka."

"Man, bring y'all asses up these goddamn stairs, and be on point."

We hit the top of the stairs, and realized that there were five laid out bedrooms up there. Then it dawned on me – when Crystal was in the salon, she made mention of havin' two kids. We didn't stop to consider if those little motherfuckas were home or not.

"Check the bedrooms," I whispered.

"Ain't no need, doggie. While I was duct tapin' the bitch and this nigga was fingerin' her pussy, she told us that her kids were still at summer camp. Ol' boy is up here by himself; in fact," Ill stopped to look at his watch, "the bitch said he usually stays asleep until nine PM - it's twenty past seven right now, doggie. The big bedroom on the end is theirs."

We quietly chambered our bangers.

Before we made our approach toward the master bedroom,
I whispered in Gooch's ear tellin' him to go to the garage and bring Miss No Panties upstairs. Before he ran down the stairs, I grabbed Gooch by his arm and told him we didn't have no time for his personal porno dreams.

"Bring the bitch right upstairs!"

Face/ Fetty Boy

As Gooch spun off, Illy-Ill was already inside the master bedroom. Seven-thirty at night, and this nigga Marcus was up here asleep wearin' some Superman tighty whities. We didn't have a chance to laugh at the nigga. The only sound I heard was the flesh of this nigga's face jigglin' after Ill smacked him back to life.

"Wake yo bitch-ass up, nigga!" Ill shouted.

Ol' boy jumped up like we dumped cold water on him or some-thin'. The nigga was almost as black as me, but his face was white and wide-eyed like he had seen a ghost. He kept blinkin' his eyes and shakin' his head from left to right.

"This ain't no dream, nigga," Illy-Ill said after putting the steel right against the nigga's bottom lip. "A nightmare, maybe, but it ain't no dream."

"I'ma tell you what this is," I said. "This is your one and only chance you get to be a prosecutor." Even scared out'f his fuckin' mind, the nigga Marcus looked at me like I was crazy. "A prosecutor decides what a nigga gets charged with - they're the ones who control why niggas like you and me get sent up the river. Ya dig? So, you get to decide... right now. What are my menz & I gonna get charged with - robbery slash home invasion? Or a robbery, slash home invasion, slash two counts of murder? It's all the same to us, nigga. With the criminal jackets we sportin', the robbery alone will have us locked up in them mountains until the sun burn out. So, you could get wit' this," I rubbed my two fingers together symbolizin' the money sign,

"or you could get wit' that," this time I pointed at Gooch with his pistol up the bitch Crystal's ass. "The choice is yours."

The nigga was shook like a flagpole in the wind. Motherfucka even started to sob. He was a big dude, too; that shit confused me, until I turned around and saw Lil' Gooch standin' there with Crystal draped over his shoulder. Her mouth, hands, and feet were all duct taped; it was almost like Ill and Gooch used the whole roll on her. Another thing I definitely couldn't help but notice was that Crystal was butt-ass naked, and Gooch

Face/ Fetty Boy

had the nozzle of his heater right up the bitch's asshole. I thought to myself, "Nasty, but effective..."

The muffled sounds of Crystal cryin' through the duct tape caused the nigga Marcus to cry right along with her.

"O-o-okay," he murmured. "Y... you can h... have it all!"

In two seconds flat, the nigga was out the bed. He dashed over to a portrait of him and his bitch hangin' on the wall; typical, I thought out loud. He snatched the picture down, then almost shitted on himself when Illy-Ill pressed his gun to the back of his head.

"This ain't the motherfuckin' forty yard dash, doggie!" Ill shouted. "Slow yo' ass the fuck down and get the combination right the first time around."

The nigga's hand was shakin' the whole time, but he got that shit open in one try. I don't know what it is about wealth that hypnotizes a person, but me and my niggas damn near had a hard on when Marcus peeled open the door to the safe. The stacks were so many I couldn't count'em. We didn't even need to turn the lights on 'cause the jewels in the safe were sparklin' like wine in ice. Diamond necklaces, Rolex watches, and of all else, an assortment of handguns.

There was an envelope with papers inside that turned out to be the titles to his cars and deeds to all this nigga's property.

When Gooch walked in with the gun in ol' girl's butthole, I noticed a Prada napsack hangin' over a hook on the closet door. I dumped the shit out, then started emptyin' the safe. My heart was beatin' so fast, I felt like I just got finished fuckin' Nina's sweet pussy.

We took everything. When I say everything, I mean everything! I tossed a gun or two over to Ill, along with some watches and other jewelry. Gooch was still fixated on Crystal's ass and pussy to give a fuck about his cut right then. After forcing Marcus to sit back on the bed, I put all the titles and deeds in the waistband of my jeans. What happened next reminded me just how much of an authentic nigga Illy-Ill was.

Face/ Fetty Boy

He walked over to Marcus and put the gun under his chin, "This was an inside job, doggie. Somebody tipped us off about who your bitch was. Where she get her hair done. We even knew that your ass would be up here sleepin', doggie. So, don't think we don't know about the drop-in safe with the coke, nigga! Where that shit at?"

Ill was bluffin' the hell out'f this nigga. Hey, fuck it. The only time a bluff don't work is when a nigga calls it. If you can bluff'em, you can beat'em every time.

I joined right in. "We want the drugs in the drop-in safe, nigga. We get that, we out. You only get to charge us with robbery, Mr. Prosecutor. If we don't get it, my manz back there is gonna put some dookie on a bullet, ya dig?"

Crystal started to squirm around at the idea of bein' shot directly in her asshole. Also, I could tell that Marcus didn't really give a fuck if Gooch killed the bitch or not. But I don't care how much you hate a bitch, if you got kids with that bitch, those kids mean the motherfuckin' world to you.

"All that money you spendin' at that Catholic school for them two little niggas you raisin' is about to go to waste. Now, I know you know what that shit means."

Without the slightest bit of hesitation, "The pool," Marcus quickly said. "Outside... the pool. There's a ten by fifteen foot crawl space beneath the drain. The remote is underneath the back of the diving board." Marcus really struggled with his next few words, "There are... fifty keys in the crawl space. All of'em are in waterproof duffel bags.
They're yours; just please leave my kids alone."

"Ill, go check that shit out," I said.

"Promise me you won't hurt my children!"

"I ain't a monster, nigga. I'm not gonna hurt your snotty-nosed-fuckin' kids. Besides... I might need to use'em as leverage again if me and my niggas ever decide to come back to Rockland County."

Face/ Fetty Boy

11 The Drought is Over

It was the heist of the century.
    We came off with so much shit that it felt like we robbed an armored truck. As soon as me, Ill, and Lil' Gooch made it back across the bridge, we stopped and hit Tiff off for a job well done. I gave her close to five grand in cash, plus all of the bitch Crystal's jewelry that was inside the safe. It was a come up for Tiff on some real shit.
    I only blessed Ill and Gooch with a little somethin' at first; I told them I wanted to wait a couple of days before we divided everything up. Besides, they knew my aphorism, and my statement of truth I lived by without question was: "to whom much is given, much is expected." I also wanted to make sure that that nigga Marcus wasn't on some "federally" shit before we flooded the strip again. Any nigga munchin' the way he was had to be in bed with some dirty cops - fed or state niggas. Who knows? But, I wasn't about to flood the strip until I felt comfortable.
    Besides, we hit that clown for one hundred and eighty-five thou' plus all his squares - fifty of them damn things.
    When we made it back to the hood, I instructed my goonz not to tell anybody what it was hittin' for. As far as the rest of the niggas on the block knew, the drought was over. We went back to business as usual. I was known for findin' new connects, so other jokers like Ron-G n'em came through to cop. Me and Ill had the birds hidden in different stash houses, but nobody else knew where - not even Freez. We even copped a little condo spot over in Engelwood; there ain't nothin'

Face/ Fetty Boy

like havin' a spot where you could get away from it all every now and then.

Every time a nigga came to cop weight, I'd take their money, then me, Ill, Freez, and Gooch would go across the bridge into Harlem like we were goin' to pick up orders. We weren't doin' nothin' except chillin'. My girl Tiff kept her ear to the ground inside Sasha's and let me know that Marcus and Crystal ain't have no idea who we were.

Way before we came off with the big score from Marcus, me and my crew would go across the bridge lookin' for out'f state plates, so it wasn't nothin' for us to gank five or six jokers in one week's time. It was easy licks; there's only one reason why out'f state niggas would go into NY early on a Friday evening; they were going to purchase drugs. It used to fuck me up how none of those so-called hustlers were smart enough to travel with a trail car; you know how the saying goes: "a fool and his riches shall soon part ways."

Before I went down the Berg, I stayed jackin' niggas. My nigga Freez used to do the drivin'. I had no problems with that cause he was a bonafide wheel man. With him maneuverin' the V, we came off with cash, money-belts, coke, dope, rings n'things. Some dudes had weapons, but I would always toss them shits into the Hudson - ya never know if they had bodies on'em or not.

Whenever we was in beast mode, the only thing I knew was grindin'. I wasn't out there to be chillin' - I didn't wanna hear nothin' from no bitch. Beast mode is beast mode - this is why my money was never funny. But ever since the heist in Rockland County, we only went into Harlem to chill, or for Ill to cop his leak leaves from Big-L n'em over on 140th & Lenox. If a nigga mixed the leak with the high grade chronic we got from the pet store on 124th & Madison, it was a motherfuckin' wrap! Talk about high! Shyiit! We were so zooted out, I'm surprised any of us could remember our own names!

"That's a new Ack right there," Ill said. "There's two

rice n'bean eaters in that new Ack right there." Ill always repeated himself whenever he was fucked up. "Yo, Fetty, we ain't got nobody in a while; let's get dem niggas, yo. We ain't got nobody in a while. They got Connecticut plates, doggie."

    I let Ill soup me right on up. We were already sittin' on a shit load of yayo and cash, even though we sold more than half the birds to the niggas in and around the 4th Ward for almost next to nothin'. Still, there wasn't no need to be out here robbin' niggas right now. "Follow them niggas, Freez," I said. We was so zooted that day, I would have told Freez to follow an armored car while I tried to rob that motherfucka with nothin' but a slingshot.

    "I'm on it, my nigga."

    When we reached the light at the Polo Grounds exit leading to the ramp to the bridge, the same game plan we had used in the past went into effect.

    Me and Ill were always the ones to hop out the whip and creep up to the car. When we got to the Acura Legend, Ill tugged on one'f the back door handles, but the shit was locked.

    I pulled out the Glock Nines.

    The sun was startin' to go down, but I could still see the shine from the chrome on Illy-Ill's .357 Magnum,.

    We hit the passenger's side and the driver's side at the same time. And that's exactly when I started kickin' myself in the ass for smokin' that goddamn wet...

    It happened so fast.

    One second Illy-Ill was aimin' into the car window, the next second he was bein' spun by a bullet to his right shoulder.

    I stared at him.

    You never really know how much love you have for a nigga until you see him on the ground leakin' and his body steamin'.

    When he crawled his way next to me, I knew he was alright. Before I took cover behind the Acura, I caught a glimpse of the chubby-face lookin' one in the driver's seat; he was pointin' his gat out the window tryin' to get a clear shot at me or Ill.

Face/ Fetty Boy

I peeped the hand signals he was givin' to his partner. These Spanish niggas wasn't goin' to buy no fuckin' drugs; they were DEA agents squattin' on niggas like me and Ill.

I peeked my head up for just a second.

I heard the shot, then felt the bullet whiz pass my ear.

The fat-ass driver squeezed off at me. One of the many things The Almighty blessed me with was twenty/twenty vision; I peeked up, saw what I needed to see, then ducked back down before the nigga could peep me. Watchin' the spark from the bullet scrapin' off the asphalt snapped me right out'f my high. I breathed in and out three quick and sharp breaths. After calmin' my nerves, I reached up and shot out the back window of the Ack. The glass shattered everywhere like a chandelier was being dropped off the Empire State Building.

As soon as I shot out the window, I got to my feet, staying hunched over to avoid being shot. I snuck up on the passenger's side and let off two shots - one went right in the passenger's head, and the other ripped through the driver's lower jaw. I caught'em both with their heads down after they ducked when I put one through the back window. That was just a distraction, suckas - y'all ain't the only ones who know how to get one up on a nigga.

Just as I slumped both DEA agents, Freez was on point and pulled the whip right up to where Illy-Ill was on the ground bleedin'. Ill struggled a little to get to his feet, but he made it. He limped his ass into the car holdin' his shoulder, then Lil' Gooch pulled him all the way in. I kept the ratchet smokin' as I backed up toward the ride. I knew I hit both'f them pigs, but I kept shootin' anyway... blam... blam...

Once I was inside the car, Freez spun off doin' a buck or better all the way to Orange General Hospital. It's a wonder we didn't take chase. Thank God Ill didn't die on me. Still, that was a wrap for us and our reckless, wild adventures.

* * * * *

Face/ Fetty Boy

The game was wearin' on me, heavy!

We was robbin' kats when we didn't need to. I stayed smokin' them dust blunts with Illy-Ill out of desparation. The shootout with those DEA agents forced me to lean back a little. Chasin' that paper while tryin' to get a hold of the game had me missin' classes on the regular.

On late nights, I hugged the strip like the block was the finest piece'f ass in the world. Dead Eye and the crew burnt it down during the day. Even with me playin' the block heavy, I still found time for Nina and her sweet, tight, little holes. She didn't mind me playin' the block so closely just as long as she was being looked after.

All the drugs we came off with from up in Rockland County were gone. Like I said, we damn near gave the birds away so we could bring the 4th Ward back after the drought had hit. But I made sure to leave at least fifteen of them things stashed away. When I went to go check on'em, all that shit was gone!

I knew right out the gate that it couldn't have been Illy-Ill who took'em; I had told him to stay off the block until his shoulder healed up. Me and him were the only ones who knew where the shit was. It's possible somebody could've followed us to the spot. Maybe ol' girl Tiff thought she deserved more than five G's and some jewels. Her pussy was iller than the wet we were smokin'; she could've tossed that ass at Lil' Gooch and got him to find out where the stash was. Whatever the fuck was goin' on, I gotta take my ass up to Harlem and holler at Pedro, the boss of my new connect.

Ever since the drought hit, these niggas were gougin' the prices. There was too much hand-to-hand and foot-to-mouth shit goin' on. If the prices went up for us, that meant the prices went up for the fiends. That also meant I was gonna have to spend more time on the block 'cause the fiends needed more time to come up with the money for a fix. I wasn't tryin' to hear that shit.

Face/ Fetty Boy

August was almost over and I still haven't gotten my new whip yet. The drought had shit movin' slow. And smokin' that leak had me fuckin' my money up - I was splurgin' on stupid shit, not focusing on what the fuck I wanted and needed to do. My only choice was to game Pedro the same way I gamed my last connect. Shit, before coke reached a record low of twenty-two a gram, they were gettin' me with these ridiculous-ass prices; ain't no way in hell I ain't gonna get these motherfuckas back. They say a hard head makes a soft ass. But, in my head, Pedro's hard white was gonna make me cold, hard green cash.

I had tricked my eighty large I had stashed away down to forty. The only reason I was able to pay the young boys who worked for me was because of the Rockland County heist. Plus, I was gamblin', playin' C-low, hostin' motel parties... dumb shit. Yo, that wet will have your mind fucked up! We were supposed to be stackin' chips to start Freez's rappin' career- that was our plan to get out'f the game, but we were nowhere near our goal... not even close.

Damn, nigga! I shouted inside my own head. I was drivin' Freez's ride over to see Pedro, and it occurred to me that I wasn't even close to buyin' my mama a new house. I ain't have no choice; I gotta game this pussy. I got forty G's on stash, and forty-two large for the re-up on two birds. The sun don't shine forever; gotta make my move now or it's never.

I made it to the spot early. If a nigga wanted to holler at Pedro directly and not one of his flunkies, you had to get there early. As soon as I parked the car, I noticed Pedro sittin' on the steps in front of the building he ran his operation out of.

He looked at his watch, then nodded at me like he was surprised to see me at that time of day. I nodded back and walked up on him as casually as I could so he wouldn't get the wrong idea.

"Pedro, my man," I said. "I'm glad I caught you, poppa."

"Heeey! Jersey, my mang!" he shouted. Everybody who came across the bridge was named Jersey to this guy. Yet,

Face/ Fetty Boy

here he was screamin' like we were best friends. I knew what it was really hittin' for, though - he was hollerin' so his shooters inside the building would know somebody new was on the block.

"Wassup wit' you mang? Talkeeng to me what's wrong. You lookeeng like someone kill your dog. You no likeeng the pedico, huh?"

"Come on, Pedro, yo. You know you got the best coke New York has ever seen, man." I sat right next to him on the steps like we had been friends for years. He offered me a cigarette. I refused him 'cause that shit with Illy-Ill made me think twice about smokin' behind everybody. "Nah, I'm good, yo."

"You good, huh? If it's not the pedico, it must be the prices, eh?"

I might as well throw this nigga some bait 'cause he is fishin' hard. "Nah, it ain't the price either, Pedro."

"Well, talkeeng to me, mang. Talkeeng to Pedro."

"You know, the last time I came up here I got pulled over with three of them things in the ride. I mean, I was lucky; they never searched my shit, they just gave me a ticket. Shit has just been crazy for me in Jersey, Pedro. A bunch'f ups and downs; you know how it be out there. What I'm sayin' is, I've been spendin' with you for a couple of months now. I was kind'f hopin' you would toss a little somethin' my way. You know? A little consignment? You could at least front me what I've been spendin'."

I could tell by the look on Pedro's face that he wasn't the average nigga out here wholesalin' drugs. He ain't say shit to me. He just stared at me It was as if he could tell where I've been and where I was goin', all with one glance. The shit started to creep me out. It sort'f gave me the feelin' you get at a poker game when you have to fold a bad hand.

"I buy two, you front me two-"

"Lemme stop you right there, poppa." I knew he was gonna go in sooner or later. But I ain't know he was gonna proposition

Face/ Fetty Boy

a nigga. "I've been hustleeng in these streets since I ten years old, poppa. Ju'know how long dat is?"

"Nah, Pedro. How long is that?"

"Dat almost thirty years, Jersey - thirty years. Ju'know what change out here in thirty years?" Before I could even answer him, "Notheeng," he said. "Notheeng change out here...except me. I get smarter, poppa. Ju'know Lu Lu? He from Jersey, like you."

"Yeah, I know him," I answered. "Somebody smoked him last week. His wake is tonight at the funeral home on my block. Why?"

Pedro laughed lightly, then flicked the ashes from his Newport onto the steps. "Not 'someone', poppa," he said. "It was me. I... how you say... smoke 'dat fool?"

"I don't get it, Pedro man."

"No? Well, get this, Jersey. Lu Lu and his main mang Scientific come to me with that same basuda you talkeeng. Only they talk it to me better, ju'know?"

"Yeah, I know that fat nigga Scientific, too," I said.

"Well, poppa, my shooter only catch Lu Lu. The other one get away. He hideeng with fifteen kilo belongeeng to me. Now, you take care of the madicung for me, I pay you five kilo. I no care about the fifteen kilo, poppa. It is the principle. I let him get away with my cocaine, every chocolo in Jersey will try me, ju'know?"

"Yeah, I know," I said sarcastically. And this nigga done figured out I'm one'f them chocolos.

"You do this, I pay you five kilo. And I also forget you come to me talkeeng basuda, too. Deal?"

Pedro reached his hand out so I could shake it. I was leery than a motherfucka. Not only did this nigga peep my scheme, but he was gonna pay me twice the amount I was tryin' to game him for just so I could do a job for him. But what else was I gonna do; I need them motherfuckin' birds so my shop could keep runnin'.

After shakin' his hand, "You gotta deal, Pedro. That's

literally an offer I can't refuse. Plus, I would have murked that nigga for one; I never liked Scientific or Lu Lu." Truth was... We didn't like any of them Dog Pound niggas. I did have a little respect for Lu Lu, only 'cause he was dubbed the king of beatin' connects. "We definitely gotta deal, Pedro. But dig this. I got forty-two large in this bag right here. You give me seven of them things and I guarantee ol' boy won't see the sun rise. If not, you can send your shooters and make it dark for me, too. I never was good at hidin' no way. On top of that, I'm a man of my word."

I gave Pedro the bag of money. He thumbed around inside it until he realized it was holdin' forty-two stacks.

"All 'Benny Franks' in there," I said. I already knew Pedro liked nothin' but hundred dollar bills. I watched him as he took the cigarette from his mouth and whistled out sharply one time. Almost immediately, one of his workers bobbed his way toward us; I don't know where this nigga came from. He handed me a brown paper bag with seven of them things in it; it made me wonder how the fuck this spick knew exactly how much to bring.

YEAH! I shouted inside my own head. Once again, it's on! I know just how I'm gonna murk this nigga Scientific, too. I'ma put this plan into effect, then take my ass right over to that Lex dealership. Scientific, you may be the new king of beatin' connects, but "uneasy lies the head who wears the crown" in my town, nigga.

Chapter 12: The Set Up

I took it easy on the drive back; not too easy, though them State Troopers will pull your ass over quick if they see you drivin' too slow. The whole time I was tryin' to concentrate on the road, Nina's ass was pagin' me 911 behind her home number. She probably didn't want nothin' except some money to get her hair and nails did. Then again, I don't think she ever paged me nine-one-one before. It had been a few days; she could just be missin' me a little somethin'. Whatever she wanted it was gonna have to wait. I only had a few hours before Lu Lu's wake started, and I knew his right-hand man Scientific was gonna come through to pay his respects.

I'll have to call Nina back after shit slow down a little. Right now, I need to track Ali Mu's ass down - ASAP! I need him for somethin'. He's probably over at crackhead Felicia's house gettin' his dick sucked as usual.

Before I get with Mu, I gotta stash these seven bricks, then hit the strip; I need to tell everybody to rock their army fatigues tonight at the wake.

Track down Ali Mu...
Stash these squares...
Get with my boys on the strip...
Call Nina...

With all these thoughts spinnin' around in my mind, I

almost didn't realize that I was over the speed limit on Route 4. Slow down, Fetty, I said to myself. Too much shit is on the line right now.

* * * * *

Ali Mu was this ol' head fresh out the Federal Penitentiary A.D.X. in Colorado. He was one'f those types of niggas that did bids in different Fed joints across the entire United States. This last bid he did was a thirty-year stretch. Pht - imagine that shit!

You can learn a lot in life from people who have walked a hard long path like Mu. He grew up on G.G. Ave. He loved tellin' niggas that the last time he was home was when Reuben "The Hurricane" Carter was just a little punk motherfucka. Ali Mu used to take his lunch money when they were in grade school. But, after all the shit "The Hurricane" went through dealing with this fake-ass American justice system, Mu ended up havin' all the respect for him in the world. Pound for pound, Ali Mu thought Reuben "The Hurricane" Carter was the best boxer to ever come out'f Jersey.

Mu had been out the pen for a week, and most of the time I would see him coppin' nicks down on the strip. Always straight money with him. He didn't look like the usual pipe head, so I cut into him one night while we were all chillin' on the block. It turned out Ali Mu was nothin' but a real-live-old soldier. He would only cop the crack just so he could get his jimmy waxed by Felicia or one of them other basehead bitches.

From time to time, people would see Mu chillin' with me just kickin' the willie bo-bos. He would beat me down about guys in the pen - guys like Larry Hoover, Pistol Pete, King Blood, O.G. Mack, the Uni-Bomber, Wayne Pray... just guys he had ran into during his travels in the system.

The truth of the matter was Ali Mu always gave up some trill-ass game. I remember this one time he told me that I was too flossy and flashy.

Face/ Fetty Boy

"Young Fetty Man," as he would call me, "you learn in the basics that light radiates heat; ya dig, young brother? You need to get out the limelight or else you gonna get burned. You either gonna end up with a long prison sentence like I did, or you gonna be a victim of a vicious n'violent murder, baby boy. This game is cold-blooded, jack!"

Not only would Ali Mu drop a drink on you, but he was also good at what he did. If you had the proper street etiquette, and if you ever had a conversation with Mu, you would see he had potential to be a hired gun; and that's exactly why I cut into'm - for nights like this.

Mu was old enough to be my father - fifty, but looked like he was my older brother. He was only five-feet-six-inches tall. But he was a chiseled-rock-solid one hundred and seventy-five pounds. His guns were up, chest was up; this man could probably wash boxer shorts on his eight pack. He was a fifty-year-old ex-con, built like a war machine and ready for whatever.

"When you gonna give me a 'sting' or a 'hommy'?" Mu would always ask. A sting or a hommy wasn't nothin' but slang talk for a robbery or a homicide. When I asked him how much it would cost for a hommy:

"For you, Young Fetty Man, just give me whatever it's worth to ya. But, for anybody else, ten large ones or better."

I just told him to be patient and that his time would come to earn his keep. I let him know that if he needed anything, to come and find me A.S.A.P. If I wasn't on the strip, then get whatever he needed from Dead Eye.

"Young Fetty Man, you the best nigga I know out here, man. You like the family I no longer got."

It's not everyday a nigga will tell you some shit like that. I understood where he was comin' from, though. He outlived his entire family - his entire generation done past on. Now, all he knew was crack-smokin' Felicia, her crack-smokin' friends, and of course... Young Fetty Man.

Face/ Fetty Boy
* * * * *

Before I went lookin' for Mu, I hit the strip. I took Freez his bird I had copped from Pedro, then told him to spread the word about the dress code for the night's activities. Of course, he asked all his usual questions, "Wassup, my nigga? What's goin' on? Somethin' gonna jump off?" Like he was the host of Jeopardy or somethin'.

"Just spread the word, nigga. And make sure you out here with your shit cocked - it might get ugly tonight." I said the words, but the truth was, if Ali Mu did what I needed him to do, my plan would be smoother than a baby's ass. "Right now, I gotta take care of somethin'; I'll catch up with y'all later."

* * * * *

I first checked Felicia's house after tellin' Freez what to do. I knew I could find Mu there or somewhere close by; it was only two blocks over from G.G. Ave down on Auburn Street. I hated comin' around this motherfuckin' spot, but I needed to find Mu like yesterday!

Her front door was wide open.

Little Bey-Bey Kids were runnin' around with their diapers hangin' - knowin' Felicia's trifilin' ass, the diapers were probably full of shit.

As soon as I stepped foot on the porch, I could look in and see Felicia sittin' on the couch in her bra and panties that looked like bean bags. Tryin' not to throw up from the sight of her and the smell of diapers, "Yo, Felicia, where Mu at?" I asked.

"Oh, hey, Fetty. Mu just walked out the door. He headin' to the liquor store to get him a drink. Motherfucka just got his S.S.I. check his mama died and left him. The nigga ain't hit me off, yet!" I know this bitch lyin' 'cause Mu is always hittin' her ass off. Felicia used to be one of the baddest dime pieces in the hood until this Puerto Rican kat flipped

Face/ Fetty Boy

her whole shit up-side down with crack. She was handlin' the shit at first; she started off by lacin' blunts. Now, she's suckin' that pipe like soda through a straw, and it's startin' to show... bad! I don't know what Mu saw in her ass; sympathy, empathy... only the Lord knows fo'sho'. "Fetty, you got somethin' until he come back? He's supposed to give me a few dollars." That's lie number two, but I needed Felicia's ass gone by the time Mu got back so I could lay my plan down to him.

"Felicia, you know damn well I don't ride around with that shit on me like that. And you know I don't do no hand-to-hand, unless it's after one A.M. - take this fifty, though. Go see Dead Eye right quick; he got them big-bag nicks again." As soon as I said the words "big-bag nicks", Felicia's ass was so excited, she wanted to come up out'f them fucked up drawers she was wearin'. But, I damn sure wasn't fuckin' her nasty ass.

"Oh, shit! Y'all back to sellin' them? Them nicks is the shit!" she said. Then, out of left field, She asked, "Fetty, where your girl at, huh? You got a wifey for lifey?"

Maybe ten years ago, bitch, I thought to myself... maybe!

"Felicia, get yo' ass out'f here. And, if you run into Mu, tell'm to hurry up 'cause I'm here waitin' on'm."

Felicia skipped out the door, singing and dancing; she was happier than a punk down Marti Gras! It wasn't even five minutes before Ali Mu popped up with his Jack Daniels in hand.

"What's hapnin', Young Fetty Man?" he asked.

I didn't give Mu a chance to sip his drink, "Yo, Mu, you know that thing I'm always tellin' you to be patient about?"

"Right on," Mu said. "You talkin' about the hommy."

"Well, I need you to make that happen tonight."

Mu smiled his old-head smile. He sipped the Jack Daniels for five whole seconds, then wiped his mouth with the back of his hand. "It's 'bout time!" he shouted. "I was startin' to get bored 'round here. I was 'bout to take my show on the road 'cause this crack-sniffin' bitch is becomin' a pain in my ass,

Young Fetty man!"

"Nigga, you know you ain't takin' no show on the road without takin' me," I told him.

We laughed and shared a drink. Before Felicia had a chance to come back, I laid my whole plan out to Mu. I could see the killer instinct of the wolf come alive in his eyes. "Cold blooded," he kept sayin', "this motherfuckin' game of life and death is cold blooded!"

I wanted to get up out'f there before Felicia's ass came back, so I handed Mu my sky-pager, then jetted out the door. Before I hopped in the car, "Remember, Mu, this shit needs to be like clockwork," I said.

"Young nigga, I've been sendin' niggas on their way since the Plymouth Rock days! You just hold the tail," he said, "let me fuck the cat. I got this. Cold blooded, jack... cold blooded."

* * * * *

Now that Mu was all squared away, I finally had time to go and check on Nina's ass; find out why she had been pagin' me 911 for the past two hours or so. I decided to go home and shower before givin' her a call.

"Nina, waddup, baby girl?" I said into the phone. She went right in on a me.

"Where you been?" she screamed. "I've been pagin' you 911 for fuckin' ever!"

"Whoa, whoa, breathe easy, ma. What's wrong?"

"What's wrong? Why you ain't call me back? That's what's wrong!"

"Nina, I was really tied up, yo, on some real shit. Plus, I thought you would have sent me a direct message on the sky pager if something was seriously wrong."

By this time, Nina was in tears. I had too much shit on my mind to be listenin' to some spoiled-brat's sobs comin' through the phone. I really wanted to hang up on her, but I didn't want to come across too insensitive.

Face/ Fetty Boy

"Come'n, Nina baby, just tell me what's wrong."

It was just like Nina's fine ass to drag this shit out. She cried for about five more minutes on some real-live-moaning shit. If I didn't know any better, I would've sworn it was that time of the month. She kept goin' on and on about how her life was all fucked up. How her dreams of havin' a career and whatnot was goin' down the drain. I didn't know what the fuck she was talkin' about, especially with all the scratch I had been shellin' out since I met her ass - her mama's bills, her school tuition, her high maintenance habits... Nina must've lost her goddamn mind.

"Yo, I literally have no idea what's goin' on right now," I said. And that's exactly when she dropped the bomb on me.

"I'm pregnant, Franko!" I pulled the phone away from my ear 'cause she screamed that shit like a hell demon. "I'm not keepin' it either! I told you before we got together that I had school to think about, not to mention my career. On top of that, you out there runnin' around with all your boys and shit and ain't got no time for me!" Yo, Nina's mouth was on a marathon, but the only thing replayin' in my head was the word pregnant.

"My mother went through this same type'f shit, Franko! I told you all about my father doing time! Do you know how hard it has been on my mother raising me by herself? Do you? I ain't goin' through that shit! What if you leave me?"

"I ain't goin' no..." I tried to give Nina a little reassurance, but her ass wasn't havin' it.

"What if you get locked up?" she continued. "You don't think I hear the stories about you out there killin' people and shit?"

When she paused to let out some more sobs, I used the moment to ask her, "Who the hell said some shit like that?"

"It don't matter who said what; it matters if it's true or not!"

"No, that shit ain't true, girl. I ain't killin' nobody out in these damn streets. And you damn sure ain't killin' my baby! I'm comin' down there at around ten tonight; we'll

Face/ Fetty Boy

talk then."

The long silence and soft crying on the other end of the phone already told me what Nina was about to say, "Ain't nothin' to talk about, Franko." Then she hung up.

I laid back on my bed, and my eyes found a spot on the ceiling; I was lookin' at my ceiling posters - Pac, N.W.A., Scarface, Brand Nubians, L.L. Cool J - soon, my life is gonna outdo all them niggas; but right now, my mind was starin' out into my whole existence. Nina ran that not-having-a-father shit down on me. I couldn't get mad either 'cause I grew up without a father my damn self.

Still... that don't give Nina the right to be talkin' that she-ain't-keepin'-the-baby shit. I don't give a fuck if she look like Cleopatra or not, I'll hang her high if she even think about killin' my seed.

I wonder if it's gonna be a boy, though?

What if that little mothefucka look just like me - a little black baby with a big-ass dick - ha, yeah!.

What am I gonna name that little nigga, though?

Ah, hell... I got plenty'f time to think about that. I'm just really lookin' forward to tellin' my moms that she's finally gonna be a grandmother.

But right now, the main thing bubblin' to the surface of my mind was the thought of that nigga Scientific gettin' hit in his mug in just a few hours. You know the drillie!

Face/ Fetty Boy

Chapter 13: The Wake

I always liked Greg's Funeral Home. It was a grimy establishment located on Graham Ave between the one-way blocks of Godwin and Hamilton. I'm familiar with the spot 'cause me, Dead Eye, and my thug niggas would usually hang out at the pizza joint right across the street from Greg's; either that, or we would shoot pool at the pool hall just down the strip.

The main reason why I dug Greg's Funeral Home was because they took care of the dead folks in my hood for a low and affordable price - in the 4th Ward, a dead person was a dime-a-dozen; people popped up dead on the regular, and the funeral costs would become a burden on their families. But Greg's would take your body and bury you for next to nothing; you gotta appreciate havin' a spot like that in this fucked up ghetto America.

And don't let it be a ghetto celebrity that got pushed. It would be like a block party up and down them one-way streets. We never liked that dude Lu-Lu, but he was known in the hood. That meant everybody and their mama was gonna be out this motherfucka tonight - just the type of shit needed for my plan to go smooth.

By the time 8:30 p.m. rolled around, shit was moving just how I had expected. Real dudes, fake dudes, bitches, niggas,

Face/ Fetty Boy

bitch-ass niggas, kats from other projects, out-of-town dudes, out-of-state dudes... everybody was out that motherfucka. You would have thought Snoop or Pac was comin' through to tear down the stage or somethin'.

As instructed, all my dudes from the strip was in attendance, rocking their fatigues. Actually, we had all been there settin' shit up since a little before eight o'clock. Me and Freez were chillin' inside the pizza shop. Everybody kept coming in askin' me what was goin' on; rightfully so, whenever everybody hit the block rockin' the same gear, that meant that something you ain't want no part of was about to go down.

I just kept tellin' everybody, "Just be on point, y'all. This is Lu-Lu's wake, and don't nobody know fo'sho who killed him. His people might just think we did that shit 'cause we always beefin' with them niggas. You never know. That's why I told y'all to dress for the occasion... just to let them fools know we ready for whatever."

Of course, I was lying to my niggas. I knew who killed Lu-Lu, and more importantly, I knew that another body was gonna be droppin' at this wake. But Dead Eye and Freez were in the dark on this one - everything ain't for everybody.

As expected, the liquor store on the corner was packed. People were gonna be tossin' back the Henn-Rock and pouring some out in honor of Lu-Lu. The inside of the funeral home was filled to capacity, and there were about three times as many people out in the streets. I squinted my eyes in order to scan my twenty-twenty in and out'f the crowd, but there was still no sign of that fool Scientific.

I was staring through the shop window as I took a bite from my slice of pizza, and that's when we noticed the white Suburban Truck pull up out the corner of my eye. I think everybody noticed that shit; it was already dark out, but the truck's chrome Spreewell rims were spinnin' and shinin' brighter than a prison guard's flashlight. I continued slyly watching as these four dudes hopped out the truck. "Pussy-hole," I said

Face/ Fetty Boy

to myself just above a whisper - my Jamaican accent coming to life - after noticing Scientific was one of the four dudes.

They were all dressed similarly - like money ain't mean a damn thing to'em - but Scientific was sportin' a plain-white tee, designer-blue jeans, a red Yankees fitted cap, and that nigga's wrist was smilin' with diamonds and his chain was swingin' left to right with every step he took.

Whoever was driving pulled off - I guess to go find a place to park - and Scientific and his crew strolled right past the shop. This nigga looked through the window right at me. Our eyes locked in a squint for a brief moment, then Scientific gave me a head nod as if to say, "Whaddup?" I returned the gesture by shruggin' my shoulders and taking another bite of my pizza.

Scientific and his entourage made their way inside Greg's. He wasn't gonna see nothin' but a bunch'f females - young chicks and old ladies - huggin' and cryin'. Lu-Lu's family members were probably gonna beg this nigga to find out what happened to their loved one. Ha - little did they know, they were gonna need somebody to find out what happened to Scientific's ass!

After they disappeared inside the funeral home, I just continued to eat my slice. Freez, as expected, never left my side. We just sat there eating, while scopin' all the people in front of Greg's. We were just crackin' jokes on all the bitches who were attending the wake. Most of them females didn't even know Lu-Lu's ass; they were just out here chasin' the 3D's: dick, drugs, and dollars.

"Oh, shit!" Freez said suddenly. "There go Yolanda's fine ass. I ain't seen her in a few months. I wonder if she wanna hit the telly after the wake?"

I cracked a phony smile, then said, "You ain't gonna find out sittin' over here with pizza sauce all over them greasy-ass lips, my boy. Go ask her what the fuck she got planned for tonight. Find out if we can jump her?"

I knew Freez would take the bait. The bitch was lookin' good, but I ain't give a fuck what Yolanda was plannin' on doin'

Face/ Fetty Boy

after the wake. I just put a battery in Freez's back 'cause I needed him gone for a few minutes. I watched him wipe the grease from his mouth as he stood from our booth seat. The look in his eyes told me that he knew I was up to no good.

Before Freez was able to reach the door, he looked out the window and saw Scientific and his bodyguards stepping out'f the funeral home. After seeing them huddle up in front of the building smoking cigarettes, Freez had forgotten all about the donkey stickin' out the back of Yolanda's skirt. He was trying to have my back like he always did, but I needed him to step away just for a quick minute.

"Yo, brah," I said while looking at my watch, "go order me two plain slices and a soda to go; I'm 'bout to go see Nina in a minute."

After looking at me leerily for just a few seconds, Freez said, "Aight, my nigga. Two plain slices and a soda... cream soda, right?"

"Yeah," I said.

"Got it; I'll be back."

As I listened to him tellin' the counter girl what to get, I took out my burn-out flip phone and dialed a number. When I heard the operator's voice for the instant message service, I immediately said, "Baby, please drop off that new white tee, them blue jeans, and the red fitted... the outfit is outside on the front porch. I'ma rock that with my diamond watch and matching chain tonight."

* * * * *

Old Head Ali Mu was in the cut squattin' like Khalif when the sky pager I had given him started to buzz off. He read the message, then eased from the shadows of the alleyway he had been squattin' in. Sportin' black sweatpants with the hoodie to match. He pulled the hood over his head with his hands calmly tucked into the hoodie's front pocket - gripping a big-ass 44-Bulldog.

Ali Mu quietly emerged from the cut, looking down at the

Face/ Fetty Boy

sky pager one last time, "White tee, blue jeans, red hat," he said to himself, that's that nigga right there. He tucked away the pager, then tossed Scientific a mean mug before shouting, "Yo, nigga! Why the fuck you put your goddamn hands on my daughter?!"

All the people in the street who had come to mourn Lu-Lu's death stood still like mannequins in a clothing store window. A lot'f crazy shit goes down on the regular in the 4th Ward. But, it didn't matter if you were a gangster, hustler, pimp, whore, crackhead, or just some bitch-ass wanna-be... there was one rule everybody agreed on... nobody fucked with the kids.

Scientific and all his menz and'em flicked their cigarettes to the curb. They turned around to see who was shouting, and since he was their so-called leader, Scientific started to run his mouth first, "Yo, who the fuck you talkin..."

Boooom! Boooom!

I bet if he knew those were gonna be his last words, he would've chosen something different to say. Before the end of the sentence could escape his mouth, two bullets crashed their way into Scientific's skull. That nigga was a goner before his body hit the ground. Red hat and all, I could still see the blood start to ooze from his head. His cronies were stuck on stupid and caught off guard. They didn't even duck for cover right away like everybody else in the street. All Ali Mu had to do was squeeze off three more shots into the air before these fools decided to dive to the pavement.

Me and Freez stayed right in our seats watching through the pizza shop window as if nothing was going on. We watched the whole thing unfold like a midnight matinee.

People screaming.

Niggas and bitches squattin' behind parked cars.

Scientific deader than a door knob.

His menz done fled the scene afraid they were gonna be next.

Me and Freez? We in the shop ain't worried 'bout nothin' 'cause at least a hundred motherfuckas came in and out'f the establishment and saw us sittin' there.

While running the scenario through my mind, I could hear the sirens closing in from a distance. The tires of cop cars were screeching to a halt. The lights atop the cars lit up the dark sky. Hidden within the hysterical commotion of all the people, me and Freez walked off heading toward the hoop ride we had parked on Hamilton Ave.

Freez waited until he pulled off before he said, "Yo, you's a cold-ass nigga, bruh."

"Nah," I said. I had the ice grill on staring out into the sky, but I was smiling inside my own head. "I keep tellin' you, yo... this motherfuckin' game cold. You gotta stop actin' like a rookie, nigga. You ballin' with me, but your mouth is bigger than your heart, dawg."

I know that nigga felt it when I said that shit. But he just sat in the driver's seat maneuvering the V as if my words hadn't fazed him.

Freez breathed out sharply, then said, "I'm just sayin'... Lu-Lu and Scientific were like generals out this motherfucka. Who was that nigga wit' the gun anyway?"

Generals? I said inside my own head. This nigga must be crazy. "Yeah, brah? Well, guess what. Generals Patton and McCarther just lost their motherfuckin' stripes. End of story. Why is it end of story? 'Cause sucka-ass niggas turned into goners gets no rap... them niggas gone!"

A few more blocks had passed before Freez opened his mouth again. "Aight, them niggas gone," he said, "but, why did you have all of us dressed for war if all along you were gonna have somebody else kill the nigga?"

I had to take a pause after he asked that question. A nigga that's been in the game as long as Freez has should be able to do the knowledge to this shit. "Use your fuckin' head," I finally responded. "There wasn't nothin' but a bunch'f snitch-ass bitches, old ladies, hustlers, and hard-working civilians out there tonight. All of'em ain't nothing but potential witnesses. And the only thing they witnessed was an unknown man dressed in black shootin' a known drug dealer. When they give their detailed descriptions to the cops, our whole team will be in the clear 'cause we were rocking the opposite of what the shooter was wearing. In fact, the only thing ringing in everybody's ears will be a story of how some father was out there gettin' revenge for his daughter. Do the one to the shit, nigga."

"What if someone from the strip suspected somethin'? What if they say some shit that might lead back to us?"

"Looky here, brah... me, you, and old Head Ali Mu... that's all who know about what went down at the wake - us and the connect who paid me five pies to pull this shit off."

I knew Freez's eyes would spring to life when he heard I was sittin' on five of them things. "Five birds?" he said.

"Yeah, nigga. And one'f'em is yours. I'm giving Ali Mu a half and ten stacks for the work he put in. And stop worrying about them goofy-ass niggas on the strip. Ain't nothin' to tell 'cause you can't tell a crime boss a motherfuckin' thing. You know it. These bitches know it. These candy-stick niggas know it. They also know not to play with me, son; especially when I know where they mama live. They kids live. They grandparents. Nigga, I'll get their pet fish in the fish tank; Fetty don't give a fuck. So all that 'what if' shit you cryin'... you might as well cry me a fuckin' river, then build a bridge and get over it, dawg. Ain't nothin' on my mind, except flipping these squares and coppin' something pretty from that Lex Dealership. By hook or crook, I'm coming the fuck up. You wit' me or not."

"Fo'sho, Fetty," Freez responded, but I could hear the doubt in his voice.

"And as long as Pedro, or who the fuck ever is willing to pay me five birds to off niggas, I'ma have to change my name to "one-a-day" out this motherfucka 'cause that's how many bodies I'ma drop to get my hands on them millions.

Face/ Fetty Boy

Now... pull this shit over and get the fuck out, nigga. I need to head over to Nina's crib to take care of some shit."

* * * * *

Freez called one of his freak whores to come and pick him up, while I hit the Uey heading to Nina's apartment.

Ever since I started taking care of her and her mother, I made sure that I had gotten my own key to the place. Ms. Mary didn't really care 'cause I kept the lights on in the crib; plus, I think she more or less enjoyed the male company. Truth be told, I kind'f reminded Ms. Mary of her late husband. I ain't sayin' Nina's moms was lusting after me or nothing like that. I'm just saying she probably misses having somebody around who can take care of shit.

By the time I parked the car and stuck the key in the door, it was already 10:45 p.m.. I entered as quietly as I could 'cause all the lights were off and I didn't hear a damn thing. I tiptoed my way to look in on Ms. Mary, but she wasn't in her room.

"Probably at another card game with her girlfriends," I said to myself.

I eased down the hall and opened the door to Nina's room. She was sound asleep atop her bed with the covers pulled slightly to one side. She was wearing this little nightgown thing that I like - it was a tanktop and skirt set. What I liked about it was that Nina never wore any panties with it. One of her cinnamon-colored ass cheeks was sticking out teasing the shit out'f me! I looked down and saw my dick bricking up beneath my jeans. Shyiit... you ain't gotta tell me twice! I came up out'f everything I was wearing quicker than a virgin's first nut!

I walked to the side of the bed in the direction where her face was turned. I was tempted to wake her up by slappin' her on the cheek with the cockasaurus. She's already pissed at me, that shit might not go over too well. Instead, I just

Face/ Fetty Boy

stood there - dick on solid like a rock - bangin' to the right and strokin'm from the helmet to the balls.

I ran a single finger across Nina's lips.

No response.

I caressed her lips again, only a little harder this time.

Her eyes yawned open.

Waking up to the ungodly sight of me strokin' on the King Kong ding-dong almost caused Nina to jump out the bed. I had this fucked up Kool Aid smile on my face, too... I know she was spooked.

"What the fuck, Franko!" she shouted.

She sucked her teeth and rolled her eyes. Then she turned on her side facing away from me as if she wasn't beat for my affection With all the grinding I was doin' in the streets, I hadn't tapped that ass in a few days. She can play "keep away" with the pussy all she wanted; I was gettin' up in them guts one way or another... even if I had't take it!

I knew she wanted the dick just as much as I wanted the pussy. She trying to act like she mad over this being pregnant shit. I don't know... every time I get to bangin' her back loose, she always screamin' for me to cum inside her, talkin' about she wanna have my baby. I dropped the seed up in her and now it's a fuckin' problem?

I eased into the bed next to her, until my third leg started to press against her ass crack.

Bingo!

She spread her legs a little bit, and that's when I knew I was about to punish the pussy. I reached my left hand underneath her and grabbed her throat. She yelped when I snatched her head toward my mouth so I could whisper in her ear, "I'm 'bout to fuck your ass until you can't walk n'more!"

I could feel her body shivering when I gripped her hip with my other hand. I pulled her onto my dick as I thrust forward at the same time. She screamed and grunted so loudly, I thought I broke the poompum. But, then she reached back and grabbed my ass cheek so she could pull me deeper inside her.

Face/ Fetty Boy

Her juicy love-fruit of a hole gripped and swallowed my third leg to the fullest.
"I can feel it in my stomach, Franko!" she shouted.

That's all I needed to hear. I started long stroking to the point where Nina's butt cheeks were slapping against my pelvis. By now, we were both puttin' our strength into it. It almost felt like the $1,800.00 bed set I had bought her was about to fall apart.
I had her pussy fartin' and the titties floppin'. Nina was screamin' all kinds of freaky shit while she threw it back at me.
"Oh, shit, Fetty! I... missed youuuuu... soooo much! Fuck this pussy! It's yours... fuck this pussy!"
She started begging for every inch of me, so I lifted her leg higher and drilled her with the deep, quick strokes, on some all the way in and all the way out type shit!
"Ooooh, God!" she screamed. Sounding as if I was punching her in the belly from the inside out. "I'm gonna... I'm gonna cum on your... big black... dick, Franko!"
You ain't the only one about to cum, I thought to myself. As soon as I felt myself about to bust off, I slammed my dick all the way inside Nina's hole and held it there. I knew it was all the way in because her body seized up and she screamed louder than a white girl in a scary movie. I squeezed off so hard inside her I thought my jizz was gonna start oozing out'f her ears.
I knew she had popped off already because she had dug her nails deep into my lower back.
The night was long, yet so was my dick. We just repeated the process over and over hitting every position in the book. She even got on top and fucked a nigga until she caught a cramp in one of her hamstrings.
"Oww!" she screamed.
I laughed and said, "I told you you wasn't gonna be able to walk by the time I was done with you." I kept drilling her and she kept throwing it back until we were both sweaty and exhausted. At one point in time, while we were taking a rest,

Face/ Fetty Boy

she had the nerve to say that she wanted me to give her some space. I looked at her like she had lost her damn mind. I flipped her over face down ass up, and said, "As good as this pussy is, you can have space, a galaxy, a universe... you can have a motherfuckin' spaceship!." Before I knew it, she was moaning again with the sound of my balls slappin' against her milky-way.

When we bust off this time, I just flopped right down on top of her. I didn't know how much time had passed, but I know I definitely put that twerk in; not only that, but Ms. Mary had to have come home by now, even though we never heard her come in. I was so tired, I started to fall asleep with my dick still on solid inside Nina's cum catcher.

I'm uncertain, but I could've swore Nina said that she didn't care how much I fucked her brains out, she was still gonna get an abortion. Like I said, I was tired. I ain't even feel like responding to that shit... yeah, aight... abortion my ass...

Face/ Fetty Boy

Chapter 14: Spaceship

A few days had passed since that long night of beatin' up Nina's oochie-wallie. I was chillin' at my rest laying in bed staring up at the ceiling posters again. My eyes shifted back and forth from BIG to Pac, BIG, PAC, BIG, PAC... staring at the two of them had me thinking about the condition of my beautiful black people.

The concepts of regicide and fratricide came about because of our conquerors - European-whites or Spaniards. Our people were kind-hearted kings when those savage-ass Europeans came through raping and pillaging everything - and they got the nerve to call us uncivilized. They took the crown from atop our heads and put it beneath our feet. Now, anytime we see a Black Man on top of his game, we wanna try and knock'm off his square. If a Black Man's ride is better than mine, I'ma jack him. If his girl looks better than mine, I'ma fuck her. If he got more money than me, I'ma rob him... and that's exactly where the fratricide comes in. 'Cause, the only way for me to stay on top and keep other brothers off my ass is to kill a motherfucka... a motherfucka who look just like me... in other words... my brother.

As I stared up at Biggie and Pac, I realized shit was exactly the same with the people I idolized. Fratricide in hip-hop started with them two - don't let nobody tell you nothin' different.

On September 7, Pac was gunned down in Las Vegas Nevada, however, he refused to say who shot him, or to die

Face/ Fetty Boy

right away. But when he did die, the back and forth feud on wax had people assuming that Biggie and his camp were responsible for Pac's assassination. Brilliance rules the world and the ignorant suffers the burden; even though there was no proof to the assumptions, and all evidence pointed to a gang banger from out West, the media wanted our people to believe that Pac died due to an East-coast West-coast rap war.

They promoted the concept of fratricide with their many reports on the incident. In my hood, there is a saying - you're only as good as the last nigga you took down. I guess this was true because Biggie was crowned king fo'sho' when Pac died seven days after gettin' hit up. Layin' on my bed this morning, I realized I was staring up at two of the truest definitions of fratricide and regicide. Welcome to ghetto America, where everything positive a Black Man does, is frowned upon by another Brother.

* * * * *

A few days later, my born day had arrived. It was just past Labor Day, which meant the Lex Dealer was gonna be closed until after the four-day weekend. When Tuesday rolled around, me and Freez went straight to the car dealership on Route 17. I was snatchin' a fully loaded silver Lexus 450 Land Cruiser truck. They had just dropped, and the dealership's owner had already told me that only a few had been sold in the New York area. I was gonna be the first person in Paterson whippin' around in one of these bad boys.

Even after signing all the papers, I couldn't complete the purchase without my moms as a cosigner. She wasn't gonna be able to get off work until the next day. So, I came up with a plan for the dealer not to report the large cash purchase. We would both make out if he followed the script; the dealer would get to keep 6 large plus an additional 4 G's for the cover up. A cash purchase of 10 G's or more would have the FBI and IRS clockin' on my doorstep.

The deal went smooth; the dealer got his taxfree commission, and I was cruising the strip in a ride suitable for a crime

Face/ Fetty Boy

boss with my main-man Freez playin' shotgun.

"Godayyum!" Freez shouted. "This shit feel like we ridin' in a motherfucken spaceship, my nigga!"

"Niggaz already sick out here, now they gonna throw up," I said.

"Oh, yeah, Fetty... I almost forgot to tell you... you remember that project chick Yolanda?"

"Who? The one that got your nose wide open?"

"Yeah, like the way Nina got you sprung," Freez shot back at me. Leave it up to him to spit some bullshit.

We laughed a bit before I said, "Yeah, I know that hoe. Why?"

"She called me a few nights ago. Talkin' 'bout be careful, or some shit, cause them project niggaz saying we had somethin' to do with the hit on Scientific."

"Yeah, what else that bitch say," I asked. The way Freez was explaining this shit to me made it seem like his gut was tellin' him he knew this nonsense was gonna happen.

"You know how these fake-as-fuck niggaz be, they talkin' that somebody gotta die shit."

While Freez was giving me the low-down, my thoughts started racing. Thinking about how, not too long ago, I was just down Jamesburg juvie joint. I stayed in some shit down there. Then, got out and hit the block full speed. In a matter of months, I had killed a few niggaz, plotted the murder of another nigga, pulled off a few major jooks, bagged a queen and got her pregnant, put a team together and beat a couple'f connects, then copped the dopest ride in New Jeruz. Only real niggaz do shit like that with such swashbuckle attitude. The problem is when real shit happens on the strip, people know that real niggaz are responsible for it. Fuck it... it's elementary.

"Death is the inevitable, my boy," I said, "just as long as it ain't you or me dying before our time." I pulled the car to a stop at a red-light, waiting to get onto Route 46.

Face/ Fetty Boy

That was a perfect moment for me to drop somethin' heavy on my nigga. "Dig this shit here, Freez. The only thing guaranteed in this world is change. The night gonna change into the day and the day back into the night. The young will become old in the body, and the old will become young in the mind. The last stop is when life turns into death. Some niggaz believe that there's life after death, but I ain't never seen that shit. The point is... as sho' as the earth is turnin' and souls is burnin', death is gonna happen. But that shit gonna happen on my terms. Ya feel me?"

I put the car back in motion before Freez could answer. I knew his head was fucked up by what I had just told him. We talked about how we were gonna move the rest of the work we were sittin' on, and about findin' a new connect. I knew fuckin' with Pedro was now out'f the question 'cause he had paid me to carry out a hit. That meant this Goya beans and rice eatin' motherfucka got dirt on me now. I told Freez that I wasn't feelin' doin' business with a nigga holdin' somethin' over my head.

"I feel that, Fetty."

"True," I said. Then I asked him, "Yo, how much cash you got put away?"

"About seventy large, plus them two things you gave me."

"Aight, yo. Hurry up'n move that 'cause it's time we put our paper and our heads together so we can take our show on the road. This shit here ain't no forever plan, Freez... we need a way out. And your skills wit' spittin' them bars is the perfect exit strategy." I had Freez gassed up; I could tell because his eyes doubled in size when I started droppin' that good shit on'm. "That Jay-Z dude and his crew were just like us. They took risks - big motherfuckin' risks. But with great risk comes great reward, my boy. We just gotta be smart about our shit. And believe me when I tell ya, I'm damn sure gettin' my moms that house up in Englewood Cliffs, even if it's the last thing Fetty does out here." I reached over and Freez gave me a pound on my fist. "Who says crime don't pay," I said with a smile.

* * * * *

After the much-needed pep talk, we just rode on laughin' and jokin'. Mad chicks passed us on the highway eye'n the new ride. Freez pulled out a glass jar of that Bronson Hydro and rolled up some of the best grass I had ever smoked in my life.

Eleven minutes later, we had finally reached Paco's, this little rim shop we liked to go to. I figured I'd get Paco to get my rims spinnin' and hook up some 6-inch TV monitors in the headrests. When we pulled up in the spaceship, I spotted a pretty-ass white-on-white 911 Porsche modelling with a cocaine-white-leather interior. The license plate in the back was a temp; it was like the owner just walked off the lot like I did.

"Look at that shit, my nigga!" I said after grabbing Freez's arm.

"Dayyuum!" Freez whistled. "That's a pretty motherfucka right there! Them shits go for like a hundred and twenty-five bills fully loaded."

We walked by on some cool shit 'cause, on the real, the whip I had just copped was just as fly - or it was about to be once Paco got finished with it. Just before we reached the entrance to the shop, the door swung open... out came a face I was definitely happy to see.

"Oh, shit! Pretty-motherfuckin'-New!" I shouted. "Where you been hidin' at, potnah?"

"Ah, you know... here, there. I got bustahs, hoes, and the poe-poe watchin' me, man. You know I duck and dodge while niggaz is shootin' and lootin'."

New's vernacular was still slick as I had remembered it, plus he was dressed like someone out'f a Players Ball! He was rockin' some lyme slacks and a matching button-up shirt with

Face/ Fetty Boy

some olive-green gators. His chain was blingin', both his ears were bling-bling, his wrist was like SPARKLES!... my nigga had even grown his hair long enough to keep it in a ponytail. I almost didn't recognize none of that shit 'cause of the thick-ass blonde headed white girl rubbin' all over New's chest.

"Damn, New, you doin' white bitches now?" Freez asked.

"Man, black bitch, red bitch, green bitch, white bitch, any bitch can be the right bitch! I'll take a bitch that look like a pig, give her a wig and a gig, ya dig!" After me and Freez bust out laughin', he said, "But you can call this one here Turnpike cause you gotta pay to get on and pay to get off, my nigga. Not you though, Fetty Montana; I fucks with you, so you gets to fuck with my bitches." Pretty New looked over at Freez, then said, "And you? Just 'cause your name is Freez don't mean the pussy is cheap. KRS-One had that shit wrong, nigga; the crack cost money and the pussy do, too!"

"Goddamn, New!" I shouted while holding my stomach. "You still a funny motherfucka, yo. And you done turned into an overnight pimp out this motherfucka!"

"Yeah, well, I figured I done fucked skinny bitches, white bitches, fat bitches, Spanish bitches, other niggaz bitches... I might as well do somethin' to keep these hoes laughin' and the pussy percolatin'. Shyyiit, you should see my bottom bitch, that hoe look like Kiesha Kentay."

I knew it was a joke, but I had to ask, "Who the fuck is that, New?"

"Kuntah's sister, nigga!"

We laughed a bit more before Freez asked, "So, what you doin' out here, New?"

New reached his hand out, then the white girl put somethin' in it. I didn't see what it was, but then New said, "Triple L, my boyee... triple L - look, listen, and learn."

He pointed his hand toward the Porsche me and Freez were lookin' at when we first pulled up, and that's when I noticed he was holdin' a remote control. He pressed one button, then the sound system started bumpin' louder than when the three

Face/ Fetty Boy

of us had went to Broker's night club a little while back.

"Goddamn!" I shouted. The bass was so loud we could see the windshield vibrating like that shit was about to bust! There go that nigga Jay-Z again, I said inside my own head. I think the song was called Cashmere Thoughts or some shit like that. "You know man, I'm just dealin' that hoe money... You know hoe money is slow money... but it's sho' money... Caviar and silk dreams, my voice is linen, spittin' venom up in the minds of young women... Life's short so play hard and stick hard... And the only time you love'em is when your dick hard."

That nigga Jay-Z was spittin' some slick shit on that tape. I kept thinkin' to myself that my nigga Freez can spit fire just like that... maybe better.

"That's your shit over there knockin' like that?" Freez shouted.

Pretty New turned the music back down and handed the remote back to Turnpike, "Money, pretty cars, pretty hoes, and clothes is all Pretty New knows," he said.

"I ain't know you was grabbin' like that over on Governor Street," I said to New.

"Nah, woadie. Pretty New in and out'f town wit' it. I be in PA, Delaware... them country boys payin' $90 a gram out there." Pretty New swiped his whole hand between Turnpike's ass crack and sniffed it before sayin', "And, as you can see, I'm doin' my pimpin' on the side."

This white girl's fat ass cheeks had me mad distracted. I ignored the mounds under her tight-ass skirt by askin' New about the connect we used to fuck with, "Yo, still fuckin' wit' Jose and'em?"

"You ain't heard what happened to Jose ass?" New asked.

"Nah, put me on, New."

"Man, that clown went and bought a new 500 Benz flossing a little too hard on them Bronx Niggaz. He forgot that ya can't

Face/ Fetty Boy

dangle a raw steak in front'f some hungry wolves and not expect them wolves to take a bite. Well, them niggaz sure did take a bite - they took his car, his rings, his Roley and his life... not necessarily in that order, either."

"Say word, New!" Freez said with his bottom lip almost hitting the cement.

Pretty New looked over at me as if to say, Yo, Fetty Boy, is this nigga Freez for real? Instead of clownin' Freez, he said some more slick shit, "Duck and a truck, my dude."

"What?" Freez said. And my facial expression was asking the same thing.

"Duck and a truck, my nigga." I watched New grab his white chick between her mountainous ass cheeks again pulling her closer toward me and Freez. "Tell'em what that shit is, baby," New said.

Turnpike spit her gum out onto the parking lot pavement, then licked her pink lips, "A duck and a truck," she repeated, her voice sounded like she knew how to fuck a brotha brains out,

"If he tells you that a duck can pull a truck... hook the duck up to the truck, and watch the duck pull the motherfuckin' truck."

Before me or Freez could say shit, we watched New stick another piece of gum in the white girl's mouth. He patted her on her ass telling her to step aside, then he turned to us and said, "That nigga Jose had just fronted me twenty pies, too." He winked his eye toward the Porsche and cracked a smile."

"I hear dat," I said. "New, you done really came the fuck up."

"Well, you know, even after you hook the duck up to the truck, you still gots to get the butter from the duck when you can."

"Yeah, sho' you right, brah. I just came from picking up one of them new Lex Lands." I gestured with a slight head nod over at the silver spaceship.

"Damn, my nigga! "New shouted. "That shit too big for the hood, man. "You better take a page out'f Jose's book. Be careful out there, woadie."

"I hear you, New. I got the right niggaz watchin' my back, though. Besides, I'm only gettin' some deep-dish rims put on her. Paco's gonna hook up the sound system and the TV's in the headrests, then I'ma call it a day."

"I hear that hot shit you spittin', my boy," Pretty New said. "I hear that shit so well, I can hear the spit steamin' when it hits the ground."

That was another laugh New gave us before we had exchanged numbers and parted ways. As me and Freez headed into Paco's, I said, "You see that shit right there, Freez? Pretty New doin' his motherfuckin' one-two thing. That nigga ain't chasin' the paper, the paper chasin' him. You gotta love and respect his game."

I thought to myself, G.G. Ave niggaz congratulate and never playah hate.

Face/ Fetty Boy

Chapter 15: Wolves

After a few days of shittin' on the town in my new spaceship, I had ran into my nigga E-Rick. Really, I was out creepin' late night with this bad-ass young fox named Kimberly. I took her to this place called T.G.I.F.'s up in Wayne on Hamburg Turnpike- none of Nina's nosy-ass friends hung out up that way.

Youngen damn sure didn't act her age, though; we had barely hit the highway before her head disappeared in my lap. She even scrapped her fingernails underneath my balls while slurpin' her thick lips up and down the diznick.

"Easy, ma! Godammit," I said while trying to concentrate on driving, "you make him too excited and he gonna throw up in your mouth." That young girl ain't hear a word I said. She gave me brain the whole way to the restaurant and on the way back from the restaurant... I even pulled into the parking lot behind the skating rink and stretched out her tight, moist twat. Kimmie had the spaceship's tinted windows foggier than a little bit.

After digging her back out for nearly an hour, we cruised through the strip to see what was jumpin'; and that's when I saw that nigga E-Rick hustlin'. Like always, his clientele was flocking all around him. He basically had an unemployment line going up and down the block. He was still rockin' his usual button-down shirt with some Capri dress slacks. He

Face/ Fetty Boy

always looked like he just stepped out of an office building somewhere.

"A'yo, E!" I shouted after rolling down the window, "don't go nowhere, I need to dolla at you!"

"Aight, you better hurry up, though. I'm almost through pitchin' these jums. And you know I don't play this block for too long. No hangin' or bangin', just strictly slangin', lil' bro."

E always had something smart to say whenever he was in the paint gettin' his cheesy bread. For as long as I had known him, that's just how he did him. I chalked it up as just being the make up of his charisma. "I'ma drop my shawty off over on Park Ave," I yelled, "I be right back, big bro."

From the strip to Park Ave. and East 18th Street, then back to the strip took less than five minutes - especially how I was whippin' it. When I came back, I parked the ride on the corner of Hamilton Ave and East 18th Street. Then, walked up the block to Graham Ave. and hit the right. Like clockwork, E-Rick was about to close up shop.

"I told you I'd be back, old head."

E-Rick looked at me, then his watch, as if he was surprised to see me, "Damn, Fetty... where you park at?" he said.

"Down Hamilton Ave. you know my shit too big for this strip. Plus, I don't need the heat right now."

"I feel you, my young gee, but I ain't feeling being on this block this late. You got something to say? You need me to do something? Talk slick and make it quick, lil' bro."

E was a slick huslitn' dude, but I knew I could trust'm. Any nigga that could come out on the block for years grindin' solo without crossin' anybody not even once... you know you can trust that man. I put it to'm straight about what had went down with Pedro; After all, E-Rick was the one who put me onto Pedro in the first place. I told him about the five birds I was paid to duff the nigga Scientific. As carefully as I had planned the whole thing, I laid it out for E-Rick. What I didn't tell him was about Ali Mu being the one to actually pull the

Face/ Fetty Boy

trigger. Didn't have to, either; the streets talk just as much as they be watchin'. And E was able to fill in the blanks like the O.G. he was.

Still, I had convinced him to tell Pedro that I did the job I was paid to do, but to also tell him that I had gotten knocked for a ratchet. I told E-Rick to make up some story about how I had gotten a high-priced attorney and plead out to a 5 with a 3. "If he buys it, he buys it," I said, "If he don't, he don't."

Which ever way it went, Pedro wasn't going to be seeing me again. Those five keys signed and sealed all of our dealings.

E-Rick said, "Yeah, I got you, lil' bro. Pedro's ass probably would love the fact he wont' be seeing yo' ass again, too. And the fact that you got the job done might even land me a better price wit'm." E-Rick rubbed both his hands together as if he was trying to shake off some excess dirt; really he was telling the rest of the fiends on the block that he was closing shop. He took the toothpick out his mouth, then flicked it to the ground. I watched him take his glasses off and polish them with the end of his Versace shirt. He hopped into his hooptie ride, an old BM, and pulled out of his parking space. He rolled the window down, then said, "I like you, Fetty. You know why? Because your young, wild, crazy ass is a wolf. This game is gonna always need wolves out here to keep the eco-system intact."

"Fuck is a eco-system?" I asked.

"Look at it this way, lil' bro, wolves like you are needed to keep these other animals in check. If the wolves die off, all the other animals start acting other than themselves. Shit would be all rearranged out here. The rats would be chasin' the cats. The cats would be chasin' the dogs. And while that's going on, the snakes, them niggaz you be hanging with, still gonna be slitherin'. They gonna start thinking they are the lions of the jungle. Your raw energy is needed in this game.

Face/ Fetty Boy

You gotsta know your worth out here, lil' nigga. You gotta know what moves to make and when to make'em. Otherwise, your emotions and loyalty will be your demise. And it makes no goddamn sense that a nigga would bring about his own destruction." E-Rick pulled off leaving me with his final words, "Glad to see you ballin' and not crawlin', lil' bro. And don't worry about it...I'll handle that for you."

After watching E speed away from the griminess of the strip, I headed back down Godwin Ave so I could get off the block my damn self. As soon as I dipped past the dark open field where all the pipe-heads be at searchin' for niggaz stashes, I heard a weak, but familiar, voice cry out, "Young Fetty Man... Young Fetty Man... over here, Young Fetty Man." I almost didn't hear it 'cause the jewel E had just dropped on me was still running through my mind.

Young Fetty Man? I repeated inside my own head. Don't nobody call me that except for old head Ali Mu, and that nigga is too much of a thoroughbred to be sounding like some cracked out dope fiend.

"Young Fetty Man," the voice said again. I looked further into the darkly lit field. I ain't see shit but a bunch of garbage tossed everywhere. Empty alcohol bottles and plastic bags. That's when I noticed a slender figure standing about ten feet away from me.

"Ali Mu?" I said. But when I saw Ali Mu standing there looking like he done smoked up everything he could get his hands on, I called his name out with the voice of one'f them R&B singers. "Is that you, Ali Mu?"

"Yeah. It be me," Mu answered. "Come here, Young Fetty Man." I stepped further into the littered field and immediately wished I would've kept it moving. Mu looked bad... fucked up bad! That nigga had sores all over his face and white blisters jumping off his ashy lips. I stepped closer 'cause I couldn't believe what I was lookin' at. Why the fuck did I do that? That nigga smelled like pure-D-shit!

Face/ Fetty Boy

"Damn, Mu!" I said while placing my hand over my nose. "What the fuck happened, yo?" The sight and the smell made me wanna throw up in my own mouth, but on the inside, my heart was completely broken. I always had mad love for Mu. Seeing him like this fucked up my state of mind. My mentor, my friend had fallen victim to the pipe. Did Felicia's crackhead antics have him strung out like this, I asked myself. Maybe it was that half'f bird I had hit him off with? Damn, don't tell me I fucked my ol' head up like this?

"Man, you know how it go, man," Mu finally said. "Fuckin' Rick the Ruler got me. But I'ma get this monkey off my back sooner or later, watch. In the mean time... you got anything on you, Young Fetty Man?"

I just stood there. Straight fucked up by the sight of what was in front of me. I ain't even bother asking Mu what happened to the blow I paid him with two weeks ago.

On some real shit, the thought crossed my mind to slump Mu with two head shots right there in that dirty-ass field. If he out here runnin' like this, there's no tellin' what he'd do to get his hands on some of that shit - including snitchin' on a nigga like me. I could put two in his head just like Mu did to Scientific... that'll definitely get the monkey off his motherfuckin' back. Nah, on second thought, that's a bad move right now. I'll take a rain check on that.

"Nah, Mu," I answered. "I don't have nothin' on me. But hold this and get yourself cleaned up." Before I had found Mu in the worst of conditions, while kickin' it with E-Rick, my nigga Ren slipped me a mean knot. I peeled off the first five bills - all hundreds - and gave'm to Mu. "Meet me out here tomorrow," I said, while placing the bills in Mu's hand, "I need you to handle somethin' for me, main man."

"Aight, Young Fetty Man! You got it! You the best nigga I know, man!"

When I put that five hundred in Mu's hand, that nigga disappeared into the dark quicker than a penis in a whore's mouth. Right then, I had decided to have my top lieutenant, Illy-Ill,

Face/ Fetty Boy

leave Mu's ass stinkin'. I had told Ill to put Mu down as soon as he got the chance. For a live wire like Illy-Ill, as soon as you get the chance meant right fuckin' now.

* * * * *

Two weeks ticked off the clock, and I hadn't seen Mu around the block. He usually never hung out on the strip anyway, but since he had turned into a crackhead, where else would he be? I dipped past Felicia's place. Her kids were still runnin' around with shitty diapers and she was still tryin' to suck me off for a quick fix. Of course I told that bitch to sit the fuck down and shut the fuck up. When I asked about Mu, she said she didn't know where he was. Supposedly Mu had left town and went down south or some shit with his aunt he always spoke about.

That's when I knew that Illy-Ill had put Mu in his final resting place. Ill and I both learned the rules of murder a long time ago... never speak about the shit you already got away with. He slumped Mu and didn't even tell me. I respect the game and Illy-Ill enough not to ask him what he did with Mu's body. Hopefully, it's somewhere never to be found. Rest in peace, Old Head Ali Mu... rest in peace.

Face/ Fetty Boy

Chapter 16: To the Top or Broke

It's a damn shame what happened to Ali Mu, but I couldn't dwell on that. A man has to walk his own path, and he's gotta do it solo. My path was leading me in a whole 'nother direction.

For starters, all the work Freez had been sittin' on was gone, finished, finito. Me and my team were left with a few ounces at best. I never talked shop with my menz n'em, except for Freez; they ain't know if I was sittin' on a few grand or a few hundred large. Truth was... I wasn't sittin' on nothin' near close to what I'm supposed to have!

Week after week, we were flossin' at parties, buying out the bar at clubs; on top of that, I had copped the spaceship. Not to mention, Nina's high-maintenance self, who, as far as I could tell, was still havin' my baby. I kept her under my wing and spoiled her ass rotten down to the core. It didn't matter where I was going, I had Nina with me showing her off and lettin' my family and friends know that I was about to be a father. Starting a family may have been just the thing I needed to get my mind focused on what I was supposed to be doin' out in these fucked up streets.

* * * * *

A few Sundays back, my uncle Coppa-G, who lived and drove a taxi in the Bronx, had come by my mom's house.

Face/ Fetty Boy

Whenever my moms made her rice & peas with oxtails, Uncle Coppa was definitely gonna show up sooner or later.

I remember he was tellin' me about these dudes in the Bronx called the Shower Posse. Don't even get me to lyin' about what that shit mean, but my uncle said these niggaz had work for cheap. I ain't really pay attention at the time 'cause I had just came up off the jooks, plus I still had the five birds Pedro had paid me. All that shit had me feelin' like a millionaire. The game move so fast, yet niggaz always thinking that the shit they sittin' on ain't gonna ever run out. You heard what Diddy said - "The Sun Don't Shine Foreva..."

I recall my uncle tellin' me, "Mi a show you, Frankie; de mon, dem big star, dem have pure shyit str-8 from yard! Dem Spanish bwoy you a deal wit no have dis, nephew, mi a tell yuh."

My uncle Coppa-G was a straight Patwa talkin' yardee-type dude. He had been in this country for over five years now, and still spit that shit like he was back on the island. I love it when he comes around 'cause it gives me a chance to kick it in the language that all the bitches love.

"Alright, Uncle Coppa," I said, "me ago check it out inna few weeks zeen an if it a de real ting, yuh done know mi ago tek care a yuh, u'hear?" Uncle Coppa-G just smiled at me and shook his head up and down. He liked it when I kicked it with him like a true Yardee Jamaican. Any other time I'd be soundin' like a straight Yankee bwoy, as my mother would say.

"Yeah, mon," Coppa answered, "just mek me know and mi a carry yuh go check de big don dem."

That conversation was three weeks ago, and now it was time to put these rude bwoys to the test and see what a gwan, I thought to myself.

Momma-P was cooking oxtails again today, so I knew Uncle Coppa would pop up to get his eat on and tell us some jokes. My favorite unc rolled through at around quarter after six in the p.m.. Freez had came over, too; I told him to stop

Face/ Fetty Boy

by so we could hear about these Shower Posse dudes together - plus, Freez loved my mother's cookin'.

While the rest of the family was occupied, me, Freez and Coppa dipped onto the porch so we could scheme about these Jamaicans in the Bronx who was lettin' it go for $18,000 a pie.

"Uncle Coppa, what a gwan, puppa?"

"Wassup, mi nephew? What you and dis criminal up to?"

Me and Freez laughed before Freez responded by tellin' Coppa, "Damn, Coppa-G, you gettin' mad fat, mon!" Me and Coppa ain't say nothin', but inside our heads, we were laughin' at Freez's fake-ass Jamaican accent.

"Yeah, mon," Coppa said, "mi a fat 'cause mi a eat steak and a stay up late wid yah muddah!" He loved joking around with me and my friends. And, truth be told, all my friends loved Coppa to death.

"Yo, Unc, mi know you 'bout to get your eat on, but when you done, you tink you could tek me to link up wid dem Shower dudes tonight?"

"No, mon. Good ting you did wait, 'cause the Feds hole on pon a few a dem and dem shut down shop for now."

"Bumba ras claat!," I said. It was like all the air seeped right out of my plan. But, just as quickly, Uncle Coppa brought that shit back to life.

"Don't worry 'bout a ting, nephew. Mi a have someting betta dan dat. All it tek is some money and legwork. Mi bredren tell me how the coke mek it ova yah from yard. So, if you want, we can cut out the middle mon dem and go get dat mi self fi yah."

"Blat fire; hell, Yeah!" I damn near shouted that shit. I had to remember that we were chillin' on my mother's front porch. I put my finger in front of my mouth tellin' them to be quiet when I was the one loud as fuck. "Yeah, dat sound sweet, Unc. How da whole ting work?"

"Well, Frankie, all we haffi do is liquefy each key we buy in Jamaica and put it inna de white rum bottles. We ah wait til de whole ting clear Customs. Den mi ah mix the proper solu-

Face/ Fetty Boy

tion that will bring the coke back from de dead, mon. Dis will change the whole ting back from liquid to powder."

"How you mean, Unc?" When I asked the question, I looked over at Freez and that niggaz eyebrows were crinkled; Uncle Coppa had him just as confused as I was.

"Well, mi gal work a one bakery inna de Bronx, and dem send fi five case loads a rum once a month. You don't haffi worry 'bout dat end, me a have it curry n'crisp, mi yute."

"So, how many kilos can you ship at a time?"

"The rum come inna twenty-four bottles. Dem usually get 'bout five cases of it to bake da rum cakes for de month. Mi a tink 5-bottles we load up inna each case won't look suspicious. Dat's twenty-five kilo ah come cross the boarder str-8 to us."

Yo, I think I started droolin' out that motherfucka; that shit sounded so good. "Yo, Unc, how much a kilo in Jamaica?"

Uncle Coppa smiled and leaned forward in his seat before sayin, "8-10... give or take. The ting pure as snow."

"Eight to ten G's!" Freez shouted.

I elbowed him in the chest before sayin', "Nigga, shut the fuck up!" I ain't blame'm, though. That shit had me screamin' inside my own head, too. "Yeah, mon, dat sound sweeter than candy, but only one ting."

"Wha de i'deal wid?" Coppa asked.

"We need work now... right motherfuckin' now. Who gonna go to Jamaica and put all this into play, Unc?"

"Don't watch dat, mon. Yuh no hear me say? Mi a fly down next week fi go deal wid de ting. Mi done tell yuh, say mi have it all program properly. All yuh haffi do is put up the money and mek sure me eat a food for my time and troubles."

"Shyiiit, Uncle Coppa, if all goes well, you ago eat more than steak. Try lobsters with some mobsters!" I said, and gave Freez one of our flashy handshakes.

"Dat mi a talk about, mi bwoy... dat me a talk about, star."

* * * * *

Face/ Fetty Boy

It took a few days, but we put the loot together. After all the gamblin', trickin', and flossin' me and Freez had been doin' over the last few months, we were only able to put together enough for twenty pies. Add to that Coppa's air fare and travel money, we shipped $200,000 to Jamaica stashed in a barrel filled with clothes and appliances. We tossed Coppa another ten grand for himself to cover his expenses. That put me down to my personal stash of about nine G's. Still... the shit was worth the risk. In this case, it would've been a bad risk not to take the risk.

"Yo, Freez," I said, while sittin' in the passenger side of Freez's whip, "it's to the top from here on out, my brotha. We gonna have the purest and cheapest shit on the East Coast. Miami won't even be able to fuck with us if this works out."

"And what if it don't, Fetty?" Freez asked. I gotta admit, I wasn't prepared for a question like that. But Fetty Boy was always the type of nigga to keep shit real. And, if the plan failed, then it was back to the basics for me and my niggaz- pullin' jooks, beatin' connects... whateva it took.

"If the shit fails, then we broke again, my boy. But the reward makes it a risk worth taking."

Face/ Fetty Boy

Chapter 17: "Dramacidal"

"Heavy is the head that wears the crown..." I think that's written in the bible somewhere. On Nas's joint, "It was written", Nas said, "I'll knock the crown off the so-called King of the town and lock it down..." His alter ego, Escobar, also spits on the same album, "Street dreams are made of these, niggaz push beams and 300E'z, a Drug dealer's destiny is reaching a key..."

I guess me and my team were ahead of our time 'cause, for us, it was more like: "cash, weed, cars, ghetto celebrity, hood movie star." Esco rhymed about all that on a track with his Queensbridge heads, Mobb Deep. Nas left out one thing, though; it's cash, weed, cars, ghetto celebrity, hood movie star, and drama!

* * * * *

After me and Freez had sat and kicked it with Uncle Coppa, there was really nothin' left to do but sit and wait. The anticipation alone was a killer. I had called Coppa a few times to make sure things were going smoothly down in Jamaica. All Unc said was, "Don't worry about a ting, mi nephew. De ting soon come; everyting criss. De ting got hold up 'cause de mon dem a wait pon de Colombian dem fi come wid a shipment. Just cool, mon. Me have it now and a put it together, everything curry!" He kept assuring me that shit was all good, but I was impatient like a motherfucka.

I never really had much tolerance for the bullshit. It

Face/ Fetty Boy

was just that the strip was dry and my team was bleedin'. Me and Freez couldn't wait to get our hands on those keys so we could flood the streets. But the Lord works in mysterious ways... ain't that what they say? We ain't have no product, so we had no reason to play the block. That made the narcos madder than a motherfucka when they came rollin' through. They went crashing through the doors of all our trap houses. They started snatchin' niggaz off the strip questioning them about all types of shit allegedly involving me. The good thing was the narcos didn't find any drugs; they couldn't, it was like ground zero out there. They didn't find no guns either. The only thing they found that could have possibly gotten their dick wet was about fifteen hundred in cash and some empty drug paraphernalia out of a single stash house.

One Time ain't like that shit at all. Them suckas came to my mom's house and searched everything from the freezer to the shoe boxes in my bedroom. I had already taken whatever little cash I had left over to Nina's crib so she could put it up for me. The only thing those clowns left with was my body to take me downtown for questioning. Y'all know how it is in Urban USA; a nigga is guilty before his ass even get in the cop car.

* * * * *

The precinct had changed since the last time I was there. It's cleaner. The cops are younger. It's more females wearin' badges now. Even got a few new black cops up in the place. But, for the most part, the D's of the Paterson P.D. were still white as that powder they tryin' to stop me from slingin'.

The first detective to come at me with the dumb-ass questions was Detective Meyers out'f Homicide. I knew when these jokers first started runnin' down on the strip that this shit wasn't about no drugs. Wasn't nobody doin' shit 'cause the streets was dry. With no drug dealers to catch, the authorities had more time to look into unsolved murders. And, if I'm sittin' here, that means somebody is out there runnin' their fuckin' mouth about what they think they know. Oh, well... time to play the white man's game.

"Where were you the night of the shooting in the Broadway building?" Meyers asked. In my mind, I'm like, are you serious? This fat-ass white man sittin' here in a shirt and tie that only his fucked up salary could afford; I was goin' in on him inside my own head, but he just kept on with the questions. After ignoring his first question, he asked me about Lu-Lu's wake, but still, I just looked at the fat cracker like he was speakin' Russian. A few more cops entered the room; they called themselves starin' me down on some tough-guy shit. That made Meyers' punk ass a little bolder. He blurted out the words,

"Old head Ali Mu, we know you got him to do your dirty work, you piece of shit!"

"You got the wrong guy," I calmly answered. "I don't know any of these people or nothin' about the shit you talkin'." My face sported a smile so big I'm sure this pig was countin' all of my teeth. Then... he hit me with the bombshell.

"How much did the Dominicans in New York pay you, huh?"

My smile disappeared quicker than a motherfucka when he asked me that bullshit. Niggaz was definitely watchin' out in them streets; they even talkin' now - maybe even kats from my own camp.

"Nothing to smile about now?" Meyers said. "We can't prove any of this shit yet; hell, we got witnesses that say some old lady shot up the Broadway building, but we know it was you! We'll get ya, you fucking scumbag. We always do." Meyers waved his hand at one of the other detectives in the room telling him to open the door so I could leave. Just as I was gettin' up, he said, "Just tell me one thing... what did you do with Ali Mu's body?"

Damn! these clowns even suspect that I had somebody get rid of Ali Mu! Somebody in my circle definitely got diarrhea at the mouth. "Man, I done told y'all, I go to school and mind

Face/ Fetty Boy

my business. I wasn't nowhere you said I was. And I don't know nothin' about nothin'."

Just as I started to walk out, this fine-ass redboned bitch was entering the interrogation room Meyer's had me in. I heard one of the other cops call her Detective Benson. Talk about a body! This chick will make a nigga lip synch! Her jetblack hair spilled down to the small of her back, and her hips and ass were straight out'f this world! Her skin looked like someone had poured a caffe latte all over her. As soon as she walked in, she captured the room with her apple-scented Victoria's Secret body lotion. I imagined hand cuffing her to the interrogation table and fuckin' her doggie style right then and there.

I was quickly snapped back to reality when the cop chick started bombardin' me with questions. There was no doubt that Meyers set this shit up. Just 'cause I'm a big strong black nigga, he think I'ma start runnin' my mouth just 'cause some pretty bitch walked in. They must think I'm a sucka or a cornball or some shit. I can't even front, my first inclination was to start tryin' to kick it to the bitch. She had me. But all that shit went out the window when she started asking me the same questions as them other fools.

"Miss, like I told your boy'n'em, I don't know shit. I suggest you call my lawyer, Paul Bergen; I know the procedure."

Yeah, I knew that shit would get all these cop's attention. Whenever a nigga start spittin' the "L" word, law enforcement starts taking on a whole new demeanor.

* * * * *

Even after they're supposed to let you go, the cops will try to keep a nigga sittin' in the bullpen for a few hours. I had been runnin' these streets for too long not to be prepared for something like that.

While sittin' on one of the dusty-ass benches, a thousand and one thoughts were wrestling around in my head, I wondered if Nina was gonna have a boy or a girl? Is Uncle

Face/ Fetty Boy

Coppa-G gonna be able to pull off the deal? I wondered what my nigga Hubby is doin' in the Afterlife... probably down there makin' the Devil shit himself. Damn! Who the fuck could be snitchin' to the jakes n'shit?

While I was sittin' there questioning myself, these other dudes in the bullpen started talkin' loud as fuck. When the jakes first put me in here, there was only two or three other people; now the shit was turnin' into a pen party.

"Man, I swear I'm done smokin' that shit!" I heard one of'em say. By the drawn-out sound of his voice, I knew he was a pipehead from down the hill. That nigga probably say the same shit every time the pigs stick his ass in here. "Yeah, Ray-Ray, I'm fuckin' done, I tell ya. I'm gonna take my ass to A.A. as soon as I make this $5,000 bail."

I laughed inside my own head 'cause this pussy is soundin' silly as hell right now. First of all, if he did get five G's, he'd probably smoke the shit instead of using it for bail. And secondly, he needs to take his ass to N.A. 'cause A.A. ain't gonna do shit for'm. He so high, he don't even recognize that the nigga he's talkin' to is higher than him! This Ray-Ray dude is just sittin' there with his mouth open starin' down at his shoes.

"I'm straight up this time, Ray-Ray," the crackhead continued. "But sometimes it seems like if it wasn't for bad luck, I would have no luck at all. I swear, it could be raining pussy outside and I'd walk out there and still get hit right over my head with a big fat dick! I woke up this mornin' after scorin' a few bucks to buy a little 'Rick the Ruler', then end up in this raggedy-ass joint. And I know the judge is gonna make love to me 'cause this same shit happened to me up the hill two weeks ago."

Yo, this nigga funny as hell. I guess his luck is bad if there's pussy floatin' around and he keep runnin' into dicks. And he right about the judge makin' love to'm; if he's a repeat offender, the judge just might fuck'm down!

Face/ Fetty Boy

I needed that little time out. Listenin' to that pipehead made me stop thinkin' about all the bullshit that's goin' on right now. Hmph - I guess that geezer was my fix for the day. Once that bullpen therapy was over, I needed to find out who'd been runnin' their fuckin' mouth to the cops. I stepped outside the station and breathed in the mild air. It relaxed my mind a bit and made me think more clearly. Maybe it was E-Rick who was snitchin'. Nah, it can't be that nigga, man. He got too much shit goin' on. Plus, the last time I saw him, he was ballin' harder than the rest of us on the strip. It could be Freez doin' all the talkin'; he know just as much as I do. Nah... hell no... no way.. not my nigga... me and Freez go back like Tony and Manolo. It can't be my nigga Illy-Ill, he too much of a goon for that shit. Please don't tell me I'm blinded by love for these niggaz! I'll figure it out in due time. Nothing stays in the dark for too long. I just gotta make sure to stay on my P's and Q's. It's plain as day the jakes is on me. But they ain't find shit; all they got is information from some rattin'-ass bastard. It's gonna come to light... believe that.

* * * * *

I needed to get away from the strip for a while. For the past few days, I had been creepin' with my little shawty Kimberly. I stayed away from the block, my mother's house, even Nina. The only one who knew where I would be was Freez just in case he had heard from Uncle Coppa before I did.

Me and Kimberly were up in the telly on Rt. 4 one day, and my pager started buzzin' like crazy. The pager made the same sound that it always did; I could just feel it in my gut that this page was gonna come with more drama.

Of course, it was a 911 page from Nina. When I called her back, she said she needed to holler at me and that I should pick her up from work at 3 p.m.. She usually drove to work

Face/ Fetty Boy

herself, so I just figured that her mother was using the car.

I ain't gonna front, I was type nervous. What the fuck she wanna talk about now? Then again, I could be just feelin' the effects of all the stress I had been under lately - the jakes snatchin' me up, no work on the strip, niggaz on my team yappin' to the captain... waitin' on Uncle Coppa. On some real shit, I'm glad Coppa-G was movin' like a turtle. If he had made the deal jump off earlier, the narcos would've ran down and knocked us off with the mother load.

I ran all these thoughts through my mind while driving to the bank where Nina worked at part-time. After thinkin' it all through, I figured she was just missin' me; I was lookin' forward to sexin' her down later. Thinkin' about that wet, pregnant pussy had me doin' eighty all the way to Ridgefield Park. If anybody could ease the weight on my shoulders, it was Nina.

Nina working part-time as a bank teller was a good thing. Her mother always told her that I wasn't gonna be around forever to do all the heavy lifting. She kept tellin' her that she needed to focus on her own life. Her own career. Miss. Mary was right in a way, but I already had it set up what would happen if I ever went to prison - Nina and my baby would be well taken care of. Me and Freez swore to each other that we would look out for each other's family if one of us ever got knocked or killed. Besides the game, Nina was my life. And born or unborn, the baby she was carryin' was my life, too. They were my motivation to go hard in the hood. My every thought about the future included Nina - a house with the picket white-fence, marriage, kids, I'd retire after makin' them M's, and she'd probably still wanna work a 9 to 5... or not.

Thinkin' about Nina made the time tick off the clock like Nathan. I pulled the spaceship up in front of the bank at about ten to three. Nina came bouncin' out the door in her little sexy-girl strut twirling her hair around her finger and chewin' on some bubble gum.

After she hopped inside the truck, I asked, "You said 3

Face/ Fetty Boy

o'clock, it's ten of... why you so early?"

"My boss let me leave early," she said. "Besides, I ain't want you out here waiting too long."

As I eased the whip out the parking lot, Nina just sat back in the passenger seat staring out the window. We talked about this and that, but she was actin' a little nonchalantly. I knew her better than the back of my own hand; even better than the back of a hundred dollar bill. She was tryin' to tell me somethin', but didn't know how. Either that or she was pissed about some shit she done heard. I figured I'd just be quiet and let the silence of the car ride frustrate her into tellin' me what was goin' on.

Maybe she was mad 'cause we weren't makin' all of our regular trips to Barney's and Sak's 5th Avenue - shopping in the mall, hittin' Bloomies and Neiman's. I don't know how she could complain 'cause I was hittin' her off with enough money for her and her cousin Sha-Sha to do them. They was hangin' out together while I was out there grindin'... or what I liked to call, "Scratchin' and Survivin!"

After five minutes of the silent treatment, I had turned onto the Rt. 80 ramp; that was the quickest highway back to Paterson this time of day. I decided to ask, "Yo, how the baby doin'?" I reached over and gave her belly a rub like I was rubbin' on a crystal ball. She giggled a little 'cause she was ticklish, then playfully pushed my hand away.

"Stop playin' so much, boy!"

"Whaddup, then? You throwin' up n'shit? You startin' to eat crazy shit like hotsauce on your ice cream? Ha ha..."

It felt good jokin' around with Nina. Even though I had been creepin' with Kimberly, my mind was constantly on my true love. I loved bein' with Nina. I loved everything about her, even her feisty-ass attitude. Sometimes it felt like she was the only chick that could figure me out. She reminded me of my mother in that regard. But, just like my experience has always been with females, a bitch will flip the script on you in a heartbeat.

Face/ Fetty Boy

"I went and had the abortion, Franko."

When I heard those words, all that playful joking shit went right out the window. It was like my heart had stopped beating. It felt like The Man Upstairs was holding a huge remote control and had decided to press pause on my entire life. My first thought was to just backslap Nina and make her ass do a backflip right out the spaceship. That was my first, second, and third thought.

A few seconds went by before my mouth found the words,

"What the fuck did you just say to me, yo?"

"What did you expect, Franko? You out here involved in all types of shit. What if you end up in jail? My moms raised me while my father was doing time. I'm not trying to go through that with you! Plus, I got school and work to focus on."

I hated callin' her a bitch, but right now I ain't give a fuck. "Bitch, you ain't think about none'f that shit you talkin' when you was beggin' me for the dick and spendin' my goddamn paper!"

"Yeah, your sex is more than good, Franko! And, apparently, you giving that shit away to other bitches!"

There goes the heavy hitter, I thought to myself. I swear niggaz in the hood talk like a bunch'f bitches! I said, "You always listenin' to some bullshit your busted-ass girlfriends be tellin' you!"

"Don't even try it," Nina shot back, "because Sha-Sha told me everything." She wasn't screamin' at me anymore; in fact, she returned to her nonchalant shit. "She told me how you be sneaking around with your little young bitch named Kimberly."

Goddamn, niggaz run they mouth too motherfuckin' much!

"Who the fuck is Kimberly?" I asked tryin' to fake the funk.

"Frank, you good, but you ain't that good, nigga. I bet your ass ain't know that Sha-Sha moved into the same building as this Kimberly bitch over on East 18th. She walked right

Face/ Fetty Boy

up to Sha and was talking about how she go with Fetty from G.G. Ave and how she be sucking your dick. The bitch even said she pregnant."

Woah! I came to a sudden stop at a red light. It was definitely possible my pretty-young thang was pregnant 'cause I damn sure been puttin' sperm in every hole that bitch got!

"Listen, yo, I don't care what your gossipin'-ass pigeon cousin done told you, that don't give you the right to kill my fuckin' seed! How I'ma look now? I'm goin' around tellin' everybody that I'ma be a father! My mother gonna be a grandmother! I guess now I got the dumb look, huh? The jokes on me, y'all." Nina tried to say some shit, but I kept goin' in on her ass, "You's a low-down-dirty bitch, Nina... fuck you! Fuck yo' ass and everyone you cool with, including Sha-Sha and your mother!" Alright, maybe I ain't mean to say her mother; Miss Mary was actually good people. But Nina had me feelin' hurt like never before. The words were just comin' out my mouth on their own. In the streets, a nigga would welcome his own bloody murder rather than experience disloyalty on this level, especially from his so-called soulmate. My world was being ripped apart, and I was helpless. I could already tell that time was going to be the only cure for this type of hurt. Damn, Nina! I said inside my head. Shoot me! Stab me! Send my ass to prison forever! But don't kill my fuckin' baby! Some scars can never heal!

The rest of the ride back to Nina's house took alot longer than usual; actually, it was the same ten minutes as always, but the silence in the whip made the clock tick slow as hell. We didn't do much talkin' after she dropped the bullshit on me. I mean, I would blurt shit out here and there. Like, "I should kill your fuckin' ass! You wanna kill my baby n'shit! Let's see how the fuck you like it!" I cut into her pretty hard, too. Then told her that my mother had told me not to trust her ass. That she was just like the rest of these gold-digging whores out here in these streets. "Just 'cause yo' ass act smarter than these other hookers don't mean you any different - fuck you, bitch!. You don't wanna have my baby? I'll find somebody who will. Maybe I'll go check out this Kimberly bitch you talkin' about; she already pregnant with my seed, right?"

I took shot after shot at Nina. All she did was sit there and take it. She kept wiping her tears every time one rolled down her pretty little cheeks. I acted like I ain't give a fuck she was cryin', but really, I couldn't stand to see her so sad. That's why I was glad we had finally reached the Towers.

Usually, I would go up with Nina and chill for a while. Not this time. I pulled the spaceship right up in front of the building and came to a stop in the fire lane. "Bitch, get the fuck out my shit!" I yelled. The look of shock in her eyes almost broke my heart, but I kept the screw face on and even reached over to throw the door open for her. "Get the fuck out! I'll call yo' ass and let you know when I'ma come get my shit! All that shit you got at my mother's house, I'll drop that shit off when I fuckin' feel like it! Now, get out... and fuck you str-8 like that, bitch!"

A few project chicks were hangin' out in front of the building. They just stood there after I screamed on Nina, eyes wide and mouths dropped to the pavement. For Nina, it was like a nightmare. I don't even think she realized what was goin' on. The tears kept spillin' down her face, and it took her almost two minutes before she could find the strength to get out the whip.

Getting out the spaceship, she turned around and asked with a shaky voice, "You not comin' up?"

"Goddamn, yo... you supposed to be the smart one! What part'f this shit you don't understand!?! I'm done wit' yo' retarded ass!" I don't know what Nina said next 'cause I reached over and pulled the door shut, then shot right back into the street. Everybody outside the building turned and looked at me 'cause my tires screeched all the way until I reached the next block.

Face/ Fetty Boy

* * * * *

I couldn't lay low like I first intended after hearing about the abortion. I played the strip heavy for the next week or so without a care in the world; spazzin' on niggaz, hard too, on some bully shit. It was like I had lost my sense of direction. I kept trying to tell myself that sacrifice was necessary in order to be great in this world - Nina was just one'f those sacrifices.

Still, I missed the hell out'f her. I was questioning myself about whether or not I was too hard on her. She was on my mind 24/7. And if I wasn't alone ruminating about Nina, then I was talkin' to all my boys about her. They were probably sick of hearing her name, just like I was sick of missing her.

She even rode through the strip one day in her mother's car. I was sittin' on a milk crate chillin', while my menz'n'em were shootin' dice. Lil' Goochie looked up and said, "Yo, there Nina go right there, Fetty."

Styling like I ain't give a fuck by sayin' "Fuck that stinkin'-ass bitch. I stared right at her while she paused at the stop sign. She must've read my lips; the look in her eyes gave her the same sad appearance she had when I first told her to kick rocks.

"Stop frontin' on that girl, yo," Lil' Gooch said, "you know you love her."

Just like I had been snappin' on all my menz, I snapped on Lil' Gooch, too. "Mind yours and I'ma mind mines. Translation... stay the fuck out my business, Gooch. If I say fuck the bitch, then that's what it is str-8 lace.. fuck the bitch."

My team backed off me a little 'cause they seen that I was feelin' some kind'f way. Nina or no Nina, I was still king of the strip. I was just missin' my queen frontin' like the shit was all good.

But I still had to harden my heart towards her. I was

Face/ Fetty Boy

drinkin' and smokin' cess more than I needed to. I started long dickin' all the hoodrats that I never fucked before on the strength of Nina. I wanted to drink, smoke, and fuck the pain away. It worked for a while; but my desire for Nina wa a lot stronger than I wanted to admit. I should have never put the brown sugar before the dirty green cream.

Face/ Fetty Boy

Chapter 18: "Some Say the Ex..."

Two weeks can seem like an eternity when you have things to do; that's exactly how long it had been since Coppa-G went to Jamaica. I had heard from him once or twice, but it had been a few days since our last communication.

I was never a patient type of dude. Neither was Freez, even though he was handling the waiting better than me. We needed that work to land so we could get back to doin' what we do. All the drama we had faced over the last two weeks had us on tilt. We thought that if we idly hopped from club to club, we could keep our minds occupied until the weight landed. We didn't achieve nothing except blowing more of the paper we were sittin' on - paper that was gettin smaller by the minute.

We definitely played the strip more than we needed to. The bad part was we were out there just bullshittin'. Drinking and smokin' that chronic. Sittin' on milk crates kickin' the willie bo-bo with our menz n'em. There were even rumors going around that me and Freez were broke and that the cops had taken everything from us. I even had one motherfucka named Justice ask me if I wanted to sell the spaceship. It almost took my whole team to talk me out'f killin' that hating-ass nigga. Freez, Ron Gotti, Dead Eye, Lil' Gochie, Illy-Ill... it took a hot minute for all of'em to calm me down. They did run Justice's bitch ass off the strip and made him relocate down the hill somewhere. The way Justice was actin' made me think he was probably the one that was doin' all the snitchin'. I don't know what to think right now. All this waitin' shit got my whole program fucked up.

* * * * *

That same night, I had finally gotten the call from Uncle Coppa. Uncle or not, I wasn't in the mood for all the pleasantries.

"Yo, nephew!" Coppa shouted. "The ship set sail already. Mi a call you last night, but you no answer. What a gwan?"

"Nuff fuckery a gwan, unc. When you drop back inna de place, me will reason wit you zeen, star," I answered. "What time your flight fi tomorrow, unc?"

"Mi flight four in the evening, nephew."

Before we hung up, I confirmed with Coppa that he would be coming on a Continental flight landing in Newark. The moment I snapped shut my flip phone, it felt like all the stress had been lifted from my shoulders. I was in such a good mood, I immediately rushed out my mom's house to head over to Freez's place, so I could give him the good news. We would always discuss business in person, one of the reasons we survived so long in this game.

When I pulled up in front of his house, I caught sight of this white car roundin' the corner. Right away, I started thinking about Nina. She drives this little white Toyota. So, every time I saw a small white car, my mind flipped right back to thinking about Nina's ass. I ain't got time to be wasting thoughts on her right now. I went up to Freez's door and rang the bell. It took my nigga three whole minutes to answer the door. When he finally let me in, I realized he took so long 'cause he was just getting out the shower.

"Good news, my boy" I said while closing the door behind me.

"Yeah, tell me somethin' good, my nigga," Freez said.

Face/ Fetty Boy

He was in and out the bedroom getting dressed like he was heading to the club somewhere.

I sat on the white leather sofa and snatched up the remote to the TV. I reached for Freez's weed stash that he kept in a hidden stash spot beneath the sofa's cushions. I waited until I rolled up two fat spliffs before I said, "Uncle Coppa-G will be back tomorrow. Everything is everything. The work left yesterday ahead of him. That means, in a few days, we'll be back in business stronger than ever."

Freez had this big-ass Kool Aid smile on his face. He finished rubbing some lotion on his ashy elbows, then sat next to me on the sofa. I handed him one of the blunts, and we sparked both them shits with one match. "That's a lot'f work coming ourway," Freez said after blowing some smoke rings toward the ceiling.

I inhaled until my lungs filled out my entire chest, then blew a smoke ring that made Freez's rings look like little Cheerios. "It ain't shit Fetty Montana can't handle," I said with a smile.

* * * * *

I woke up the next morning like a kid waitin' on Santa Claus. My head was a little clearer, but even after the good news, I found myself still thinking about Nina. I went over to this little soul food spot I liked to eat at called E & A on Straight Street. It was only 7:30 in the morning, but this spot stayed open 24/7. I ordered my usual breakfast - whiting fish, scrambled eggs w'cheese, and some grits. Eating my favorite breakfast was a good way to clear my mind of Nina. As I sat there licking my fingers like a hostage, I caught myself staring out at my truck. Right away, I remembered that I had a bunch'f Nina's crap in the back seat. Just like that, I had found an excuse to go over and check in on her.

I had barely touched my food before gettin' up and dialing Miss Mary's number.

Face/ Fetty Boy

"Good morning, Miss Mary," I said after hearing her voice; I was glad Nina's mother was the one to answer the phone. "How you doin'?"

"I'm fine, Franko. Where you been, huh? What's going on with you and my daughter?"

"You gonna have to ask Nina that, Miss Mary. She didn't tell you anything?"

"I know how women are, boy" Miss Mary shot back. "I'm asking you."

"No disrespect, but you're gonna have to ask your daughter about that." The way shit was sounding, It seemed like Miss Mary didn't have the slightest clue that Nina was even pregnant. that meant she damn sure didn't know anything about her daughter having an abortion. "Miss Mary, I'm over at E & A gettin' my eat on. Can I swing by right quick and drop off Nina's stuff, please? Plus, I gotta few things in her room I wanna pick up."

"Well, you better hurry up. The both of us are getting ready to leave for work pretty soon."

"Be there in a few, Miss Mary."

* * * * *

It wasn't even eight minutes later I was letting myself into Nina's building - I realized I still had her key on my key-ring when I was locking the doors to the truck.

At the top of the stairs, I reached to slip the key in the hole, but at the last second, decided to knock instead. I had gotten lucky before with Miss Mary answering the phone. But not this time. Nina opened the door immediately. I was still in the process of knockin' when the door flew open. She took a half a second to look me up and down, then she shot straight back to her room to finish getting dressed for work.

She ain't say shit to me and I ain't say shit to her. I just threw her things on the couch, then made my way to the

Face/ Fetty Boy

kitchen table and sat down like I owned the place. Barely seconds after sitting down, Miss Mary came out the back room with a huge smile on her face.

"What's up, boy?" she said while reaching to give me a hug. "What you done did to my daughter?"

I hugged and kissed her back, then said, "No, Miss Mary. You need to ask your daughter what she did to me." I didn't give Nina's mother a chance to respond. Really, I was just hoping she would chill with asking all the questions. If Nina didn't tell her mother what was goin' on, then it wasn't my place to say anything. I ain't no stoolie; I wasn't trying to blow Nina's spot up. "Here's your key back, Miss Mary. And there's Nina's things on the couch."

"Both of y'all are crazy people," Miss Mary said with a smile, "which meant the two of you are perfect for each other." Me and Nina's mother sat together at the kitchen table and joked around for a few minutes. She seemed happy, which was important to me; after all, she was almost going to be my mother-in-law.

While she was explaining to me what had been goin' on with her job and everything, we heard, "Ma, I'm walkin' out the door. See you later."

"Okay, Nina," Miss Mary turned and said. "Drive safely, baby. I won't be back until around 6 o'clock because I'm going somewhere with Mrs. Scott after work. Okay."

"Alright, Mom." Without even looking back, Nina marched right out the door.

Miss Mary smiled at me and patted my hand once or twice, then went to her bedroom to finish getting ready for work. I stayed seated in front of the TV watching Good Morning America. It was a good program on about the so-called War on Drugs. The government was redirecting a lot of its funds to beef up the number of DEA agents in the field. There was speculation that the CIA was using its close ties with Afghanistan to help fund their secret agendas. I laughed to

Face/ Fetty Boy

myself while watching and eating my breakfast from E & A. I laughed because Afghanistan is the heroin capitol of the motherfuckin' world.

Five minutes into enjoying the program, I jumped to attention because I heard the front door bust open then slam shut. In walks Nina with nothin' but attitude all over her face.

Miss Mary came from out the back and asked, "Nina, what are you doin' back here? D'you forget something, child?"

"No, Ma. I'm just not goin' in today; I really don't feel too good. My stomach is bothering me for some reason."

You sure it ain't got nothin' to do with that motherfuckin' abortion? I joked to myself. After a few minutes of Nina playin' her sick act, Miss Mary came over and kissed me on my cheek. While she headed for the door, she told me not to be a stranger.

"You know I love you, Miss Mary. I will always come and check on you." She gave me a finger wave, then left the apartment leaving me and Nina alone.

Nina ran so quickly into her room, I thought she was a new member of the Jamaican track team. I waved my hand at her like I couldn't be bothered with her bullshit, then went right back to watching TV. I swear it was no more than fifteen seconds, Nina marched right back into the living room wearing a pair of the shortest pum-pum shorts I had ever seen! Fuck ever seen; I ain't even know she owned no shit like that! My dick bricked up instantly. Yeah, yeah, I said to myself, she wanna fuck. She must be missin' the diznick.

I kept my eyes on the TV, or at least pretending to, while Nina paraded her thick, lil' ass around the apartment. She went from the kitchen to the living room, back to the kitchen again. Then she finally disappeared into her room and closed the door.

Without even thinking twice, I went to the front door and snapped the chain lock into place. Afterwards, I shot straight to Nina's room and barged in without being invited. Of course, she tried to put up a fight by giving me some attitude.

She was lying on the bed emotionless when she mumbled,

Face/ Fetty Boy

"What you want? Get out, boy."

"Bitch, get the fuck out'f here with dat. Where my shit at?" I said. Then made a beeline to the bottom of her closet looking for the black Prada knapsack I had given her weeks ago with all my loot in it. Imagine my surprise when that shit wasn't there. "Stop the games; where my paper at, yo?" She didn't answer. She didn't have to. With all this new shit I saw sprinkled around her room, I had come to the conclusion that she spent my shit. "You know what, keep it, you sheisty-ass bitch." I said.

"Your mama sheisty!" she shouted back.

I shot straight to the bed and grabbed her pretty little ass by her throat. I lifted the sexy lil bitch right off the bed with just one hand and stared into her fuck-me eyes. Without being told, my hand just kept squeezing her neck. I only snapped out of it when I heard her gag. I eased my grip, but kept Nina on her knees at the edge of the bed. "Bitch, what the fuck you say about my mama?"

She had this terrified look in her eyes, or maybe she was trying to match the look of intent in mine. Whatever the case, I knew I was about to run up in that ass somethin' terrible. I kept my hand around her neck and used my other hand to pull at them little tight-ass shorts.

"Franko, please don't do this!" she shouted. "Please don't!"

With every word she yelled, my dick grew an inch longer. I was so tense, I thought I was gonna bust off right there in my pants before I had a chance to get hers off! She kept beggin' me to stop, while tears streamed her face at the same time. I ain't give a fuck about none of that shit. The bitch wanna kill my seed and spend my paper; the way I see it, Fetty done already paid for the pussy.

"Franko, please... I'm sorry!" she yelled.

"Oh, I know you sorry, bitch!" I kept my hand on her neck while finally pulling her shorts down exposing her cute, little olive-shaped backside.. "Why you kill my baby, bitch?" After the question, I shoved her ass down to the bed. I didn't even

Face/ Fetty Boy

bother gettin 'undressed. I unzipped, pulled out my pre-cum-drippin' dick, then pushed it in her until her eyes almost popped out her motherfuckin' head. Goddamn, that pussy was more moist than a warm breakfast muffin and wetter than papaya juice! All the while, Nina was crying, "No, Franko... no! Don't do this! Please!" That shit ain't do nothin' but make me more aroused. I pushed my dick so far up in her that I knew immediately when I hit Nina's spot. Her whole body tensed up, and all those No! No! No's! turned into Yes! Yes! Yes!

Normally, I would be able to stay up in the pussy all night, but Nina's shit was feeling too good! I threw her legs over my shoulders and started jack hammerrin' that pussy! Five minutes ago, she was hollerin' for me to stop, now she was beggin' me to cum inside her. Little did she know I was already cummin'. I exploded inside her walls like a fire hose!

I flopped down on top of her, and that's when I realized that she was giggling at me. "Minute man," she jokingly said. I couldn't do shit but smile back at her. That pussy was the truth!

I told her that, in a little while, I'd be headin' out to the airport to handle some business. I let her know that when I got back I was gonna pick her up to take her out and do something special. I think B.I.G. said it best, "Some say the ex make the sex spectacular!" Or maybe this bitch just got me pussy whipped!

Face/ Fetty Boy

Chapter 19: Them M'$

The birds, me and Freez was waitin' on landed smoothly, just like Uncle Coppa said they would. Twenty pies of the purest product New Jeruz has ever seen. The initial plan was to split the pies down the middle like the Red Sea. Then Coppa would collect a stack off each kilo - ten G's from his favorite nephew, me of course, and another ten from Freez. The thing was, as soon as all that weight was within my grasp, I had began to formulate a new plan. Fuck Jersey; time to take over the world!

Me and Freez was in our new stash house in Passaic, NJ; a short drive from Paterson. I was just about to lay my plan down for Freez when he turned and said, "Damn, my nigga, I'm glad we did take the risk! Coppa-G came through like a motherfucka!"

With my eyes hypnotized by the twenty pies, I responded, "The greatest risk in life is not taking one."

"You are absolutely right about that shit. If it wasn't for our risk taking, we'd still be buyin' bullshit work from them wet-backs. Plus, this coke is the best fishscale I ever seen with them little pink sparkles n'shit."

I smiled to myself at Freez's excitement, also because he had no idea what those pink crystals meant. "The 'pink sparkles', as you call them, meant that the coke was pure, Freez. One hundred percent uncut."

"I hear. So, what's up? You wanna cut it?"

That gave me another laugh at my dude's expense, "Nah,

Face/ Fetty Boy

nigga," I said. "We ain't cuttin' or cookin' this shit." I could tell by the raised eyebrows on Freez's face that my new plan was gonna bring him into a new arena. He was so used to sellin' base and not powder that his own mindset was placing limitations on him. But, for me, ain't no limits in my DNA. I told him, "It's time to corner the market and change the game out in these streets. I keep tellin' you that I'm not trying to do this shit all my life. My moms needs a house and you got a rap career to focus on, dun. That shit cost!"

A huge question mark was now painted across Freez's forehead to go along with those raised eyebrows. "So, what's the plan?" he asked.

I smiled, then laid it down. "Peep game. You know them nickel weed bags they sell on the boulevard?"

"Yeah. Them cheap shits I be buyin' when I'm tricking off with a hoodrat."

"Those be the ones. We're gonna stuff them weed bags with this raw, good shit and let 'em go for nickels. We can let the smokers cook their own shit. Once the word gets out about this perico, all the sniffers will be coming out the woodwork. And, all the while, we'll be behind the scenes sellin' weight at the same time."

Freez looked at me like I was wearin' polkadotted gators or some shit. "I don't know about this, Fetty," he said.

"Listen, nigga, who's the brains of this shit; me or you?" I didn't let Freez have a chance to answer, "Use your goddamn head for once. As soon as one of them crackheads cook up a 58/58 sized bag, they gonna end up with a twenty sack instead of a nickel."

I think that's when Freez's wheels really started turnin'. His eyes popped open and his jaw dropped down, like he was about to start eatin' some ass, then said, "Oh, shit! Now I get what you sayin', bro! That shit gonna shut the city down, my nigga!"

"Exactly. Plus, them Puerto Ricans over on 17th Ave. are the only ones pushin' raw coke for all the sniffers; them days are done. It's all or nothing for us... you in?" I asked Freez, but I didn't allow him any time to answer, "'Cause if you not ready for this, you can take your cut from all this shit and roll. But don't look to re-up with me and my team. So, let me know now, nigga."

All the doubt, all the timid shit Freez was displaying before went right out the window. He turned to me and said, "Hell yeah, I'm in, my nigga." We embraced each other in a gentleman's hug, then we both turned and stared at the work laid out on the table in the middle of the living room of our new stash crib.

"Aight, then," I said, finally breaking the silence. Put the word out on the strip. Let everybody know we havin' a meeting later on. Make sure they know it's gonna be new rules to this shit." Freez gave me a head nod right before I said,

"It's our time for them M'$, my nigga. We climbing the ladder of success escalator style."

"I'm wit' dat," Freez said, "but what if the niggaz on the strip ain't wit' it?"

"That type of shit ain't never been a problem for me, my boy. We just play big bank take lil' bank. Anybody puttin' up resistance can be layin' up in Greg's with a suit and tie on getting their motherfuckin' die on. You feel me? Wolves don't run with sheep or shepherds, remember?. I'll be damned if we gonna compromise or negotiate with a bunch of cowards. It's just like I said... it's our time to shine. We gonna get them M'$, then make our exit from all this shit."

* * * * *

It took a few weeks before the strip actually started jumpin' again. At first, the pace was slower than a turtle at Jones Beach. But, after the word had gotten out, everyday out that bitch was like the Greek Fest!

Long-ass lines of customers coppin' coke stretched farther than five blocks in any direction. The strip was under a new regime; just one hustler, two lookouts, and two shooters on each shift who changed their locations every thirty minutes. It was a wrap for all that idle hangin' out bullshitin'. It was like a straight zoo out there filled with zombies coming from all over. If we ever ran out of work, we would haul ass to one of our stash houses to re-up. While we were gone, the fiends would stagger around the strip looking like a scene straight out of The Walking Dead!

All the new traffic drew mad attention from "one time", but that never turned out to be a problem. Whenever the cops rolled through, the lookouts would be on point with walkie-talkies and, my team would get ghost with the quickness. The cops knew that something had drastically changed on G.G. Ave., but they ain't know exactly what.

The other hustlers in the town had to stop selling coke/base and started pumpin' either nick-knack weed or smack. Some of them niggaz simply had to take on a day job. Me and Freez had shut the city down! You rarely saw us out that motherfucka either. Shyiiiit... it was rare to even see us anywhere in town!

Illy-Ill was now el capitan, and he damn sure ruled with an iron fist. All me and Freez had to do was collect the ends from the stash house; a stash house no one knew about except us and Illy-Ill.

Every few months, Uncle Coppa-G would handle his handle and cop some more of them things for us str-8 from Yard. He had set things up with the suppliers so he wouldn't have to travel back and forth to Jamaica. All the plane rides would have definitely drawn too much suspicion. All Coppa had to do was ship a barrel bearing gifts and loot to the suppliers, then the suppliers would do the rest. The operation was brilliant if I had to say so myself. I put that shit together like a stack of Legos. But, for now, it was all about stayin' low and stackin' them M'$.

* * * * *

Face/ Fetty Boy

With the product practically sellin' itself, there was more time for us to spend in the studio working on Freez's mixed tapes. The loot was so bountiful, we just kept recording hours in this studio up in Englewood, NJ. In fact, it was said that the Sugar Hill gang had recorded and produced mad hits in the same studio back in the 80's. The spot was laid back and close to New York. It had all the latest equipment; it was so upscale, on any given day, you could've run into artists like Raeqwon The Chef, L.L. Cool J, DeLa Soul, Black Street... not to mention a host of producers and DJ's who stayed rippin' up the airwaves.

When me and Freez stepped in the place, everybody was wondering who we were, especially when Freez started lacin' them tracks. We was rockin' much better gear than all the celebrities. Our jewelry was rockier. Whips were more exotic. Our swagger forced the music industry to accept us right away. Almost immediately, we were getting shout-outs on Hot 97 from that fly-ass Latino chick Angie Martinez. Artists started mentioning our names on S&S and Flex mix tapes. Nobody had an after party without giving us an invite. Our names started to ring bells. And it all stayed under the illegal radar 'cause Freez's music was beginning to earn steady paper, so the Feds ain't have no reason to fuck wit' us; at least not right then.

We stacked the money we were making from the strip and did all our flossin' with the studio cash. One of the first things we bought was a pair of matching double-head lights GSXR Kawasaki bikes from this place called the Motor Mall on Route 46. On the weekends, we'd put on a daredevil show up and down 8th Avenue poppin' wheelies, then we'd tear the pavement up racing down Route 80 with our loud pipes. I gave the spaceship to Dead Eye and copped a Bentley GT with a creamed out paint job and interior - the dude at the shop called it hazelnut. Freez splurged on a marine blue 600-Coupe.

The better life wasn't all about us. I finally got my

moms that house I always wanted to get her. I moved her right out of Paterson and into Engelwood Cliffs. At first I had gotten her a condo in P-town. But Moms kept complainin' about some white dudes who stayed parked outside the condo all day. I could tell that not knowing where the money was coming from worried her, so it was off to a three-story house in an all-white neighborhood. The back yard was so big it looked like a public park for little kids. The house had three floors, including a basement and an attic. The garage could fit three whips inside, but I only bought my moms two cars - a Beamer Station Wagon and a Range Rover Truck; both of'em ocean-pearl white.

   She was loving her new toys, but she was still stuck on the thought of them white dudes that were parked in front of her old condo. I told her that she was in a new neighborhood now and that there was nothing to worry about. But, my moms ain't stupid, not even a little bit. She didn't say anything, but she knew it was probably the Feds trying to create a case on me and Freez. That's exactly why I had instructed Freez to keep his ass in the studio. His music was keeping us in the clear. All the people we hung out with had celeb status; they were making us look like legitimate entertainers. But, just to ease my mother's mind, I decided to keep my head low for a little while... way low.
   I called my cousin G-Man down in South Philly. The next day, G was in P-Town. I showed him my stompin' grounds for a little while, then me, him, and Freez went to have dinner at an upscale restaurant in Upper Saddle River. Lobsters, steak, and shrimp was spread out across the whole table before anybody said a word about business.
   I told G-Man how I wanted to get low and take my show on the road. His response was like music to my ears.
   "Dig, cuz, a few of my homeboys makin' it hot down South Carolina. Shit, with what you got goin' on, you could supply them niggaz down there. The criminal element kind'f thrives

Face/ Fetty Boy

down that way 'cause the one-time move much slower than they do up here. Ya feel me, cuz?"

I always liked my cousin G. He was a big nigga, too; about an inch taller than me. Plus, he kept his weight up. Even while having a conversation with someone, he would keep his eyes roaming around the room. He always sat close to an exit in case he had to break camp in a hurry. He knew when to stay strapped or when to have the heat layin' nearby. He was a motherfuckin' criminal... that shit just run in my family.

"That sound like some shit I could get into, G," I said. "My strip in Paterson goin' lovely, but it's time for me to take this show to new heights. I need to expand my operations; you heard?"

My cousin G-Man sipped his drink almost choking on it before he asked, "What... you lettin' the strip go, cuz?"

"Lettin' it go?" I repeated like I couldn't believe what I was hearin'. "Shit, cuz, you ain't listenin'. I'm expandin' my shit. The strip is too small for a nigga like me. What me and Freez got can't even be called a team no more; we a motherfuckin' crime family. Freez and my other manz will oversee the town. I just need a new spot where I can chill while I eat. Keep my business off the radar. You know how this thing go."

"I feel you," G said. "My homies down bottom come up at least once a week to cop in NY; usually on Fridays. They hang around til about Sunday night so they can blend in with the Monday morning traffic."

"I can dig it," I said after dipping a jumbo shrimp in some garlic butter sauce. I had tasted some good cookin' before, but the steak, shrimp, and lobster we were eatin' was the best shit I ever had. I don't know if it was the food, the classy atmosphere, or if it was the fact that everybody around us (mainly white folks) was shellin' out more currency than an ATM. Sittin' in that restaurant with my nigga Freez and my cousin G had me feelin' like a motherfuckin' super star. It wasn't like I had never seen money before. Truth be told... gwat always found its way to my pockets. I used to spend that shit like it wasn't nothin', then I'd have to struggle to get back on top. Not anymore. I'm makin' them M'$. Niggaz in my squad makin' them M'$. Shyiiit, even our money is makin' money. Ain't no stoppin' the champagne from poppin', the drawers from droppin', or them haters from watchin'.

By the time dinner was over, G-Man had already hit his southern goonz up on the cell. He plugged me in like it wasn't nothin'. Them country boyz jumped on my offer like virgins diggin' into some wet pussy. I knew they would, too. They were goin' over the bridge coppin' for $23,000 a pie, but I was offerin' it for $20,000. And my shit wasn't stepped on. Only a fuckin' imbecile would turn that deal down.

* * * * *

When Friday rolled around, Cousin G's menz was right on schedule. C-Bo and Curve Ball - even their names are country than a motherfucka. They were two-big-black from-the-swamp lookin' niggaz. After kickin' it with them for a few, I discovered that they were originally from South Philly. They had just been living and hustlin' down Spartenberg, SC, for over a decade now. A decade too long it seemed, 'cause these niggaz dressed country and talked even more country. Both of'em had long ponytails and they rocked Versace shirts with straight-legged jeans and Stacy Adams shoes.

Attire aside, them boyz was the real deal and about that money. When we met up, it was str-8 to business. I had rented an apartment for my little young'n Kimberly over in Lodi. That's where I took C-Bo and Curve Ball so they could sample some of the product. Freez asked me why I didn't use one of our stash houses. I just shrugged him off 'cause that was one'f the dumbest questions I ever heard in my life. Just because Cousin G trust these niggaz don't mean I do. I already told myself that I was gonna meet these country kats somewhere neutral, then take'em to a spot that really ain't mean shit to me. It's

Face/ Fetty Boy

not like I was sayin' fuck Kimberly or anything 'cause that little bitch's neck game was ridiculous. But she was just one of those things that I could drop in a split second if I had to get ghost for any reason; either that or I could easily replace her.

I laid a key on the black glass coffee table, then bust it open for them so they could have a taste. Judging by their reactions, I ain't know if they were the fiends or the dealers.

"Damn, dirty!" Curve Ball shouted. That was another thing; everybody's name was "dirty" to these guys. "Miami ain't even got scales like dis, dirty!"

C-Bo, the elder of the two, stuck his pinky into the freshly split package, then took a long, hard sniff. I know he regretted that shit 'cause it gave him an instant nose bleed. "Godayyum, dirty!" he blurted. "Where the fuck you get this pure shit at? This shit got to be straight from Colombia or Peru, boay!"

After I laughed to myself, I said, "Yeah, you could say that. It's a lot more where that came from, too... depending on what y'all bring to the table."

"Shyiiit, dirty; we came to get five squares at 22 each. Now, what you gon'do?"

I swear, these kats' country accents were off the meter. 'I can do better than 22 this time around," I answered. I'll let you have five pies at 20 per being as though y'all fucks with my cousin. Better than all that, y'all won't ever have to travel for work again 'cause I'll be down your way with my next shipment."

"Shyiiit, dirty, you alright, boay," C-Bo said. "That there sound sweeter'n a Georgia peach. When your next shipment comin'?"

These dudes were turnin' out to be cool, but not cool enough for me to give out information. "Soon," I said with a smile. "Real soon."

"Well, you got our number, dirty," Curve Ball said. "Get at us. And get ready for some Southern hospitality when you reach down bottom. ya heard, boay?"

"And bring a money machine 'cause it's more'nuff paper

down bottom, dirty," C-Bo added. "Sky's the limit."

Them two country niggaz was growin' on me. We sort'f clicked from the door. But the fact remains... in this game, love and loyalty could be the thing to get you killed.

I have to really feel these dudes out. Keep my eye on'em. They got the Southern swagger, but they're originally from Philly. And it ain't no secret that alot'f slick niggaz come from PA.

I've found that if you really wanted to see a nigga unwind and let his guard down, you gotta get that liquor up in'm, then take'm to where there's a bunch'f bitches. Bad Boy Records was having a birthday party for Ma$e at Club Tribecca in Fort Lee, NJ. Of course, from being in the studio all week, Freez had gotten us some V.I.P. tickets. We invited my cousin G-Man and the country boyz to come along. Now I get to really see what they about when shit get turned up.

Chapter 20: Easy on'em!

Just like the music, the fashion trend remained on a constant change. The playahs and ballers were now rockin' Iceberg, Pelle-Pelle, Coogi, Averex sweatshirts and jackets, North Face, DKNY... everything high-end fashion was now everyday gear. Even the females came steppin' out in stilettos that didn't say nothin' except, "Come fuck the shit out'f me." They were rockin' their little cowgirl hats, Chanel, Dolce & Gabbana; hell, some of the broads were dressed like dudes. Basically, whatever the hottest emcees were spittin' about on their latest albums, that's what the hood was wearin'. Bad Boy, the Lox, Jigga... they had us on some serious fly-fresh shit with the danglin' shiny platinum chains. Foxy Brown and Lil'Kim on the other hand had all the bitches wearin' shorts that looked like panties out that motherfucka. It didn't even matter if it was cold outside the club, hundreds of females would be out there sportin' knee-high boots, a skirt or pair of shorts that couldn't cover one ass cheek, let alone a whole ass. And a sexy blouse tied at the waist just to show off their pierced belly button and tattoos.

That's exactly how shit was when C-Bo and Curve Ball rolled up at the Juice Bar in Harlem, NY. They came through in a mid-night blue GS 400 Lexus with BBS rims. The windows were thirty-five percent tinted. I ain't gonna front, that shit was tough. The sound system them country boyz had was louder than the music comin' out'f the Juice Bar. They ended up parking across the street from this spot called Willie

Face/ Fetty Boy

Burgers. A nigga ain't have a hamburger until they ate a Willie Burger.

I think C-Bo and Curve Ball were tempted to head up in there until they spotted us chillin' in front of the Juice Bar. We were all loitering in front of a banging-ass stretch Lincoln Navigator Limo. Freez rented it earlier in the day just to show niggaz how much loot we were bringing in. I also heard Freez tellin' Illy-Ill that he wanted to roll up at Murdah Ma$e's party in the stretch limo just so he could get the bitches creamin' in their underwear. There were gonna be plenty of females at Tribecca fo'sho'; Bad Boy was having a $5,000 prize strip tease contest.

Club Tribecca was off the first exit over the G. W. Bridge. the ride from Harlem back to Fort Lee was a mere five minutes, The limo driver got us there just in time to see Junior Mafia headin' inside through the V.I.P. entrance. Lil' Cease, the hottest rapper in Junior Mafia, looked over and saw me and Freez steppin' out the limo. He hollered for us and waved his hand at the same time tellin' us to come on so we could take some pictures and head inside together. Freez and Cease had grown tight after bumpin' into each other so many times at the studio. We'd all hit the weed spots together, then spark up that good ganja while blowin' plenty of paper in the local gamblin' joints uptown.

Lil' Cease whispered something in one of the bouncer's ear, then peeled him off a yard. The bouncer was bigger and blacker than B.I.G. I might have to shoot that nigga instead of givin' him the fair one. Just like I thought, Cease must've told him to let everybody in the white limo truck come in through the V.I.P. entrance.

"Gollee! Dis what the fuck I'm talkin' 'bout, dirty!" Curve Ball said. "We is high rollin' with some real live ballahs up in this bitch! Dem hog-mog eatin' niggaz down bottom ain't gon believe dis here!"

I cut in tryin' to sound country, too, but I know I fucked that shit all up. "Looky here," I said, "y'all don't spend

Face/ Fetty Boy

a red penny in there tonight. Everything on me. I'ma show y'all how P-Town niggaz play up top, dirty!"

"Now dat right there is what the fuck I'm talkin' 'bout, whoadie," C-Bo responded.

I gave the limo driver a gee, then told him to keep his cell phone on. Like everybody else, we wanted to get inside the club. And, as expected, the inside was just as live as the outside. The same Biggie Smalls lookin'-ass bouncer escorted us to a private booth. What fucked me up was that the booth was right next to the Bad Boy camp's. Mad ladies from all over kept stumbling up to us askin' dumb shit like, "Who y'all? What song y'all did? Where y'all from? Can y'all take us to the Holiday Inn after the club? We'll give y'all a after party that you'll never forget!" Freez really enjoyed that shit 'cause the nigga Hoffa was just across the joint with his entourage. Hoffa had become Freez's rap nemesis. Anytime Freez could floss in front of that nigga, he was gonna take the opportunity.

On some trill shit, the ladies in Tribecca were mega hot! But there were far too many skeetos up in the club to just jump on the first piece of ass that came sniffin' after the paper. We just played the club on some smooth nonchalant shit. The night was goin' good; that is until Freez pushed things a little too far...

Normally, if you send a bottle of Moet over to someone's table in a night club, you're just trying to show them a little warmth in this cold game. But Freez decided to send Hoffa and his BX crew three bottles of Moet. Not only that, but he sent Hoffa an envelope stuffed with cash... the same amount of cash Freez had duffed him for in their last rap battle - $5,000.

Hoffa just sat in his V.I.P. booth with a serious screw face. After about five minutes, I watched him motion for the bar maid to come to his table. He had her send the Moet back to our booth along with the envelope. Then, he and his menz made their way to where we were sitting. Hoffa was sippin' from a bottle of Don-P, spilling the shit all over the place acting and sounding like a straight-up clown.

Face/ Fetty Boy

"Moet, lil' nigga?" he said in a drunken slur. "You sent a don like me some fuckin' Moet, while y'all over here sippin' on gold bottles? Is you fuckin' crazy, nigga?"

I sat there staring at Hoffa, while peeping out the entire scene. I already saw my cousin G reach underneath his Eagle's jersey for the banger he was carryin'. The country boyz had gone out on the dance floor a little while earlier, but they were already peepin' the whole thing without Hoffa even knowing it. My nigga Freez was lettin' his success go to his head a little too much 'cause he didn't move a muscle. He just sat there, while this Nigga Hoffa and his henchmenz rolled up on us. Like always, I was gonna have to deal with the drama.

I sipped my champagne, then said, "Listen, my nigga, we just here to have a good time. And furthermore, my lil' bro. ain't mean no harm. So, you can do all that stuntin' with your Don-P or whatever, but I promise you, if you spill any'f that shit on me or any of my niggaz..."

"Promise me what, son?!" Hoffa shouted. "Promise me what?!" I ain't gonna lie, I was tight as hell that this nigga interrupted me. Plus he started talkin' that "son" shit like he was the boss of all bosses. I like to dead that type of nonsense before it catches any momentum. Set the tone from the door. That's somethin' Freez never really understood. That was evident when our homeboy Hubby got killed. Freez ain't do shit, say shit... he just waited for me to come home. And here he was again waitin' for me to handle some shit he fuckin' started. Like I said, Fetty Boy like to kill this type'f shit from the door. But Hoffa kept diggin' his hole deeper and deeper. Fuck it. That just makes it easier for me to bury his ass.

Luckily for Hoffa, when he started playin' the movie script in his head, Murdah Ma$e, Cease, and that big-ass security guard walked over. "I know y'all ain't about to fuck my born day up with this bullshit." Ma$e said.

Like the coward he was, Hoffa backed down immediately. "Nah, son," he said, "we just came over here to say whaddup

Face/ Fetty Boy

to an old friend."

"Oh, y'all know each other?" Ma$e asked with a look of disbelief on his face. From the outside lookin' in, the whole scene just looked like two camps that were eatin' in the streets were havin' a little turf issue. Truth be told, that was sort'f the scenario. But, just like Freez ain't have no business tryin' to son Hoffa, Hoffa definitely knew better than to walk up on me and Freez like the air he breathin' don't cost money. "Yo, Cease told me y'all from Jersey."

"Yeah," I said. This was the first time I stood up since Hoffa and his camp came to our booth. "We from Paterson. And, no, we don't know none of these kats. But they know us; they especially know my man here." I nodded my head toward Freez, then said, "My nigga ganked this punk-ass nigga in a rap battle for five G's at the skating rink a little while back."

"Say word, Hoffa!" Ma$e said after he bust out laughin'. He called Hoffa by name, that told me he was familiar with these Bronx niggaz.

"Yeah, he took me for five grand," Hoffa admitted. "But you know that's somethin' light. We can battle any time he's ready for five times that amount. I'll demolish all that little shit you spittin' on dem fucked up mixed tapes of yours."

"Yeah, whatever, man," I interrupted. "We ain't come here for all that. I done told you already, dun, we here for the ladies. We gonna have a good time and show Ma$e some love by spending at the bar. So, whatever you was gonna lose in that rap battle, blow it at the bar. And stop sippin' on that cheap-ass Don-P. Order some fuckin' XO or Crystal. Other than that, spin off nigga. And know fo'sho', this is a conversation we have only once."

The way I came at Hoffa and his crew's necks had Ma$e and the security standing there stuck on stupid. I done did all my talkin', wasn't shit else to be said. Then this little black nigga standing next to Hoffa wanted to start runnin' his crusty-ass mouth.

He said, "You gotta lot'f mouth wit' you, nigga. I hope

you ready to back all that shit up the next time we see you."

I ain't even know this little black-bitch-ass-nigga was here, lookin' and sounding like Hoffa's lil' security. I knew his name was Blanco Jermaine or some shit. My first inclination was to backslap this dude and make him feel like the bitch he was. But game recognize game. And I didn't wanna disrespect Mase's party by actin' like one'f these low-level thug niggaz.

"Nigga, I'm always ready," I responded. "Bet dat put your money and life on dat."

Like I knew he would, the big black security guard stepped in. I already know that Lil' Cease had told security how my mob play. These niggaz knew that once I turned it on, there ain't no turning it off until everything is dark in this motherfucka.

"Ho, ho, y'all. That's enough with all dat. Show's over. Ain't gonna be shit up in here tonight. Y'all can save all that for the Tunnel or somewhere else. Y'all niggaz is about to scare off all the bitches before we even have the strip tease contest."

That's just what I needed to get the thought of killing this nigga Hoffa off my mind. Most of the ladies up in Tribecca were more than dime pieces. I could have closed my eyes and pointed and still walked out'f there with a top-notch chick. They were all goin' the extra mile with their strip game 'cause it was Mase's born day. White bitches, black bitches, Chinese bitches... my nigga Pretty New would've had a field day up in this spot!

I even saw some of the chicks that came in with other niggaz takin' they shit off. Yo, them females stripped str-8 down to the thongs! Titties floppin'. Booties droppin'. Coochies poppin'. Shit was borderline out'f control.

In the midst of it all, I caught a glimpse of the nigga Hoffa gettin' his dick sucked by this bad-ass Puertorican bitch. This nigga had the nerve to look over towards my camp like he was doin' shit bigger than we were. I was gonna let his

Face/ Fetty Boy

earlier antics slide and blame it on the alcohol. But he takin' shit a little too far. True, Freez was out'f pocket for even startin' this stupid shit. But that's just what havin' status does to some niggaz - it makes them start actin' other than themselves. I'ma finish this shit, though... believe that.

I went to pull out my flip phone to give Illy-Ill a call. While I was reachin' for it, Lil' Cease grabbed the mic and announced that the Notorious B.I.G. was havin' a party at the Tunnel in a few weeks. Not only that, Cease told the crowd that Freez was gonna be the opening act. He pointed over to our table and the whole nine. I could see all the bitches creamin' in their panties. And all the dudes they came with were ice grillin', including Hoffa.

Right before I started to dial Illy-Ill's number, this thick-hipped cinnamon-chocolate sistah slow danced her way right up to me. The way she was movin' was hypnotic. Her lips were succulent and her bedroom eyes looked me up and down like an x-ray machine. Fuck a thong, this bitch had stripped out'f EVERYTHING! C-Bo and Curve Ball stood up and got out the way with their eyes almost jumpin' out their heads. The bitch straddled my lap and started gyratin' like she was imagining herself fuckin' me. I'm sittin' there like,

"What the fuck?"

with my cell phone still in my hand. I can't take my eyes off her big-nippled titties. Them shits looked so delicious, I just started droolin'. Still rubbin' her wet pussy on me, she took my cell phone from me. Then she licked my ear and said, "Just give me the number, baby. I'll dial it for you."

Everyone in my circle was on some, "Oh, shit... look at Fetty!" Me? I ain't know what the fuck was goin' on. I just began tellin' her Illy-Ill's number, digit by digit. This bitch fucked me up when she started dialing with her fuckin' nipples! Man, this chick had baby-bottle nipples! I can tell she was horny 'cause them shits were hard and thick and staring right at me as if to say, "Suck the shit out'f me!"

I slurped half her titty in my mouth. While I was twirlin'

my tongue around her nipple, I could hear her still dialing with her other nipple. After a few seconds she put the phone to my ear, then kept on grindin' up against my dick. She looked at me and smiled cause she could tell I was holding Mandingo style.

"Fetty?" Illy-Ill said into the phone. I wanted to fuck this chick so bad I could barely hear him. As best as I could, I started tellin' him about the bullshit that went down with Hoffa and his wanna-be-Bronx gangstaz. Every time I let the chick titty go to talk to Ill, she'd shove it right back in my mouth. My hands was all over and in between her ass cheeks. She was holdin' the phone to my ear with one hand while caressing my bald head with the other. "Yo, Fetty, you aight, nigga?" Ill asked.

I don't know how I finished that conversation with Ill; but, before it was over, I told him to gather his goonz and meet me outside the club at closing time. The last thing I told him was, "Bring wifey wit' you."

I took old girl with the cinnamon complexion into the bathroom. As it turns out, her name was actually Cinnamon. I tossed her on the sink and fucked her until her nose bled. She dialed her number into my phone, of course she used her nipples, then I left her there so I could go handle this mess that Freez done started.

I left the country boyz and their stripper dates at the table. I told Freez I was goin' outside for a minute. He nodded his head at me as if to ask if I needed him to come with me. When I told him no, that's when my cousin Gary looked me in my eyes. He knew straight away I was up to somethin'. Illy-Ill and half of the G.G. Ave. hit squad was outside of Tribecca in less than thirty minutes.

Five Ducati bikes, ten niggaz dressed in Coogi sweaters, black jeans, black flight jackets, and Black Chucker Timbs. I been told my young boys to stop with the army fatigues - that shit was played out. They had started hustlin' in whatever gear that was the latest fashion. Not only were they gettin' them

M'$, but they looked like they were gettin' them M'$. They drove whips like they was gettin' them M'$. And when the club started to let out, the crowd saw just how much paper my faculty was stackin'. The crowd stood jaw-dropped looking at Illy-Ill and the small army sittin' on bikes by our limo with the headlights illuminating in the dark of night.

Hoffa and his crew were no different. They were caught off guard just like everybody else. They started to make their way towards me. All the pump in their chest was gone. They had talked enough shit earlier in the club, but I could see it in their eyes, they were str-8 shook. Try'n to talk their way out'f the bullshit they had started earlier was their best bet.

"Remember that promise we spoke about earlier?" I asked. "Well, I don't break my promises, dunny. I tried to tell you we ain't come here tonight for beef. But you kept stylin' and profilin' like you 'bout that action. What up wit' it now?"

Silence. Not one word from him. Not a single word from his crew.

For a good thirty seconds them clowns ain't have nothin' to say. All that mouth earlier, and now niggaz act like they don't speak motherfuckin' English.

"Nah, my man," Hoffa finally said. "You got dat. Earlier wasn't about nothin'." Hoffa's talkative lil' Bro Jermaine was silent as a church mouse after seeing Ill with the chrome tray pound, the one he called wifey.

"Fetty," Illy-Ill shouted, "fuck these punk-ass niggaz. Say the word and we'll make a blockbuster flick out this bitch tonight! These niggaz can have a starring role - they can play the black niggaz that always get killed off early."

My intent was to show these Bronx niggaz that they needed to take it down and recognize they fuckin' with some real niggaz. On top of that, we didn't wanna fuck up Mase's party after the love he and Lil' Cease had shown me and Freez.

"Nah, Ill," I said after turning my back to Hoffa. "Easy on'em. They already know what it is. I just wanted to make sure they started acting like it. Easy on'em, my boyee!"

Chapter 21: In Too Deep

I was supposed to be incognito; keeping myself out'f the spotlight. But, after Freez threw Hoffa a bone at Tribecca, Hoffa and Blanco Jermaine definitely came biting. Laying my game down in front of everybody at the club drew too much attention. My plans of relocating down south for a while had to be moved up.

The first few times I went down bottom, I took Illy-Ill with me. We ripped up the highways on our bikes during the twelve-hour drive. Once or twice, we would stop at a hotel to get our rest on and fuel up the bikes. Then we'd finish off the last stretch headin' into North Carolina. Once we hit the city of Rocky Mount, C-Bo or Curve Ball would be waiting on us.

From the outside lookin' in, it just seemed like a small group of friends gettin' together for a good time. What was really goin' on was me and Ill were handing off the kilos, which we had stashed in hidden compartments on our bikes. Then we'd all proceed to Spartenburg, South Carolina - the southern boyz driving the van in one direction, me and Ill on our bikes headin' in the other.

Once we hit the heart of the city, me and Illy-Ill would

Face/ Fetty Boy

head str-8 for the projects. C-Bo or Curve Ball had already driven the stash van on a different route to a completely different location. This way, if anybody wanted to rob us out-of-town boyz or even if they decided to drop a dime, they'd get nothing but two P-Town niggaz on bikes carrying licensed guns. And, in my mind, if any of these kats down bottom wanted to try me and Ill, we'd paint the town red, then never be seen in those parts again.

Thankfully, none of our trips ever had to resort to gunplay. It got to the point where I didn't even have to bring Illy-Ill with me anymore. I started making the trip with my side-chick Kimberly. I'd be riding dolo on my bike or in the Spaceship, while Kimberly would be on the Greyhound with 20-bricks tucked in her girdle. After meeting up with the southern boyz and passing off the work, I'd spend a little quality time with Kimberly. She didn't wanna do anything except lay up in a four-star telly and let me bang her back out. I'd punish the pussy for hours, then take my dick out and put it right in her mouth. She wouldn't stop suckin' until I splashed all over the back of her tonsils. I also had shawty toting illegal guns on the ride back up North. With the way I was sexin' her, she would've smuggled a fuckin' rocket launcher in her pussy if I asked her to - not to mention I was givin' her at least two grand a trip.

My trips down bottom were becoming so frequent that my main piece Nina was startin' to catch an attitude. But her funky little tantrums were nothin' that a shopping spree at Neiman Marcus couldn't fix. After tossin' her the dick and kickin' out a few grand, all I had to say was I would be goin' down South for a few days. But Nina ain't never been a stupid bitch. She knew I was probably doin' me every time I went out of town. She just knew better than to ever question me about that type of shit again. She kept her thoughts to herself, but I knew that shit had to be eatin' her up emotionally.

While I was making things happen, the strip was bringing in hella paper. All of that was being stacked, then shipped to Jamaica.

There, Uncle Coppa would stash the loot inside this mini-mansion I was having built from the ground up for my moms. Dreams were no longer being talked about, they were being lived. Money was coming to me from every direction I looked in. I had even given a half mil to these high-power attorneys up in Clifton, New Jersey - Mike Bernstein and Paul Bergen. I called that half mil my "just in case money."

My operation was nonstop; and so was my paper. I was also making plans to cop the latest Acura NSX, a top-of-the-line sports car. That, and I had ordered Nina the new Jag she kept naggin' me for. While waitin' on the deals to be finalized, I realized that I needed to update my wardrobe. Don't get me wrong, my threads were fresh to death, but now it was time to rock the shit that nobody else was rockin'. B.I.G.'s concert was coming up, even though the date had been pushed back twice already, and I wanted me and Freez to be the ones sportin' gear that nobody had ever seen.

I didn't have much to do this one night, so I scooped up Lil' Goochie and Ron Gotti. We headed over to the Garden State Mall so we could check out if Barney's or the Eddie Bauer store had anything new. Like any other trip to the mall, me and my dudes usually hit up the food court first. There was this place that made these little cinnamon roll things with the creamy white icing on top. Man, fuck what you heard, I couldn't get enough'f them things! I had to take like three or four of them right to the face with an ice-cold chocolate milk.

Lil' Goochie had gone to the bathroom, while me and Ron Gotti took a seat over by the Wendy's. I was enjoying my food when I looked up and saw this tall, slim dude sittin' with two average looking females. If I ain't know better, I would have thought the nigga was staring at me. I tossed a head nod his way as if to say, "Whaddup, nigga? I know you?" But when the dude realized I had caught him lookin' my way, he turned his eyes and faked like he wasn't staring.

The shit didn't feel right. "Yo, Ron-G, I be right back,

dun," I said. Wiped my mouth, then headed toward the table where dude was sittin'. As I got closer, I noticed his outfit was on some other shit. He was rockin' a Versace shirt I had never seen before. If I hadn't seen it, then it must be new. I decided to ask him where he got it. Maybe the store would have some other new stuff that I could wear to see my nigga Freez open up for Biggie.

"Yo, money grip," I said, "You mind if I ask you where you copped that shirt at?" After reaching his table, I couldn't help but notice he was wearin' a pair of green alligator reptile Timberland boots. "Oh, shit, lemme see them." After inspecting his footwear, I said, "I ain't know Timbs was doin' it like that, brah."

"Nah, yo," the dude finally said. "The hip hop spot in Brooklyn, also the Apollo Express on 125th in Harlem... both spots customize boots and sneakers. And they got plenty more Versace shirts in all colors."

"Yeah, yeah, I've been to both them joints. Just ain't been up there in a while. I'll go check it out this weekend."

Dude seemed a little shook that I just came right up to him and his chicks. I thanked him for the info. and decided to let him off the hook for eyeing me the way he was. Who knows? The shit was probably nothin'.

* * * * *

I had taken a few more trips down South to get with C-Bo and Curve Ball. When I got back, I had noticed that Nina was back on her attitude shit. It was nothing she said or did, things were just a little off between us. Like, I could be balls deep knockin' the pussy sideways, and my shit would go soft on me all of a sudden. It was like my dick was tryin' to tell me that Nina's ass was up to somethin'. It wasn't just the sex, either. We could be at the movies, the mall, the restaurant, she could even be hugged up on me while shopping and I could still feel a gap between us. It was like she was with me, but not with me. Distant. Fuck it... at least that's what my mind was sayin'. But my gut told me to get to the bottom of this shit.

At first, I was gonna do some Cheaters type shit - pay somebody to follow her around. Get her on video. But I always thought that was some sucka shit. Besides, my game with these females ain't never fail me. I just decided to dial Nina and lay my game down.

"Whaddup, baby girl?" I said after dialing her number. I was at my mother's making sure there were groceries in the house. My mother was out with her bingo friends from her church. I took the moment to have a private chat with Nina.

"Ain't nothin', papi," Nina responded. "Whassup with you?" At heart, Nina was a goody-two-shoes school girl. But it turned me on to hear her talkin' like she was a video vixen.

"I'm good, ma. I just need to holler at you about a lil' somethin'."

"Holler at me about what?"

"Nothin' that can't wait til later. Plus I'm headin' over NY. You wanna ride with me? We could stop at the Fish & Chips spot on St. Nichollas and get somethin' to eat. Do a little shop til we drop type thang. You wit' it?"

It took a few seconds, but she finally answered, "Yeah, baby. I'll meet you at your mother's in about twenty minutes."

* * * * *

In no time, me and Nina had shot over to Brooklyn. Our first stop was the Hip Hop Shop that ol' boy in the mall was tellin' me about. Just like he said, they had a bunch'f Versace shirts in stock - all new shit! I let Nina pick the shirts out for me, while I picked out my footwear. I ended up with two pair of Mauri's; one pair was ash-gray and the other was a pair of three quarter burgundy crocodile soft-bottoms.

Nina left the store with so much shit, I started to lose count of all her shoes. She did get a couple'f evening-wear

Face/ Fetty Boy

dresses; when she tried'em on, she looked like red carpet or runway material.

Next we raced over to Harlem and did some more shoppin'. We stopped and got some tender vittles, all the while, kickin' the bo-bos about anything and everything. It was like everything was fine and dandy. But I knew better. My gut was never wrong about these things.

It was a comfortable and quiet drive back to Jersey. We went straight to my mom's house to kick back and relax. Nina was tired as hell, I could see it in her eyes. Normally, I would've taken her shoes off and gave her feet a nice rub down, but like I said, I needed to get to the bottom of some shit.

When we went into my bedroom, we sat on the bed and began nibbling on our leftover food. I sat my plate on the night stand and said, "Listen, Nina, I've been hearing some crazy shit. But, before I give this shit any thought, I wanna hear it from your own mouth."

It was like I had hit her with a stungun. She was quiet than a motherfucka. I had already turned the TV off. Nobody was home but us. If there was a mouse in the room, I probably would've heard it fart! Ha, old head Ali-Mu used to always tell me, "Never doubt your game, test your game, young Fetty Man!"

Finally she said, "Hearing what, Franko?"

"That you runnin' around cheatin' on me. I know it's true, too, 'cause I heard the shit from big-butt Keisha." I lied about hearing it from Keisha. But everybody knew that Keisha was nothing but a gossiping hater with a big ass and a big-ass mouth. On top of that, Nina and Keisha had lived in the same building for years and never liked each other. Throwing her name in my game would definitely get results.

"What the fuck that bitch tell you!?" Nina shouted. She tried to flip the script on me by saying I was probably fuckin' Keisha on the side. "You think I don't know you fuckin' every bitch in Paterson? You probably slingin' yo' dick all around Bergen County and the Tri-State!"

There she go with the bullshit. She ain't stupid. She know

Face/ Fetty Boy

I be gettin' mine on the side. This is the shit she signed up for. Now, all of a sudden, she gotta problem with it. "Listen, baby girl, I ain't trying to pick a fight with you. I love you to death. But, in this life I live, I need to know that I can trust you before I commit to you and only you. You ain't got to tell me, I already know I ain't perfect. And I ain't ask you about what I'm doin', I asked about you. Now come the fuck wit' it. Confess your soul to me. Is that askin' too much?" I could tell my little game was working 'cause Nina lowered her eyes to her lap. I had already stuck the dagger in, so I decided to twist it a little bit. "I said is that too motherfuckin much?!"

"No," Nina softly cried. The tears were already rolling down her cheeks and she couldn't stop sniffling her nose.

"Well then, run your mouth! 'Cause if you don't, we could end all this right here and right now!" I lied about that, too. There was no way in hell I was gonna let Nina go. Whatever she did, rest assured that I done did much worse. I ain't your average nigga, but just like any other nigga, I needed to know if the bitch I'm with is disloyal.

Nina looked up and said, "Why don't you tell me what you be doin' out there in them streets. Then we can talk about if - and that's a big fuckin' if - I be doin' anything."

I had to smile inside my own head after that last remark. She's sittin' here tryin' to match my game with some game of her own. No wonder why I loved this bitch so much. "Nina, I swear on everything I love, I will not leave you if you just be honest with me, baby." That's usually what a chick does to her man - pull the honesty card. But, when I asked Nina to be honest with me, it was like I had torn down all her defenses. She couldn't even look me straight in the eyes no more. Her lips started quivering. It was like she was afraid of me.

"Franko, you already know everything," she said. "Please, I'm begging you, don't hurt him."

"Nina, I don't know what the fuck you talkin' about. Hurt

who?"

"Shemar," she said. When she said the name, I was asking myself who the fuck is that? "He told me you stepped to him in the mall the other day."

That shit gave me the stupid look for real! I know she ain't talkin' about the nigga I asked about his fuckin clothes n'shit? But then I thought about it. The nigga was starin' at me kind'f hard in the food court. Every time I looked up, he would look away actin' like he ain't see me. The shit all makes sense now - you never see smoke without fire. Nina's fuckin' that nigga, and he was afraid I was coming up to him to push his shit back. Ain't this about a bitch?

"He's scared to death of you, Franko. Please don't hurt him."

"You been fuckin' with that tall-goofy-looking-ass nigga I seen in the mall?"

"That's Shemar, my best friend I been tellin' you about."

"Shemar... I thought that was a bitch's name! So, you been fuckin' wit' him all this time, bitch?"

"No, Franko. I swear. You was down south a lot, and I was stressing about you not being around. I was lonely, maybe even vulnerable. I went to his place just to hang out. I started to cry, then one thing led to another... it just happened."

I was lookin' right at Nina while she was feedin' me her bullshit, but after she said she went to that nigga's house, I ain't hear shit but boiling water and steam inside my head. She could tell I was fuming; immediately, she tried to make it right. "But, I swear, if you tell me to stop being his friend, I will, Franko."

"Nina, I'ma keep it real wit' you; I ain't know shit or heard shit about you and old boy. I ain't even know who the nigga was until now. This ain't nothin' but an act of God. I just knew it in my gut that you was up to no fuckin' good."

"Me? What about you, Franko? Huh? Tell me what you be doin' out in the goddamn streets with god knows who!"

"Bitch, I ain't do shit." I knew it was a lie, and she

Face/ Fetty Boy

did, too. But fuck it.

"You lyin' and you know you lyin', Franko! My cousin Keeda told me all about you and Sheema up in your Bentley!"

"So the fuck what? She was in my car... it don't mean we fuckin'! Her uncle, Tone, is my nigga up in the county jail. I was takin' her to go drop some paper off for him."

"Mm-hm," Nina said with her arms folded, "you sound just like a nigga with an excuse for everything. Well, what about this bitch named Roxy?" She fucked me up when she asked about Roxy. I don't know how she knew about her. Truth be told, I ain't even fuck Roxy - but I damn sure want to. She's this exotic Trinidadian chick that lived up in Engelwood close to my mother's new house.

"Who dat?" I asked, tryin' to play stupid.

"Nigga, don't play me! I found all her info. written on a Bennigan's napkin in your pant's pocket. Yeah, that's right, you was in here sleep, and I went through all your shit! You had the nerve to take that bitch out to eat!"

"Oh, I see how it is," I said. "I ain't nothin' to you but a low-life gangster. It don't matter that all your bills are paid, all your mother's bills. It don't matter you drivin' a better car than most doctors and lawyers. New shoes for every day of the week. Hair and nails did every goddamn day! I'm just a thug nigga to you, so I gotta be dirty, huh? You just gotta get some dirt on me. Well, watch this shit."

I went into the living room, then ran back in the bedroom with my cordless phone. I put the shit on speaker after dialing a number. The phone rang six times before Roxy's older sister, Pam, picked up.

"Yo, Pam, Roxy there?" I asked.

"Yeah, Fetty, how you?" she responded.

"I'm good I really need to talk to your sister though." Roxy was just gettin' out the shower, so it took her a few minutes to come to the phone.

"Hello," she finally said.

"Yo, Roxy, waddup?" I said.

Face/ Fetty Boy

"Hey, Fetty. What's good?"

"I gotta ask you somethin' right quick. And all I want you to do is be honest. I'll explain later... alright?"

"Boy, don't be gettin' me into no bullshit," Roxy said.

"Come'n, dead all that. Listen, did you and me ever fuck?"

"What?! Hell, no! You know I don't fuck wit no drug dealers! We cool and all, but bottom line, you's a fuckin' drug dealer. Why, who said some shit like that?"

"Nah, don't worry about it, Roxy. I'll call you later and explain, alright," I said while hangin' up the phone.

I didn't have to say shit after that. Nina just sat on the edge of my bed with the dumb look to the third power on her face. Here she was tryin' to game a nigga who had so much motherfuckin' game. Not only did I shut her little fishing expedition down, but I got her to reveal her little secret in the process. Don't get me wrong, I was definitely vexed, but I couldn't let her know that. I promised her that I wouldn't leave her no matter what. Truth is, I shouldn't have asked questions I didn't want the answers to. My gut never failed me, and right now it was tellin' me to ditch this bitch before it was too late. But, deep down inside, I knew it was far too late. I was all in. I was in too motherfuckin' deep. I had to chastise myself for not listening to my moms. I don't know how, but a mother always knows, and she told me to take out the trash months ago. I just didn't listen. She tried to teach me that blood is thicker than water. But she didn't understand that cum is thicker than blood.

* * * * *

I left my Bentley at my mother's and let Nina drive us back to Paterson. The main thing on my mind was now that I knew how Nina was gettin' down behind my back, I wouldn't even try to hide my own infidelities anymore. Doin' me meant doin' me right out in the open.

"Yo, drop me off on my block," I barked at Nina while we

were sitting at a red light.
"You not comin' to my house?" she asked.
"Hell, no," I said. "I got shit to do."
Then came the tears. Nina cried all the way to G.G. Ave.. In a crazy, deranged way, I felt sorry for her. That was probably the reason why I couldn't leave her. I wrestled with the idea over the next few days. I went around fuckin' mad bitches just to find some pussy that was better than Nina's. I thought about kickin' her to the curb and killin' old boy she was cheatin' with. But I'm the one to blame for all this shit. I'm the one who allowed myself to fall in too deep.

Face/ Fetty Boy

Chapter 22: Caught Up

Nina must be out'f her goddamn mind. I got mad niggaz in the streets gunnin' for the crown. I got a team'f young gunz depending on me to keep shit trill. I got my operations on the strip, back down Jamaica, down bottom in South Cackalacky... I got ninety-nine problems, and Fetty refuses to let a bitch be one!

A few days had went by since me and Nina had our little talk at my mom's house. I ain't really give that shit too much thought. I had other shit on my mind - like making sure my nigga Freez was ready for his big opening act tonight.

We took the Bently uptown to shop at the Apollo Express Store on 125th Street in Harlem. Coppin' our outfits didn't take long at all. The place already knew who we were and they knew what type'f bread we was gonna drop. We ended up coppin' two cranberry-wine-face Rolex watches and two 18-inch Cuban Link chains with the Jesus piece dipped in A-class diamonds. In fact, everything we bought came in twos - Gucci suits, Freez's was all white, mine was a pale lavender. We got the snake-skin Mauri's to match, plus a pair of Gucci frames. The sales chicks that worked up in the store was the true definition of Fetty Girls. They looked so good, me and Freez

Face/ Fetty Boy

started buyin' shit just to style a little bit. We had already gotten the Rollies, but that didn't stop us from coppin' two blood-red-face Movados. We had gotten everything we needed, even down to some two-toned Now & Later flavored Gators.

Somebody in the store must've called Hot 97 'cause while we were in the store, Freez's song started rippin' out the store's speakers. We were really on our way to stardom. The sentiment I felt upon hearing my nigga's song on the radio was amazing!

By the time we hit The Tunnel, anybody and everybody was runnin' up to us to have their picture taken with us. It took us forty minutes just to get in the party! Once my nigga Freez got on stage, he tore that shit down! Niggaz and bitches in the club ain't know what to do! Freez blew their fuckin' socks off Then he hit'em with some shit that wasn't on none of his tapes...

<pre>
         Yo, paper is my mission
           money, the ambition
            we type different
    thought I mentioned Fetty had a vision
      one day dreamin' 'bout money bags
           ya-know, Pyrex dishin'
            chiefin' in the kitchen
             bakin' with the soda
             call it caffeine rocks
             My hands went bad
             from liftin' them blocks
          Rollie stocky on the wrist
         caught a few blisters on my shit
   my nigga passed & I ain't been right ever since
        he the only one knew the connect
     fucked me up he went down wit' 2 to the neck
      now I spit flows, rap game new crack game
              look how I came
        Bentley GT and I came to my senses
</pre>

Face/ Fetty Boy
I'm back in the hood full of vengeance
Somethin' gotta give, my nigga
I gotta live...

He shut all them other hatin'-ass emcees down; shyiit, let me tell it, Biggie ain't even wanna go on after him.

And speakin'f hatin'-ass emcees, Billy Hoffa and his camp was in the house. They didn't come at us on no rah-rah shit 'cause they remembered when Illy-Ill and his goonies rolled up outside of Tribecca a few weeks back. Hoffa knew that all it took was one phone call; plus, he ain't know if we had some shottas scattered around the club or not.

I made my way to the unisex bathroom upstairs so I could meet up with these two Miami chicks we was kickin' it with outside the club, Tamika and Te-Te. They were two Creole klepto bitches I ran across a few weeks back. These chicks would boost your shit out the toilet before you got a chance to flush. They ran schemes all up and down the east coast - from check and credit card fraud to stealing clothes from department stores. They did it all! Their swagger was ill, too. They were the first bitches I ever seen with bangin' bodies rockin' gold teeth in their grills. They had asked me to smoke a blunt with them; some of that Bronson-$100-sack lamb spread. That shit was off the meat rack! Plus, ain't no tellin' what a nigga gonna see in a motherfuckin' unisex bathroom. Not to mention, the stalls ain't have no doors on'em; and it was dark as hell up in that bitch. Chicks got dude's balls on they chins. Broads bent over the toilets takin' it in the butt like Lil' Kim. Some niggaz eatin' pussy. Chicks doin' lines'f coke. Come to think about it, I ain't see one motherfucka in there using the bathroom!

After smoking the Blunt, I went back down to the part of the club where the main stage was. Freez had just got finished hypin' up the crowd, and Flex started playin' Mobb Deep's Quiet Storm. All it took was a little Mobb Deep to soup a nigga up.

Face/ Fetty Boy

I peeped the nigga Blanco Jermaine heading toward Freez with a bottle of Crystal in his hand. I thought the lil' nigga was about to show some love.. Next thing I knew, Jermaine spits a mouthful of the Crys in Freez's face. Then, "Wham! Wham!"

He cracked Freez over the head with the bottle. If that shit wasn't rude enough, the nigga reached into his pocket and threw a wad of cash on my dude while he was out cold on the floor bleeding!

By the time I made my way to the stage, Blanco Jermaine was backin' away talkin' 'bout, "What, nigga? What? You want some, too, you pussy-ass Jersey nigga?" Me being the nigga I am I just smiled and made it seem like he wasn't talkin' to me. It was easy to stay calm, only 'cause right then and there, I had decided that the sun wouldn't rise until I pushed this nigga shit back to the white meat. Besides, yo, that nigga knew what he was doin'. He made a spectacle in the busiest part of the club where all the security was at. They ushered Jermaine and a few of his coots outside immediately. Billy Hoffa and the rest of his team was sittin' at one of the booth tables laughin' they asses off.

Talk about pissed! These fags done fucked my night up. We had these two bad-ass Miami bitches we was gonna hit the Marriott with after the club. But that shit had to take the back seat right now... duty calls; I need to handle this shit myself.

I took Freez and the Miami chicks out one'f the back exits; a security guard we was fly with showed me where it was. The Bentley we had road in was parked a few feet from the door. I drove to the nearest hospital in less than five minutes. My nigga was in and out of consciousness and his head was bleedin' bad. I had fourty-five hundred on me, which I gave to Tamika along with my Motoralla phone. "Listen," I said,

"make sure Freez see a doctor. If I'm not back by then, y'all head to a hotel in Jersey. I got some shit to handle right quick."

Face/ Fetty Boy

I shot back to the club hoping to catch them fools slippin', mainly Jermaine's punk ass. In any whip that my team drove, we always kept a "black package" hidden in the trunk - black flight jacket, black Timbs, black gloves, and a black ski mask. I changed clothes quicker than Clark Kent in a phone booth. people were startin' to leave the club, so finding parking was easy. In a new wardrobe, I crept right up to the main entrance of the club, and sho'nuff shit, Jermaine was sittin' in his brother's champagne-colored Range stylin' and profylin' for some Connecticut chicks. I ain't want any bullets piercing these bitches skulls, so I snuck right up to the passenger side door. The window was down. I cocked the Ruger, then turned the inside of the Range into the 4th of July. My rage had taken over. The Nine was spittin' bullets everywhere. I even hit two of the chicks I was tryin' to avoid. But Blanco Jermaine was the only one who didn't see the sun rise. "That's for that sucka shit you just did to my nigga, pussy hole!"

* * * * *

Guess it's true what they say... when you're up, you're up, when you're down, you're in fuckin' hell.

I never even made it to the bridge to get back to Jersey that night. Turns out that the bouncers at the club had called the cops right after Freez got whacked in his fuckin' head. They were already on the way while I was plannin' Blanco Jermaine's murder. I out-maneuvered them for a while, so I thought. That is until I ran into a four-car roadblock on the Riverside Drive Highway. I would have definitely been in the clear if somebody wouldn't have written my plate number down and given it to the fuzz. Them faggot-ass jakes ran my Jersey plates, then set up roadblocks on both ends of Manhattan – they cornered off the Holland Tunnel and the G.W. Bridge.

Caught is caught, right? I was never the type to gamble with a bad hand. I had already pulled over and tossed the Ruger in the Hudson, so I couldn't hold court with these chumps even

Face/ Fetty Boy

if I wanted to.

"Get out the car!" one of them fools yelled. "Get the fuck out now!"

The jakes in NY were trigger happy than a motherfucka. I knew to just get out the whip as slowly as possible with my hands raised to the sky.

"Get your fuckin' ass on the ground!" The fat, white pig ain't even have to say that. I was already on my way to the pavement face down and hands behind my head - I knew what was really good wit the N.Y.P.D..

* * * * *

My ass sat on Rikers Island for six months. The D.A. reached out to all their informants, and of course, they got the word on who I be out in them streets. And because I was a Jersey nigga that did a New York crime, I got no bail. What they did give me was a goddamn speedy trial.

Nina stuck with me the whole six months. I guess me not being able to leave her ass finally paid off. She threatened me talkin' 'bout she'd be gone for good if she caught any other females comin' up to see me. That meant my little youngin' Kimberly couldn't come up to see me. But Tamika and Te-Te came on the regular; Nina ain't know nothin' about them.

On one of Nina's visits she revealed to me that she was pregnant again. That shit fucked me up. I been wanted her to give me a child, and here I am on fuckin' lock down. At first, I had to question if the baby was even mine. It could have been that nigga Shemar's sperm swimmin' up in Nina. I immediately canceled such thoughts 'cause if Nina wanted to leave and be with him, she wouldn't have stuck with me these last six months.

No question my nigga Freez came up to see me a few times. He stayed puttin' money on my books. He kept on begging me to have Uncle Coppa-G keep the kilos coming so he could give Nina my cut to put up for my seed she was carrying. He

Face/ Fetty Boy

and Nina just kept on asking about the connect. Hell, they were even asking about all the stacks Uncle Coppa had on stash for me. I couldn't let'em know anything 'cause the one time might be on to them. They could have fucked around and led the cops right to the source of my operation. Shit was just too thick right now. I had to shut all that shit down. It took me a few months to convince Freez to fall back. I reminded him about his music career. His mix tapes was movin' like big-bag nickels in the hood. Plus we were already sittin' on plenty of cheddah. Our plan was to do this shit until it was time to get out. Guess what? It's that time.

On one occasion, Freez and Nina came on a visit together. I made the mistake of reminding Freez about the millions I had stashed in my new castle down in Jamaica. When Nina heard that, I saw a certain look in her eye; the look a motherfucka gets when they think they done hit the Power Ball. Maybe that's why she was stickin' around all this time? Nah, fuck it. I had to cancel that thought, too. I know Nina loves me. She visited every week and we talked damn-near every night on the phone up until a week before my trial.

One Friday night, I was dialing her number like crazy. She wouldn't answer that shit for nothin'. Saturday came, there was still no answer. Sunday, still nothin'. Monday rolled around, and I was worried because she knew it was now a week before my trial was supposed to start.

I dialed Nina one last time.

No answer.

My next move was to give her mother, Miss Mary, a ring.

"Hey, Miss Mary. Thanks for accepting the call."

"It's okay, Franko," she said, "you know you like my own, boy. How you holdin' up?"

"Small thing to a giant," I told her. I was really fucked up behind all this shit, but I ain't wanna stress her out with my bullshit. "I start trial in a week. Lawyer says it's lookin' good."

"You know I got the church prayin' for you, don't you?"

Face/ Fetty Boy

"I know, Miss Mary. But listen, right now I need to talk to Nina. Is she around?"

"Don't worry too much about that girl, Franko. She's been goin' through a lot. I'm sure you can understand. She's in Jersey City right now with a few of her girlfriends. My daughter just needed to get away for a while."

"I can definitely understand that, Miss Mary. Do you know when she'll be back?"

When I asked the question, Miss Mary started stuttering like she had just seen a ghost or something. right before I could ask her what was wrong, she said, "Wait a minute Franko, Nina just walked in."

I listened to the phone get exchanged from one hand to the other. After a few seconds, I heard Nina's bedroom door shut, just like I had heard so many times before. Something was clearly wrong 'cause Nina still hadn't said anything into the phone. But I could hear her crying. It sounded like she had just lost a loved one.

"Yo, Nina baby, what's wrong?"

After sniffing her nose, she answered, "Franko... I... had a... miscarriage..."

As if my head wasn't already spinning. I dropped the phone the second the words spilled from her lips. I was so mad I began biting my bottom lip until that shit started to bleed. This is the second baby this bitch done got rid of somehow!

Instead of saying what was on my mind, my next words were,
"What the fuck you mean, yo? What happened?"

"I don't know, Fetty. Probably all the stress I've been going through dealing with you. I woke up last Friday with blood between my legs. I went to the doctor and he told me the baby was gone."

Man, fuck what you heard. I hung the phone up on that bitch with the quickness. I shoved a few niggaz out my way, then

Face/ Fetty Boy

made my way back to my cage. I flopped down on my bunk and used my hands to cover my eyes. I never wanted to cry so bad in my life, but my anger was boiling so much that my tears were dried up.

* * * * *

My girl lost the baby, and a week later, I blew trial. The trial lasted for two weeks before the jury came back with a guilty verdict. The two Connecticut broads ended up testifying against me. Bitch-ass nigga Hoffa did, too, 'cause it was his brother that I had shot. Plus there was some surprise witness bullshit that went down; whoever they were, they never took the stand. They just provided sworn statements under the protection of the confidential informant law. I almost back slapped the shit out'f my high-priced attorney when he told me that shit. The only thing that saved him was that I didn't get found guilty of murder, but a lesser offense of aggravated manslaughter. For the moment, my only hope was for my lawyers to appeal on the grounds that I had a right to confront all the witnesses against me. Who knows how long that shit is gonna take?

I looked back at Nina and my mother when the verdict came down. My mother's beautiful face was stained with tears. And Nina's ass was already on her way out the courtroom. She looked back just before she left, and I kind'f read the expression on her face. It was almost like she was saying fuck me and she was done with me for good. Maybe she was just traumatized by the verdict. She'll probably be up to see me as soon as she can.

* * * * *

A week ticked off the clock. I neither saw nor heard from Nina. I called her number and her mother's number one after the other, back to back... call, call, call...

Face/ Fetty Boy

Got nothin'. Not a damn thing. And I stayed dialing all the way up to ten o'clock when the jail shut the phones off. I was lost. My world was ripped apart. I ain't care about the prison sentence, I'm built for this type'f shit. What bothered me was not having Nina. Not knowing what was on her mind. Was she gonna ride it out? Was she gonna leave? She could at least hang around until I get settled into the bid and get over the hump. Or she could just be my friend.

Finally, I decided to call my nigga Freez. We had been on this ride together since day one. If anybody could give me words of comfort, it was him. I was happy as hell when he picked up.

"Yo, waddup, Fetty?" Freez said.

"Ain't nothin', dawg. But listen, I need you to go and see what's up with Nina. I can't catch her on the phone for nothin'. I think she's fucked up over my trial n'shit."

"Yeah, I hearrrd," Freez said. It wasn't really what he said, it was how he said it... like he knew some shit that I didn't.

"What you mean by that, son? What, she called you and told you what's goin' on with her?"

"Yeah, brah, she called me. And she definitely don't love you. She does fear you, though. Also, she ain't have no miscarriage, my dude; I gave her the paper for an abortion. I couldn't have my girl poppin' out no maybe baby. Feel me?"

Yo, I was str-8 fucked up from what I was hearin'! What the fuck is this nigga talkin' 'bout? I'm sittin' up in this motherfucka 'cause of his ass, and he talkin' about a goddamn abortion and that Nina is his girl n'shit! What the fuck!?!

"Yeah, so you can quit it with all the collect calls, Bee. Ain't nobody gonna be accepting them shits. It's over between y'all. I know your mouth is on the floor right now, but you's a smart nigga, you'll figure this shit out."

"Figure out what, nigga?" I said. I only asked 'cause my mind couldn't really comprehend what was going on.

"You the brains of this shit, remember?" Freez said into

the phone. I could hear that nigga snickering through the receiver. "I've been doin' my thing right underneath your dumb-ass nose. I definitely been fuckin' Nina way before y'all even met. Them birds that went missing from the stash house? That was me. The whole time you thought somebody was droppin' dime to the D'z? That was me. I thought they'd bag you after Ali-Mu slumped that nigga Scientific, that way I'd have all them keys from Jamaica to myself - well, not really to myself," he said with a sinister laugh, "I'd have to hit Nina off with a lil' somethin'-somethin'. But you managed to get out'f that, too. It was just a matter of time, though. I knew you'd do some dumb shit to get yo' ass caught up. You so blinded by this power you think you got that you can't even see what's goin' on right in front of you, dawg. Hubby had the same motherfuckin' problem... that's why I had to murk that nigga and get his ass out my way. I'm motherfuckin' Freez, nigga! Game cold, ain't it? You ain't even gotta answer that. Answer this though... who the brains of this shit, me or you?"

    Remember them tears I was talkin' about? Well, they finally found their way down my face. I cried even harder after my one-time potnah slammed dunked the phone on me. I couldn't even stand up. I just flopped to the floor right in front of the phone. I felt like I was just hit with a tranq gun. This nigga had been fuckin' my bitch even before I had came home from prison. He was the one giving info to the cops. Freez had been playin' me from day one. He tricked me into murdering the papis in the Broadway Building. Crackhead Anne even died that day... for nothin'! He told me they were the ones who had killed my nigga Hubby. As it turns out, Freez mastermined this whole shit like the Wizard of Oz sittin' behind a motherfuckin' curtain. Nas was on point when he said, "... love changes and best friends become strangers..."

    I had to remember where I was at; Rikers ain't a place for a nigga to be cryin' - other niggaz see tears as a sign of weakness. Immediately, my tears turned to blood in my eyes. And my mind became filled with nothin' but murder and mayhem! I had to think back to when I had first came home. I had suspected that something wasn't right with Freez, but my love for him blinded me; even after Illy-Ill tried to warn me about him. Still... I got a gun stashed away with his finger prints on it... a gun used in a homicide. I might have to hold onto that for somethin'.

* * * * *

Later that night, before the phones got shut off, I decided to try Nina's number again. Surprise, surprise, she picked the fuck up.

She confirmed everything Freez said. Her love for me had turned into fear. She went and had an abortion. And she was fuckin' Freez. Not only that, she had been fuckin' Freez for some time! Nina tried to blame all this shit on me! She said she couldn't raise no child while I'm sittin' in prison. She went on and on about how her mother had gone through the same shit with her father. Bitch had the nerve to tell me the only thing I meant to her was a meal ticket and some good dick.

I think that's the instant my love for her transformed into hate. The switch was turned off for good. Lights out for her, and every other motherfucka that crossed me.

"A meal ticket and some dick?" I repeated. "Yo, you ain't nothin' but a trifling-hoe-ass bitch!"

"Oh, Franko, Franko, Franko," she said making a mockery out of me, "you don't have to call me names or nothin' like that. We can still be civil."

"Goddamn scandalous tramp! I can't believe you been fuckin' this nigga all this fuckin' time!"

"If you can't be civil, I'm just gonna hang up," Nina said. "Oh, yeah... and his dick game is better than yours, too!" After that, the phone went, "Click!" I could knock the gravy out her biscuit right now!

This shit is one of the hardest lessons I ever had to learn thus far. Being betrayed is worse than knowing you're about

Face/ Fetty Boy

to die. The pain is str-8 up unbearable! They say only a blind thug will fall in love with a whore. Even with a pair of binoculars, I wouldn't have seen this shit comin'. What's fucked up is that I didn't listen to Illy-Ill when he had told me not to trust this sucka. Freez acted like he was for me, but he turned out to be a phony motherfucka. Bitch nigga wanna see me in a casket... jealous motherfuckin' bastard! The moral of the story? You gotsta play this game alone. Go for dolo or don't go at all.

If not, then you're in for a life of stress. The question I'm wonderin' is, after death... after my last breath, will I finally get to rest? Still, deep down inside I gotta be grateful for what little blessings I still got. I can't let this betrayal change who I am; gotta keep my essence. Pressure busts pipes. And, for the weak minded, that means panic is next. But there ain't nothin' weak about me. I just gotta go with what Pac said, "When you get stranded and things don't go the way you planned it, dream of riches and strive to be in a position to make a difference. If I go insane, then the game made a brother change. RESPECT THE GAME!"

Face/ Fetty Boy

Chapter 23: Pigpen

At the end of every dark night, there's a brighter day. No matter how hard it gets, I gotta stick my chest out, keep my head up, and handle this shit.

I'm lookin' at a long-ass vacation headed to them packed jails. Who knows? I might go to prison and do somethin' righteous with my life. Your destiny is sometihng you can never figure out. I can't say that the game ain't been good to me. Ain't no need sittin' here cryin' the blues over this shit... rule number one... peep game and respect game. I gotta accept the fact that I've been played. Can't let my adversaries occupy any space in my mind right now. It makes no sense feeling shell-shocked. This here is a cold-dirty-fuckin' game. Loyalty is a motherfucka... can't purchase it... can't worship it...

"Mr. Brown, said the Judge, 'do you have anything further to say before I sentence you?"

Damn. I was so lost in my own thoughts, I totally forgot this cornball-ass redneck was even sittin' here. The robe don't impress me. Bangin' the gavel don't intimidate me. People standin' up whenever the judge comes and goes don't move me. I don't give a fuck about none of these people here. The only one I care about is Mamma-P. Out of all the people in this courtroom, she's the only person who showed up to support me. There's not a seat in the house, either - the media outlets, the victim's family and nosy fools from the hood, it

Face/ Fetty Boy

was packed... I done already seen the bailiff ask a few people to leave 'cause it just wasn't enough room in here.

"Mr. Brown..." the judge started to call my name again, but I didn't wanna hear anything from anybody right now.

"Yeah, Your Honor," I said, cutting him off, "I do have somethin' I wanna say. First off, I would like to apologize to my mother for gettin' caught for this crime. Yeah, you heard me right, I apologize for gettin' caught. Everybody wanna come up in this court room and act like ol' boy was a saint. Ain't no saints left in the world. They're all dead; that's why we pray to'em. Dude was a straight drama queen. And his brother sittin' over there tryin' to ice grill me ain't nothin' but a diva. Perfect combination for a disaster." The judge kept trying to tell me to be careful of what I say, but I wasn't tryin' to hear that shit. This is my life on the line. I didn't tell him or the prosecutor to watch their mouths when they were lying to the jury. "I'm almost done, Your Honor. You can lock me up forever, but the fact still remains, I'd do the same shit all over again if I had the chance. Gettin' locked up was never part of my plans. I wouldn't wish this shit on my worse enemy. But I'd rather lose everything before I sell my soul. And, as a point of note, I think the victim's family should know that I was offered probation for this same crime if I was willing to work for the Feds and set up a certain cocaine supplier." I had to speak louder and louder 'cause the prosecutor stood up and tried to object.

"Sustained," the judge called out, but I ain't give a fuck. "The jury will strike that last statement from the record. And, Mr. Brown, I am warning you..."

"With all due respect, Your Honor, I've had niggaz with gunz threatenin' my life. You sittin' up there with that gavel ain't much of a threat at all. Like I was sayin', I'd rather die before I turn into an informant. Y'all wanna call me guilty? Truth is, I ain't guilty of nothin' except being loyal to the wrong people. At the end of the day, long after you hand down my sentence. I'll still be real. Hated by many. Loved by few.

And respected by all. Now, I'm done."

I sat back down in my wooden chair, while the courtroom erupted into a frenzy. It was so loud I couldn't tell if people were booing or cheering.

The chains on my wrists and ankles clanked against the table and the floor. I had a look on my face that said, "Fuck you! Fuck all y'all!" My mind traveled back to a place where no one existed except me and my thoughts.

This whole thing was my fault. I got caught slippin'. I trusted the wrong nigga and loved the wrong bitch. Fuck it. The most this dumb-ass judge can give me is a 15 to 30 years. I ain't never been locked up as an adult before; so, I'll definitely make my first parole eligibility. All I gotta do is stay alive in the pigpen for 15 long-ass years.

All I got from the streets right now are pictures & my memories. It's funny how memories don't leave you like people do. But, the more I remember, the more my mind contemplates revenge. Revenge is best left up to time. And time is somethin' I got plenty of. Right now, I just gotta eat this shit...whether I like the taste of it or not... I just gotta eat it.

* * * * *

The first stop was Fishkill Penitentiary. I stayed there for only two days before being transferred to this joint called Northern State. I asked the transport cop if he knew why I was being shipped to a facility so close to Niagra Falls up in the fuckin' mountains. The only response the cop had was, "Do you have any beef with anybody in the system?"

"Not that I know of," I answered.

The transport van went silent again. In fact, it stayed silent the entire five hours it took to get from Fishkill to Northern State Correctional Facility.

Reception was just like any other joint. I had to strip naked, lift my nuts, show the bottom of my feet, run my fingers

Face/ Fetty Boy

through my mouth, squat and spread my ass cheeks... this became a regular fuckin' routine. It was cold and loud in the place. First chance I got, I used the phone to let Mama-P know where I was at. My mind was still adjusting to the situation, so I didn't feel like talkin' for too long. After Mama-P, I called Illy-Ill. We had been communicatin' here and there since I had received a surprise letter from Evie-Eve after losing trial; but now was a good time for me and Ill to talk directly. We kept the conversation to a minimum...

"What up wit' ol' boy?" I asked. Ill knew I was talkin' about Freez.

"Word is he moved to Atlanta. Heard he started a record lable."

"What's poppin' wit' ol' girl?"

"Ain't seen her yet. But, when I run into her, you already know."

"Did you track Pretty New down yet?"

"Yeah. Me, him, and Coppa-G had a sitdown yesterday and chopped it up about where we go from here. Don't worry, my dude. I'ma hold you up and holla Fetty Mobb lickin' shots until I see you back on top."

That's really all I needed to hear from Ill. Freez may have crossed me, but Illy-Ill is str-8 sucka free.

After hanging up with him and wrestling with sleep because of my new environment, I finally dozed off. And, of all things, I had a dream about Freez and Nina fuckin'. I dreamt he was rammin' his dick inside her from tip to balls doggie style. And she was lovin' that shit! Fuck it... at least I got some sleep.

* * * * *

I woke up the next morning with my personal belongings waiting on me. Some cosmetics - cheap shit - but, right now I can't be choosy, towel, prison greens, new boots. I was told to get dressed because I would be seeing classification within the hour.

Face/ Fetty Boy

I discovered that the prison grounds were enormous. There were ten housing units, five on the west side and five on the east, each holding 350 inmates. There was a chapel, a big-ass school, and a college-styled gymnasium, all centered around the traffic control area. I later found out that the gymnasium was where the prison conducted the visits.

Eventually, I was classified for General population. I was also given a job inside the gymnasium - cleaning, maintenance, that sort of thing. I didn't mind it too much 'cause it gave me extra time to work out. Plus, I got to see kats from other units when they came to the gym.

Northern State was a world within itself. It was filled with corrupt guards and prison officials. Drugs came through on a daily basis. Cell phones, knives, even pussy if the opportunity presented itself. This one nigga who locked next door to me named Khalif could get his hands on anything. I got cool with him immediately.

The first month went smoothly. Most of the dudes were from somewhere in NY, so I didn't mingle much. For the most part, I pretty much kept to myself, and Khalif liked that about me. So, he cut into me one day out in the yard while we were playin' chess. I duffed off him, too! Ten games to nil! We kind'f got cool after that. Matter fact, the next day in the yard, Khalif introduced me to the person who was the number one chess player in the whole jail - this kat named Power Love, who happened to lock on the same unit as me and Khalif. I cliqued wit' him from the start. Anyone who was anybody knew and respected Power Love.

One day, the unit cop let Power come to my cell. He stood outside the locked cell door and dropped a bomb on me.

"Young brotha, you have paper on your head up in here." Having paper on your head in the joint meant that somebody took out a bounty on you. The way I was handlin' niggaz in them streets, I wouldn't be surprised if some clown reached out to his jail house peoples to have me killed. After what

Face/ Fetty Boy

happened with Nina and Freez, I wouldn't be surprised by much of anything. It might even be Freez's ass that put out the bounty on me.

"Paper on me for what, Power?"

"Only you can answer that, my brotha," Power said. "Word in the pen is you gunned down a Bronx brotha whose family is well-respected in the city. Supposedly, his older brother got ten large on you." Power laughed to himself before saying, "Shyiit, if I wasn't big on you, my brotha, I would've taken that deal myself. Ten large is a lot'f paper. Quiet as it's kept, I'm not even supposed to be tellin' you this, but my peoples say the Crips accepted the money; they waitin' to catch you slippin in the gym."

I knew Power Love wasn't supposed to be tellin' me all the info he was. While he was standin' outside my door, he kept lookin' left and right making sure the wrong people weren't lookin' and listenin'. I still had the smell of pussy on me up in the joint, but niggaz could already see that I was a Lion. Still... I was unsure of what to do. This is just like Billy Hoffa's punk ass to put a hit out on me.. all 'cause I murked his lil' brother for gettin' out'f pocket.

"So, how should I go at this shit, P?" I asked.

"You gotsta make that decision on your own, young brotha. Some kats choose Protective Custody, which means you'd be runnin' for the rest of your bid, however long that is. Or you could earn your bones and lay some'f them fools down. You do that, then you should know them Crip dudes play with knives n'shit. You might have to fight to the death if they catch you with your guard down. Whatever you decide to do, just convince yourself that it's the right thing. That's the one rule of conduct for a real man - to always do what he feels is right. It may cost you your riches. Your friends. Maybe even your life. The one thing I know for sure is you definitely gonna struggle in this joint. But you'll end up payin' a bigger price if you don't do what's right. And choose your direction wisely. It could be that you're runnin' toward a thing that will bring you harm, while runnin' from a thing that will put you at ease. Think on it, my brotha."

* * * * *

I ain't sleep all night, good thing, too, cause I ain't wanna be dreaming about Freez and Nina fuckin' no more. P-Love dropped some heavy shit on me that gave me plenty to ponder over.

The next morning, I went up to Khalif while we were on a movement together and asked him how much it would cost to get my hands on a banger.

"For you? A hunned, Fetty. I heard 'bout your little situation. I'll sell you my personal shit; a butterfly knife str-8 from the bricks."

I watched Khalif pull the knife from his waistband. The first word that popped into my head was, "Goddamn!" that shit was long and shiny. It was like the knife was just waitin' for me to stab a nigga in his neck.

"Yo, Khalif," I said after inspecting the blade, "I could have my moms mail you the money or I could pay you in cigarettes. Just let me know what's good."

"It don't matter to me, Fetty. Just keep that thing on you and stay on point when you're off the unit... especially in that gym. And one more thing... my man over on C-Unit said watch out for a white cracker Crip dude. He be rockin' a beard most of the time. He's one'f their stunt dummies they be sendin' at niggaz."

"Really?" I couldn't believe that shit, not even a little bit. "A white boy, Khalif?"

"Yeah, man. That's how it go up in here. Them gang dudes will use any throw-away gunners they can find; as long as the leaders ain't the ones gettin' their hands dirty. Most of 'dem are cowards anyway. All you gotta do is stand your ground and weather the storm. Just like the storm, this shit here will pass. And I know Power gave you some words of wisdom; make sure you listen to him. That nigga sharper than that knife. He definitely taught me a lot. The biggest lessons he taught me were these... Wise is the person who fortifies his life with the right friendships. As you grow, you and your friends will grow apart. The ones that didn't want you to climb will makesure you crawl. And you won't have nobody to blame but yourself.

"And why is that?"

I looked at him for a few seconds after he asked me that. I never told anyone about how Freez and Nina had crossed me, yet, here Khalif was using the teachings of Power Love to break the whole thing down to me like a scientist.

"I can't blame nobody but myself 'cause I would be the fool who chose the wrong friends."

"Sho'you right," Khalif said with a smile. "Power did say you were one'f the intelligent ones."

"Word, Khalif. I needed to hear that, yo. Thanks. I'm gonna owe you and Power after this."

"Nah, Fetty, you don't owe us shit more than to take care of yourself in this cold place. Them streets is cold and the game is cold, but neither one of them got shit on this place. Watch your back."

* * * * *

"He who dwells in the secret place of the Most High shall abide under the shadow of the Almighty... I will say of the Lord, 'He is my refuge and my fortress; my God, in Him I will trust.' Surely, He shall deliver you from the snare of the Fowler and from the perilous pestilence..."

Those are a few lines from the 91st Psalm. I read the entire thing over and over last night. Before I laid down to go to sleep, I had decided I was gonna handle my business.

It had to be at least two hundred prisoners in the gym by the time I got there. When I stepped inside, the guard at the entrance slammed shut the door. The usual meet & greet was goin' on. Different sets had different handshakes. I could

Face/ Fetty Boy

tell who was with who even by the way they were greetin' each other with hugs and daps.

I scanned my eyes across the gym, checkin' to see who was in what huddle. I was also lookin' for the stunt dummy white boy with the beard. As I stood with my back against the wall, I noticed one of the big homies sayin' somethin' to a gang of young dudes. I couldn't hear what was being said, but the body language of these niggaz said that some shit was about to go down.

Power Love and Khalif were right; not like I was doubtin' them, but they were on point like a sniper with their info. I tried to look casual. I even kicked it with a few jokers like nothin' was goin' on... the whole while, I got my new friend in my palm tucked up the sleeve of my Greens.

One of the young dudes went up to a gym porter and asked him to go in the back to get a new basketball. I kept my eye on him, but I didn't wanna appear too nervous. I looked away toward the niggaz playin' handball - my back still against the wall, the knife still tucked away in my hand. Just as the door buzzed open for the porter to go in the back room, I felt this small-ass fist crash into the side of my jaw right beneath my eye. It was some midget lookin' dude; actually, the little nigga looked like Bushwick Bill from the Ghetto Boyz. He str-8 snuffed me! I can't believe this little nigga is gonna be the first kat to give me a fuckin' black eye.

I ain't never been dropped in a fight, but that punch might have put me out if I hadn't been leaning against the wall. I shook that shit off, at the same time, listening to the female CO shout, "Code red! Code red!" I watched Bushwick run off to the side, and that's when I saw the white boy appear out'f nowhere.

He slashed at me with a gem star razor in his hand. But the cracker didn't realize I was waitin' on his ass. I dipped out the way, then sliced the silly prick right across his face. Blood spilled down his white cheeks and caused the sucka to freeze up. When he saw his own blood oozing, the white boy fell to his back, then I went in for the kill. I rushed toward him and dug the butterfly knife right into his belly button. I could hear the flesh tearing from his pinkish stomach as I ripped him open like I was digging for gold in his belly.

I had already made up my mind to kill this clown. I felt disrespected that Hoffa's bitch ass would send a white boy to try and take me off the map. While my rage was rippin' this white piece'f shit, I began to feel a bunch of niggaz stomp kickin' me n'shit. Some of them were punchin' me in my head. One even tried to grab the blade out my hand. But I knew that if I let go of that lifeline, it was over for me. Fuck that! If a nigga wanted this knife, he was gonna have to take my arm with it!

I found the strength to kick upward so I could get a few of these dudes off me. I was down on one knee and had to react quickly before they pounced on me again. I zeroed in on a light-skinned lookin' nigga. I Zorroed his mid section, but for some reason, this idiot decided to jump up. My knife ended up lodged into his inner thigh. After a closer look, I could see that I actually clipped the chump's balls!

The gym floor was already stained with the cracker's blood, now this nigga's blood flowed right into the same pool. Most of the so-called gees in the gym weren't built for this kind'f mayhem. They all backed away and lined up against the far wall. The look on their faces told me that most'f them were nothin' but bitches.

When I got back to my feet, I started lookin' around for Bushwick. I couldn't really see shit 'cause my eye was startin' to swell shut. I know these jokers thought this was gonna be picnic. They didn't think that a Jersey nigga was gonna bring it to'em the way I did. What these niggaz really ain't know was that I wasn't finished.

There go that midget motherfucka right there! I thought to myself. I went to chase after his ass, and he turned around and ran right into the water fountain. I caught him, slashed him across the forehead. Of course I slapped him like the bitch he was. He took off runnin' again, and I let him. I had to pay attention to the rest of these cowards. That's all they good for is jumpin' motherfuckas.

In that instance, the exit door flew open. The goon squad poured into the gym with their shields, helmets, and batons. The lead man had a super soaker strapped to his back filled with mace. Anyone who wasn't face down on the floor got dowsed with the shit. You already know I was the first nigga to be cuffed. While the CO's were tryin' to get the knife out my hand, I looked over at the white boy leakin' all over the floor. He was moaning while gasping for air. And his endtrails were on the floor along with his Caucazoid blood. As I looked closer, I saw somethin' inside the bloody mess wrapped in clear plastic with doodoo all over it.

"Is that a fuckin' phone?" I said to myself. I blinked a few times just to make sure my swollen eye wasn't playin' tricks on me. When I hit the fool in the stomach, I must've caused him to shit the cell phone out. Damn! This cracker had a phone boofed up his ass!

"Get them to Medical!" I heard the captain yell. But even I knew that the medical staff in this joint wasn't gonna be able to do shit.

"Medical?" the Lieutenant responded. "Fuck Medical... call an ambulance!"

* * * * *

I never saw the light-skinned nigga or the white Crip dude again - at all... ever! After that whole shit had happened, me and Bushwick were escorted to Medical, and an hour later, we were on the Segregation Unit. Some I.A. investigators came asking all sorts of questions. Did I owe anybody money? Did I lose a gambling bet? Did somebody pay me to kill the white boy?

Face/ Fetty Boy

"I don't know nothin'," I told'em. "I was just breakin' up a fight. Shit happened fast as hell, naw'mean?"

After realizing they were gonna get nowhere by asking me questions, I.A. sent me right back to my lock up cage.

Ad-Seg was noisier than a football stadium. Everybody was on the gate at all hours of the day and night just choppin' it up about anything and everything. They especially talked about the shit that recently went down in the gym. "It was that big nigga who just came down from Jersey!" somebody yelled out. I even heard Bushwick's punk ass puttin' a hundred on ten. The little nigga snuck me, and he back here tellin' motherfuckaz it was a str-8 up fair one... wait til I catch his ass.

I.A. came back around with more questions. That's usually how it goes; after niggaz got finished yellin' back and forth through the bars, the investigators came pokin' around with the new information the snitches done called and gave up. This time, however, they came with pictures of Billy Hoffa and Blanco Jermaine. I.A. knew it was a paid hit. They knew the whole story in fact, but I still sat there like I ain't know shit.

They offered me Protective Custody status. When I told them to get the fuck out my face, they made me sign a Refusal Order. Motherfuckin' Fetty in Protective Custody... yeah, picture that!

* * * * *

Later on I tried getting some sleep, but the noise was nonstop. Plus my eye was aching like a bitch. The ice pack the nurse had given me had melted hours ago and the pain meds had worn off. While staring up at the dim light in my cell, I caught sight of one'f the runners. He peeped his head in my cell then spun off. A few minutes later, a folded up note came slidin' under my door:

Face/ Fetty Boy

NIGGA, YOU KNOW WHAT IT IS! THIS SUUWUU DAMU TERRITORY! AND
IT'S PAPER ON YOUR HEAD! SO EITHER YOU GONNA GET DOWN OR LAY
DOWN! WE WILL BE IN THE YARD TOMORROW.
O.G. MACK!!!

* * * * *

How did Fetty get here? Was it hip hop? Was it the music that got me caught up like this? Or was it because I was "Born black in a white man's world?" Is this the shit Pac was talkin' about? I guess it's "Me against the world" fo'real. How did I go from a spoiled only child in Catholic school to "All eyes on me?" Is hip hop to blame for this? Or has hip hop actually prepared me for what's to come? The game changed me. I ain't got no choice but to respect it, even if it's "Against all odds." I'm by myself in this shit... and I love it! In one of Pac's rhymes, he wanted to know when the stressin' was gonna end. The answer? Maybe when I take my last breath. Because, truth be told, "They don't give a fuck about us. I allowed the evil of the the money to trap me." So, I gotta Respect the game!

$ $ $ $ $

Face/ Fetty Boy

How well did you connect with the story and the characters?

1. How did you enjoy "Fetty Boy, Respect the game?"
2. Did the authors use of discriptions invite you into every scene?
3. Do you think Freez and Nina stayed together?
4. Was Hip Hip a gift or a curse for the character?
5. Should there have been more or less sex scenes?
6. Was the violence believable, or over the top?
7. Do you think Kimberly kept Fetty's baby?
8. How do you think Illy-Ill silenced old head Ali Mu?
9. What role do you think Illy-Ill, Pretty New, and Uncle Coppa will play in book 2 "Lost Souls?"
10. Do you think Fetty "got down" or "got laid down?"

SEND COMMENTS AND SUGGESTIONS TO:

Etched in stone publications
c/o Fetty Boy
950 South Orange Avenue
PO Box 212
Newark NJ 07106
www.Etchedinstone-books.com
www.Etchedinstonepublications.com

or look for the Author on Facebook- Patrick Francis
email- pfrancis12363@yahoo.com

Face/ Fetty Boy

Order All books at; Etchedinstonepublications.com, Etchedinstone-books.com. All books are in E-book and kindle formats and can be purchased on Amazon.com, the Nook and I-tunes.

All correspondence and order can be mailed to;
Etched in stone publications
950 South Orange Avenue
PO BOX 212
Newark NJ 07106

Vol. #1 Fingered for Murder
Vol. #2 One in the chamber
Vol. #3 Somebody's got to die
Vol. #4 Dirty's Shot
Vol. #5 The Jasiah story

Vol. #1 Bigger fish to fry/ Money or Murder
Vol. #2 Bigger fish to fry/ Corruption
Vol. #3 Bigger fish to fry/ The Murder Game

God I finally found my way

Hood Money Millionaires

Bounce

Meat Factory

www.ingramcontent.com/pod-product-compliance
Lightning Source LLC
LaVergne TN
LVHW051548070426
835507LV00021B/2467